Rorty and Kierkegaard on Irony and Moral Commitment

Rorty and Kierkegaard on Irony and Moral Commitment

Philosophical and Theological Connections

by

Brad Frazier

RORTY AND KIERKEGAARD ON IRONY AND MORAL COMMITMENT
© Brad Frazier, 2006.

Material from Chapter 2, "The Ethics of Rortian Redescription," is reprinted by permission of Sage Publications Ltd from Brad Frazier, "The Ethics of Rortian Redescription," *Philosophy and Social Criticism*, vol. 32 no. 4 (2006) (©SAGE Publications. London, Thousand Oaks and New Delhi, 2006).

First published in 2006 by
PALGRAVE MACMILLAN™
175 Fifth Avenue, New York, N.Y. 10010 and
Houndmills, Basingstoke, Hampshire, England RG21 6XS
Companies and representatives throughout the world.

PALGRAVE MACMILLAN is the global academic imprint of the Palgrave Macmillan division of St. Martin's Press, LLC and of Palgrave Macmillan Ltd. Macmillan® is a registered trademark in the United States, United Kingdom and other countries. Palgrave is a registered trademark in the European Union and other countries.

ISBN-13: 978-1-4039-7598-0
ISBN-10: 1-4039-7598-1

Library of Congress Cataloging-in-Publication Data

Frazier, Brad.
    Rorty and Kierkegaard on irony and moral commitment : philosophical and theological connections / Brad Frazier.
        p. cm.
    Includes bibliographical references and index.
    ISBN 1-4039-7598-1 (alk. paper)
        1. Rorty, Richard. 2. Kierkegaard, Søren, 1813-1855. 3. Ethics, Modern. 4. Irony. I. Title.

B945.R524F73 2006
191-dc22   2006040578

A catalogue record for this book is available from the British Library.

Design by Newgen Imaging Systems (P) Ltd., Chennai, India.

First edition: December 2006

10 9 8 7 6 5 4 3 2 1

Printed in the United States of America.

"Remain faithful to the earth"
Friedrich Nietzsche,
Thus Spoke Zarathustra

To Dianne, Timothy, Jonathan, and Anna—
For helping me to be faithful to the earth

CONTENTS

ACKNOWLEDGMENTS

This project began as a doctoral thesis in philosophy at Saint Louis University. My supervisor was Greg Beabout. He was assisted by Eleonore Stump and Richard Dees. I would like to thank Greg, Eleonore, and Richard for their time and energy, their encouragement and support, and their thoughtful and challenging comments and questions on previous drafts of this project. I am deeply grateful to Greg, in particular, for being an exemplary mentor and friend. I also would like to thank Sumner Twiss, Jenny Overton, and Joseph Koterski, S.J., as well as the participants in various conferences at which I have given papers in recent years, for their comments and suggestions on various aspects of this project. Additionally, I am indebted to Emily Leithauser and Amanda Johnson at Palgrave for supporting this project and providing very helpful advice and assistance to me as I completed it. I am grateful as well to Josh Clark, who provided invaluable assistance with the index, and to the administration at Lee University, specifically, Paul Conn and Carolyn Dirksen, for research funding and other institutional support that greatly expedited the completion of this project.

A version of Chapter 2 recently appeared in *Philosophy and Social Criticism*, vol. 32 no. 4 (2006). A version of Chapter 4 was published in *Journal of Religious Ethics*, vol. 32 no. 3 (Winter 2004): 417–447. A version of Chapter 5 was published in *International Philosophical Quarterly*, vol. 44 no. 4 (December 2004): 465–479. I am grateful to these journals and to Sage Publications, Blackwell Publishing, and the Philosophy Documentation Center, respectively, for kind permission to use the material in these articles again here.

Finally, I would like to thank my family—Dianne, Timothy, Jonathan, and Anna—who have sustained and supported me throughout my work on this project and who fill my life with meaning and keep me grounded. I am grateful as well to my parents, Rudell and Betty Frazier, for their abiding love and support. I also have relied deeply on and drew inspiration from certain friends and colleagues during the time in which I was engaged with this project, including

Clay Dishon, Craig Howell, Emerson Powery, Todd Hibbard, Dale Coulter, Barb Searcy, and Michael Fuller, in addition to others. To all of these persons, I owe a profound debt of gratitude for their friendship and support. I have enjoyed, in particular, the many refreshing and invigorating trips that I have taken with my friends and colleagues to the "sea of irony."

BRAD FRAZIER

Introduction

We commonly seek in our lives together a mean between unreflective devotion and hypercritical disengagement. But this mean is elusive. For once we become critically reflective, it is not easy for us to pin down and observe appropriate limits to this activity. When we come to believe that we have overstepped these limits, moreover, we sometimes overreact by lapsing back into uncritical devotion.

One way to describe the critically engaged stance that we desire is to say that a person who takes it successfully combines irony and moral commitment in her life. Yet some philosophers and social commentators allege that irony is incompatible with earnestness. Commenting on the pervasiveness of irony in contemporary American culture and its acidic effects, Jedediah Purdy notes:

> Irony has become our marker of worldliness and maturity. The ironic individual practices a style of speech and behavior that avoids all appearance of naiveté—of naïve devotion, belief, or hope. He subtly protests the inadequacy of the things he says, the gestures he makes, the acts he performs. By the inflection of his voice, the expression of his face, and the motion of his body, he signals that he is aware of all the ways in which he may be thought silly or jejune, and that he might even think so himself. His wariness becomes a mistrust of language itself. He disowns his own words.[1]
>
> Today the attitude that we all encounter and must come to terms with is the ironist's. . . . Autonomous by virtue of his detachment, disloyal in a manner too vague to be mistaken for treachery, he is matchless in discerning the surfaces whose creature he is. The point of irony is a quiet refusal to believe in the depth of relationships, the sincerity of motivation, or the truth of speech—especially earnest speech.[2]

Purdy believes, then, that irony undercuts authenticity and commitment. It is a short step from this observation to the conclusion that it is unsuitable for those who are committed to fragile, moral goods.

Purdy has a philosophical counterpart in Alasdair MacIntyre. MacIntyre rejects irony on the grounds that it is an impediment to moral commitment. Some ironists defend themselves by pointing out our need for some critical distance from our commitments. MacIntyre retorts:

> If and insofar as it is necessary, in order to take up an adequately critical attitude, to disengage ourselves from our relationships and commitments and to view them with a cold and sceptical eye, then at that point we will have distanced ourselves from our commitments in a way that may always endanger those commitments. It follows that, even if there is a time for criticism, there are also times when criticism has to be put aside and to negotiate the relationship between these successfully itself requires the exercise of the virtues and a further recognition of our need for the virtues. But neither time is a time for irony.[3]

So irony, as MacIntyre understands it, is associated with a kind of critical disengagement that is inimical to commitments and relationships that hold together human communities. In that case, we should not characterize the mean that we seek between overcritical detachment and naïve loyalty as a complex stance that combines irony and moral commitment. For, on this view, irony and moral commitment are irreconcilable.

MacIntyre specifically has in view Richard Rorty's account of irony.[4] Rorty sketches his position, which he refers to as "liberal irony," in *Contingency, Irony, and Solidarity*, an eloquent and provocative work that continues to receive widespread attention.[5] MacIntyre is not alone in his negative assessment of Rorty's position. Thomas McCarthy, Jean Bethke Elshtain, James Conant, and Simon Critchley, in addition to others, take it to be plagued by a kind of breezy, moral laxity. Richard Bernstein goes so far as to suggest that Rorty's nod to the power of redescription closely parallels the perspective of the corrupt politicians involved in the Watergate scandal.[6] Elshtain alleges that to embrace certain implications of Rorty's position is to make oneself morally loathsome.[7] Suffice it to say that Rorty's position has generated considerable moral indignation among not a few of his peers.

I find this response to Rorty problematic. If we carefully and patiently analyze his position, it turns out not to be nearly as morally objectionable as most of his critics suggest. Furthermore, there are features of Rorty's position that are very insightful and suggestive, such as his account of redescription and its relation to self-creation, for instance. These often are lost sight of in the wake of the moral exasperation vented by Rorty's harshest critics. Some philosophers, such as MacIntyre, go so far as to reject irony altogether, moreover, on the basis of their critique of Rorty's account of irony. Apparently they conflate Rortian irony and irony *simpliciter*. But this move is a mistake no matter what one thinks of Rorty's position. For other accounts of irony and moral commitment are worthy of consideration.

I hope to show that Søren Kierkegaard offers us one such account. Kierkegaard extensively examines irony in his first major work, *The Concept of Irony with Continual Reference to Socrates*, and then returns to it explicitly in his most important pseudonymous work, *Concluding Unscientific Postscript to "Philosophical Fragments."*[8] A key concept in Kierkegaard's account is mastered irony. This sort of irony is irony that is employed within the boundaries of moral commitment in order to promote ethical life. According to Kierkegaard, it brings refreshment, critical insight, consistency, and vigor to ethical existence.

Purdy himself takes a position analogous to Kierkegaard's and more thoughtful than MacIntyre's when he states:

> However, there is another kind of irony, which discovers a different sort of unexpected significance. It uncovers, in what is ordinarily imagined to be unimportant or banal, something that elicits surprise, delight, and reverence. What it uncovers is richer than what the rebellion against reality produces; above all it is real. This irony is ecstatic, in the etymologically strict sense of drawing us out of our stasis. It is the irony of discovery. It moves us.[9]

Purdy's critique of a morally enervating sort of irony also closely parallels Kierkegaard's position. For before Kierkegaard posits mastered irony as an essential element in an ethical way of life, he sharply critiques unbridled, withering irony, which he characterizes as "infinite absolute negativity." Kierkegaard takes this sort of irony to be self-destructive and deeply harmful to human community.

Whether or not Rorty's position is morally lax, it is very difficult to level this charge at Kierkegaard's account of irony and moral commitment. Since critics of Rorty have seized on the moral implications of his account as their main reason for rejecting it, they at least should consider Kierkegaard's position, not to mention other interesting accounts of irony, before they dispatch with irony altogether.

My suggestion that Kierkegaard's position is worthy of careful consideration is not based on a lack of appreciation for Rorty's position. On the contrary, I take Rorty's liberal irony to be much more resourceful, insightful, and suggestive than Rorty's critics tend to recognize. Still, I find Kierkegaard's account to be more incisive and comprehensive and less objectionable than Rorty's position. Kierkegaard gets to the core of irony and reveals its vital developmental and ethical functions. There is no reason, however, why we cannot capture and appropriate the best insights of Kierkegaard and Rorty. That is what I attempt to do in my reflections.

The structure of my project is as follows. In chapter one, I explicate Rorty's account of liberal irony as he first sketches it in *Contingency*. I also attempt to remove surface-level obstacles in Rorty's preliminary account so that it may receive a full and fair treatment. In chapter two, I carefully consider Rorty's account of redescription. Not a little of the moral outrage directed at Rorty derives from this specific feature of it. I argue that most of this criticism turns on a misconstrual of a key claim that Rorty advances in regard to the power of redescription. Nevertheless, some problems remain for Rorty because he does not take full account of the implications of his endorsement of truthfulness. In chapter three, I offer an explication and analysis of Rorty's account of self-creation. I find this Nietzschean element in Rorty's position very suggestive but also problematic and in need of qualification. I argue that Rorty recognizes this problem and suggests important modifications of Nietzsche's view of self-creation, as he understands and commends it.

In chapter four, I explain, clarify, and offer several assessments of Kierkegaard's critique of pure irony as he advances it in *The Concept of Irony*. This chapter lays the groundwork for the claim that Kierkegaard is well aware of the volatility and potentially destructive nature of uncontrolled irony. Indeed, his critical analysis is as extensive and incisive as any contemporary analysis of which I am aware. In chapter five, I turn to Kierkegaard's account of mastered irony. In order to clarify and commend Kierkegaard's position, I attempt to elucidate a very suggestive analogy that he proposes between artists who gainfully employ mastered irony in their work and individuals who utilize this kind of irony to great effect in their ethical strivings. I also unpack four illuminating metaphors that Kierkegaard uses to convey the benefits of mastered irony. In chapter six, I examine the discussion of irony and moral commitment that Kierkegaard offers in *Postscript* under the guise of Johannes Climacus. Although I argue that some of Climacus's views represent a regression in Kierkegaard's thought, I also find that Climacus's position helpfully clarifies and extends certain features of the account of irony and moral commitment that Kierkegaard first presents in his thesis. In chapter seven, I conclude by offering some comparisons between Rorty's and Kierkegaard's positions. I focus especially on the different ways in which Rorty and

Kierkegaard construe irony and the stance of a person who masters irony, that is, an ethical ironist. Although a Rortian ironist's recognition of contingency is an important insight, I argue that Rortian irony is parochialized to some extent on account of Rorty's preoccupation with debunking metaphysics and epistemology. Still, his treatment of irony is much preferable to MacIntyre's hasty dismissal of it. Given certain crucial qualifications, however, I find that Kierkegaard's position is more tenable as it is more probing, disclosive, and has wider appeal. I conclude by suggesting that we look to Kierkegaard and Rorty for insight about how to understand and overcome the seemingly irreconcilable dualism of irony and moral commitment.

CHAPTER 1

Richard Rorty's Liberal Irony

Richard Rorty's account of liberal irony is one of the most prominent but also most controversial treatments of irony in contemporary philosophy. I am concerned in this chapter with explicating and clarifying Rorty's position as he first presents it in *Contingency*. After providing a preliminary introduction to Rorty's position, I proceed in four steps. First, I elucidate Rorty's understanding of contingency and its relation to irony. Second, I discuss the close relation in Rorty's thought between irony and self-creation. This aspect of Rorty's position cannot be adequately clarified apart from a discussion of Rorty's interesting and provocative concept of redescription. So after I discuss in a preliminary way the relation between irony and self-creation in Rorty's account, I turn then to an explication of redescription, as Rorty understands it, and its relation to irony and self-creation. Once these components of Rorty's account are in place, I discuss the other-regarding side of his position, that is, his commitment to and understanding of liberalism. I conclude by briefly reviewing key points in Rorty's account and by noting problems that I will address in subsequent chapters.

1.1 Rortian Irony: A Preliminary Sketch

Rorty construes irony as a stance adopted toward "final vocabularies." In regard to these, Rorty states:

> All human beings carry about a set of words which they employ to justify their actions, their beliefs, and their lives. These are the words in which we formulate praise of our friends and contempt for our enemies, our long-term projects, our deepest self-doubts and our highest hopes. They are the words in which we tell, sometimes prospectively and sometimes retrospectively, the story of our lives.[1]

So, for Rorty, the words that a person employs to form a conception of herself, others, and the world constitute her final vocabulary. The most fundamental questions she asks about her life and the lives of others will be expressed in the terms of this vocabulary and so also the answers that she comes to accept. Furthermore, as the concept is employed by Rorty, a vocabulary is final if, in addition to its having the characteristics described above, the one who employs it would have no "noncircular argumentative recourse" if she were pressed for a justification for her vocabulary.[2] So a vocabulary is final in Rorty's sense if (a) it contains the words one utilizes to understand, evaluate, and explain one's own actions, beliefs, and way of life, and the actions, beliefs, and lives of others, and (b) there is nothing—no vocabulary or set of words or concepts—more ultimate to which one can appeal in a noncircular manner in order to underwrite or justify the vocabulary.

Rorty also distinguishes between "thick" and "thin" terms in a final vocabulary. He notes:

> A small part of a final vocabulary is made up of thin, flexible, and ubiquitous terms such as "true," "good," "right," and "beautiful." The larger part contains thicker, more rigid, and more parochial terms, for example, "Christ," "England," "professional standards," "decency," "kindness," "the Revolution," "the Church," "progressive," "rigorous," "creative." The more parochial terms do most of the work.[3]

Thick terms in a person's final vocabulary thus are fairly precise and less portable from local practices and cultures to others than are thin terms. Also, thick terms do more work in our final vocabularies in that we employ them more frequently in the tasks described above. So, for instance, when a person defines herself, she utilizes thick terms in her final vocabulary more than thin ones.

If Rortian irony then is a kind of stance one takes toward final vocabularies, as briefly described above, what sort of stance is it? According to Rorty, an "ironist" fulfills three conditions:

> (1) She has radical and continuing doubts about the final vocabulary she currently uses, because she has been impressed by other vocabularies, vocabularies taken as final by people or books she has encountered; (2) she realizes that argument phrased in her present vocabulary can neither underwrite nor dissolve these doubts; (3) insofar as she philosophizes about her situation, she does not think that her vocabulary is closer to reality than others, that it is in touch with a power not herself.[4]

Among the characteristics that a Rortian ironist is said to have here, her radical and continuing doubts about her final vocabulary stand out as most conspicuous. For a person could believe that she is in touch with a power not herself, whether it is God, reality, goodness, or something like this, without thinking that her language is adequate for describing this power or is itself in touch with this power. Such a person could also believe that she is unable through recourse to arguments phrased in her present vocabulary to assuage the doubts of others and perhaps even her own doubts regarding the existence and nature of this power. She might even be impressed with the views of others who doubt the existence of this power with which she takes herself to be in touch. Yet for all this she might not have radical and continuing doubts about her final vocabulary. So although a full-fledged Rortian ironist fulfills all three conditions listed above, even at this preliminary point we can locate a weaker sense of being such an ironist. A person who meets all the conditions listed except that she fails to have radical and continuing doubts about her final vocabulary merely exhibits what Gary Gutting refers to as *epistemic* ironism. She has simply an antifoundationalist, or more generally, an antiepistemological attitude.[5] An ironist who also has radical and continuing doubts about her final vocabulary has additional concerns that a mere epistemic ironist might not share.

Rortian ironists also hold to a fairly strong thesis about the power of redescription. They believe, as Rorty puts it, that "anything can be made to look good or bad by being redescribed."[6] Of course, no one desires that her most basic values and the things that give her life meaning be redescribed in such a way that they appear bad, evil, or repulsive. Rorty notes, however, that his ironists do not deplore or regret the fact that redescription has this power. Rather, they respond to their recognition of the power of redescription with a sense of liberation on account of their believing that redescription can be employed in the production of novel and interesting forms of self-creation. For Rorty's ironists, redescription is a powerful tool for getting out from under stultifying final vocabularies.

Rortian ironists also are nominalists and historicists.[7] What these commitments amount to, for Rortian ironists, is captured by Michele M. Moody-Adams, who notes:

> The historicism involves, among other things, accepting the contingent origins of even one's most important beliefs, plans, and preferences, while the nominalism requires jettisoning the notion that in order to be fully human a person must conform to some antecedently given pattern of plans, preferences, and beliefs.[8]

A Rortian ironist's historicism leads her to think that it is futile for human beings to attempt to climb outside of their own practices and historical context in order to see the world *sub specie aeternitatis*. Her nominalism refers to her antiessentialism. Rorty explains this feature of his sort of ironist this way: "She thinks that the occurrence of a term like 'just' or 'scientific' or 'rational' in the final vocabulary of the day is no reason to think that Socratic inquiry into the essence of justice or rationality will take one much beyond the language games of one's time."[9] This belief, in turn, leads Rortian ironists to dismiss attempts to formulate criteria of choice between final vocabularies.[10]

Finally, Rortian ironists are characterized by a kind of light-mindedness. They are never quite able to take themselves completely seriously, Rorty suggests, because they are struck by the fact that the terms in which they describe, understand, and evaluate their own lives and the lives of others are mutable, contingent, and fragile.[11]

1.2 IRONY AND CONTINGENCY

As Rorty construes irony, it has a very close relation to recognizing and coming to terms with contingency. In the introduction to *Contingency*, Rorty states that an ironist is "the sort of person who faces up to the contingency of his or her own most central beliefs and desires."[12] When Rorty introduces the ironist in the middle section of *Contingency*, moreover, he notes that she will "take naturally" to the line of thought concerning the contingency of language and the human self that he has developed in the first part of *Contingency*. So we can clarify Rortian irony by clarifying what is involved, for Rorty, in facing up to contingency.

Before we can understand more clearly what facing up to contingency involves, however, we need an account of Rorty's conception of contingency. What exactly does Rorty mean when he claims that ironists face up to the *contingency* of their most central beliefs and desires? On a common meaning of contingency, according to which something is contingent if it can be or fail to be, Rorty's claim merely means that ironists face up to the fact that their most central beliefs and desires might have been very different and could be revised substantially in the future. Indeed, since ironists might not have existed, they might not have had beliefs and desires.

There is something right about this way of interpreting Rorty's claim.[13] Rorty certainly agrees that human beliefs and desires are contingent in this respect. Consider, for instance, how many of our current beliefs and desires might have been very different. We might have had very different experiences; we might have lived in a different culture, at another time, inhabiting a different language, with different parents, children, and friends, and in a society influenced by different religions. Perhaps these observations are enough to give us pause about the extent to which our current final vocabularies, and thus our self-conceptions, might have been different and are out of our own control in certain respects. Rorty intends to claim much more than this, however, when he claims that his ironists *face up* to the contingency of their deepest beliefs and desires, for it is difficult to see why any thoughtful person would *not* face up to the contingency, in this sense, of even her most central beliefs and desires. So we have not yet uncovered an important distinction between being merely a reflective person and a Rortian ironist. But surely there is one.

We begin to uncover a controversial thesis about contingency to which Rortian ironists are committed when we consider what is involved, for Rorty, in *not* facing up to contingency. If we fail to come to terms with the contingency of even our most central beliefs and desires, what have we done, in Rorty's view? We get a preliminary answer from Rorty to this question in the context of his discussion of the "strong poet" or maker, a figure who is contrasted with persons who fail to come to terms fully with contingency. Rorty states:

> Only poets, Nietzsche suspected, can truly appreciate contingency. The rest of us are doomed to remain philosophers, to insist that there is really only one true lading-list, one true description of the human situation, one universal context of our lives. We are doomed to spend our conscious lives trying to escape from contingency rather than, like the strong poet, acknowledging and appropriating contingency.[14]

We can gather from these claims that, for Rorty, contingency is to be contrasted not only with necessity but also with universality. For instance, when Rorty claims that human nature is contingent, he does not mean merely that human beings might have failed to exist and have a rather fragile existence while they exist. He also intends to claim that there is no universal human nature, no single true description of "the human situation."[15] So facing up to the contingency of one's beliefs and desires involves accepting that one's beliefs and desires are features of one's own local historical epoch and that there are no beliefs and desires that all human beings share *qua* human.[16]

This interpretation is borne out by other remarks Rorty advances in the same context about the "strong maker." Rorty explains:

> The strong maker, the person who uses words as they have never before been used, is best able to appreciate her own contingency. For she can see, more clearly than the continuity-seeking historian, critic, or philosopher, that her *language* is as contingent as her parents or her historical epoch.[17]

The "continuity-seeking historian, critic, or philosopher" to whom Rorty refers, is a person who seeks for universal features in human history, language, or the human condition. Rorty contrasts this sort of person with persons (strong makers) who see more clearly and appreciate their own contingency. The contingency of language, to which Rorty refers, concerns not just the contingency of the actual words of a language, but the concepts (Rorty calls these "metaphors") one uses to understand and evaluate oneself, others, and the world. So Rorty intends to convey that the strong maker appreciates the contingency of final vocabularies as well as the contingency of the words and phonemes of human languages. Since self and world conceptions are learned and expressed in the terms of final vocabularies, Rorty also intends that these things are contingent, that is, not necessary and not universal. We are invited to believe that local historical and cultural factors that could have been otherwise cause us to have the final vocabularies that we inherit.

Rorty contrasts ironists and metaphysicians in a way that closely parallels his distinction between strong makers and continuity-seeking thinkers. This contrast also helps him to elaborate the claim that recognizing contingency involves recognizing the local, nonuniversal quality of our most cherished beliefs and deeply seated desires. As Rorty explains:

> The metaphysician is someone who takes the question "What is the intrinsic nature of (e.g., justice, science, knowledge, Being, faith, morality, philosophy)?" at face value. He assumes that the presence of a term in his own final vocabulary ensures that it refers to something which *has* a real essence. The metaphysician is still attached to common sense, in that he does not question the platitudes which encapsulate the use of a given final vocabulary, and in particular the platitude which says there is a single permanent reality to be found behind the many temporary appearances. He does not redescribe but, rather, analyzes old descriptions with the help of other old descriptions.[18]

The metaphysician's basic blunder, according to Rorty, is that he thinks that terms in his final vocabulary track with real essences that transcend his local time and place. Rorty suggests that this problem derives from the metaphysician's failing to come to terms with the sheer contingency of his final vocabulary, especially the metaphors within it that suggest to him that he has grasped certain universal features of human existence.

Rorty also claims that metaphysicians continue to be attached to common sense. This feature of a metaphysician contrasts sharply with an ironist's attitude toward common sense. As Rorty explains:

> The opposite of irony is common sense. For that is the watchword of those who unselfconsciously describe everything important in terms of the final vocabulary to which they and those around them are habituated. To be commonsensical is to take for granted that statements formulated in that final vocabulary suffice to describe and judge the beliefs, actions and lives of those who employ alternative vocabularies.[19]

So just as Rorty's ironist will "take naturally" to his defense of contingency, the metaphysician will recoil from it, since he interprets Rorty's line of reasoning about contingency as an attack on common sense. This contrast between the metaphysician and the ironist helps us begin to clarify the connection between contingency and irony in Rorty's account.

A Rortian ironist displays a certain kind of light-minded attitude toward final vocabularies, especially her own, which owes to her nominalism and historicism and her appreciation of the power of redescription. Furthermore, she displays a facing-up-to-contingency attitude that contrasts sharply with the attitude of metaphysicians, who, as Rorty construes them, are anything but light-minded about final vocabularies, especially their own. Metaphysicians continue to talk about and argue for universal features of human existence.[20] Rorty suggests that they must overcome this tendency in order to come to terms fully with contingency.

One might conclude from this sketch that, for Rorty, a person merely needs to become sufficiently nominalist and historicist in order to face up to contingency. But there is a difference between merely recognizing contingency and facing up to it. The latter involves being aware of the deeper implications of contingency and embracing them. Rorty thinks that persons can recognize contingency and yet fail to become ironists by failing to follow out and come to terms fully with the implications of this insight. He makes this point in his brief discussion of a liberal utopia. In Rorty's utopia, nominalism and historicism would be part of common sense just as atheism and agnosticism now are acceptable common sense positions, even if they are somewhat variant forms of common sense thinking. As he explains:

> In the ideal liberal society, the intellectuals would still be ironists, although the nonintellectuals would not. The latter would, however, be

commonsensically nominalist and historicist. So they would see themselves as contingent through and through, without feeling any particular doubts about the contingencies they happened to be. . . . They would be commonsensical nonmetaphysicians, in the way in which more and more people in the rich democracies have been commonsensical nontheists. . . .

But even if I am right in thinking that a liberal culture whose public rhetoric is nominalist and historicist is both possible and desirable, I cannot go on to claim that there could or ought to be a culture whose public rhetoric is *ironist.* . . . Ironists have to have something to have doubts about, something from which to be alienated.[21]

Notice that nonintellectuals in Rorty's utopia recognize contingency but are not subsequently plagued by radical and continuing doubts about their final vocabularies. Ironists, however, still suffer from these doubts even in Rorty's utopia. The reason is that ironists have to have something from which to be alienated, something about which to have doubts. Perhaps ironists are alienated from the liberal final vocabulary dominant in their utopian culture. In this utopia, intellectuals and nonintellectuals would be liberals without believing that they have noncircular philosophical foundations for their liberalism. They would not believe, moreover, that liberalism is the right political theory in the sense that it best promotes the realization of human nature, even though they might believe that liberalism is best for promoting the flourishing of persons like themselves. Yet something about this situation bothers ironists in Rorty's liberal utopia. Perhaps they doubt the utility of liberalism or have doubts about the various ways of life that are underwritten by liberalism in their utopia. What these lingering doubts could be will be discussed in more detail below.

So when Rorty refers to the various contingencies of human existence or even the set of contingencies that human beings, *are* he has in mind not merely the lack of necessity of human language, human concepts, and human beliefs and desires, but also the local and finely contextualized quality of these things. Furthermore, Rorty suggests that there is a very close connection between being an ironist and coming to terms with these various and thoroughgoing contingencies of human life.[22] The connection is this: Rortian ironists do not flinch when it comes to facing up to contingency. They accept the fragility and mutability of their most central beliefs and desires. This acceptance gives rise to a kind of liberating light-mindedness toward their final vocabularies. But they are not distinguished from other intellectuals and nonintellectuals simply by their acceptance of the various contingencies of human existence. For Rorty believes that nonironists can accept contingency by becoming nominalists and historicists. Rather, ironists are distinguished from other nominalists and historicists by their radical and continuing doubts about their own final vocabularies. Perhaps these doubts indicate the *degree* to which they recognize and embrace contingency and are alienated.

Thus far I have focused mainly on the antiepistemological and antimetaphysical features of Rortian irony.[23] I fear that, as a result, at this preliminary point it may not be at all clear why reflective and morally serious persons would want to be Rortian ironists. After all, what is attractive about a life characterized by doubt and alienation? Based on what we have seen thus far, moreover, one might suspect that a Rortian ironist could not avoid having a cavalier attitude toward morality. Also, it is still unclear what we are to make of the radical and continuing doubts of Rortian ironists about their final vocabularies. I will address these concerns in the next two sections by developing the aesthetic and ethical components of Rortian irony.

1.3   IRONY AND SELF-CREATION

The sketch of Rorty's views on contingency above suggests that facing up to the various contingencies of human existence is a bracing and sobering task. But Rorty thinks it also is liberating. In fact, he suggests that we think of freedom as "the recognition of contingency."[24] What does this claim about freedom mean?

It is not difficult to misconstrue what Rorty has in mind. A natural interpretation of Rorty's claim about freedom is that, in order to act freely or to be a free agent, one must believe that the circumstances in which one acts are contingent in some respect. When this reading, in turn, is set in the context of current philosophical debates about free will, it quickly translates into the idea that we must have or at least believe that we have the ability to do otherwise with respect to any given choice in order for that choice to be a free choice. Or it may suggest that there has to be real indeterminacy in the world or that we have to believe in indeterminacy, in order to act freely. These possible extrapolations, however, are far from Rorty's mind. He never even so much as hints or subtly intimates that he intends his view of freedom to be understood in this metaphysical way. So, we have to be careful about how we interpret Rorty's claim that we think of freedom as the recognition of contingency.

We have observed that, for Rorty, the ironist fully recognizes her contingency. If freedom is the recognition of contingency in some sense, it stands to reason that the ironist is free or freer than persons who do not recognize contingency to the extent that she does. So we may get a clearer picture of how Rorty conceives of freedom by observing his reflections on the nature of the ironist. This turns out to be a helpful strategy. Rorty characterizes the ironist's existence as a struggle for self-creation through the recognition of contingency.[25] Consequently, for Rorty, freedom is or is closely related to self-creation.

Rorty's discussion of self-creation is one of the most interesting and suggestive features of *Contingency*. He claims that our self-conceptions are initially given to us through the final vocabularies that we inherit. The task of self-creation thus becomes, for Rorty, the task of getting out from under inherited vocabularies by forging one's own terms for describing, understanding, and evaluating oneself and others.[26] The final vocabularies that we inherit and, to a lesser extent, other final vocabularies that we encounter constitute the raw materials out of which we compose these new terms. What exactly does all of this have to do with recognizing contingency? The answer is this: recognizing the contingency of final vocabularies, especially the final vocabulary that one has inherited, leads a person to see that it is not necessary and inevitable that she understand herself and others just in the terms that have been given to her by her culture, parents, and ancestors. A person who has this realization awakens to the possibility of becoming an individual, someone who to some extent gives her life its own particular character, who exerts some amount of control over her life.[27] As Rorty states, in regard to such a person:

> He is trying to get out from under inherited contingencies and make his own contingencies, get out from under an old final vocabulary and fashion one which will be all his own. . . .
>
> The generic task of the ironist is the one Coleridge recommended to the great and original poet: to create the taste by which he will be judged. But the judge the ironist has in mind is himself. He wants to be able to sum up his life in his own terms.[28]

In a related discussion of Nietzsche, Rorty adds:

> He hoped that once we realized that Plato's "true world" was just a fable, we would seek consolation, at the moment of death, not in having transcended the animal condition but in being that peculiar sort of animal who, by describing himself in his own terms, had created himself. More exactly, he would have created the only part of himself that mattered by constructing his own mind. To create one's mind is to create one's own language, rather than to let the length of one's mind be set by the language other human beings have left behind.[29]

Rorty sums up this line of reasoning by suggesting that we view self-knowledge as self-creation.[30] In other words, when we see that the terms in which we understand ourselves are contingent and revisable, then we are more able and more inclined to undertake the process of becoming new selves through modifying, revising, and expanding these terms. So, for Rorty, the recognition of contingency is closely linked to the likelihood, if not the possibility, of novel self-creation. That is why he suggests that we construe freedom as the recognition of contingency.

Whether or not we accept Rorty's conception of freedom, perhaps we now are in a better position to understand in part why Rorty is attracted to irony. A Rortian ironist clearly perceives and fully embraces the contingency of her final vocabulary. The upshot of this, we now see, is that she experiences greater freedom and individuality. This freedom derives from her coming to take the final vocabulary she has inherited lightly enough that she is able to get out from under it by constructing out of it and other final vocabularies that she encounters her own terms for understanding and evaluating herself, others, and the world. Consequently, an ironist experiences greater freedom *from* inherited vocabularies, which may be stifling, and freedom *for* experimentation with new ways of conceiving herself, others, and the world.

Still it is possible that an ironist's inherited final vocabulary and her limited experience with other final vocabularies will not provide her with enough suitable raw materials for the construction of a new final vocabulary that adequately promotes her project of self-creation. Furthermore, she may fear that she has been so thoroughly socialized into her inherited final vocabulary that she will never really get out from under it, no matter how much she attempts to do so. Persons who turn away from the religious traditions into which they were socialized sometimes experience this kind of doubt, whether they turn to other religious traditions or away from religion altogether. Suppose, though, that our exemplary Rortian ironist is able to get out from under the final vocabulary that she inherited and construct what she takes to be her own terms for understanding herself and others. She still might continue to worry that her new final vocabulary will turn out to be someone else's or a hodgepodge of terms that she has borrowed heteronomously, that is, without any significant alteration or refinement that makes this vocabulary her own in some important respect.

I think that Rorty has these kinds of doubts in mind when he states:

> The ironist spends her time worrying about the possibility that she has been initiated into the wrong tribe, taught to play the wrong language

game. She worries that the process of socialization which turned her into a human being by giving her a language may have given her the wrong language, and so turned her into the wrong kind of human being.[31]

We have to be careful about how we interpret the phrases "the wrong kind of human being" and "wrong language game" in this passage. Clearly Rorty does not intend to suggest by these phrases that his ironists worry that they have inherited a conception of human nature that fails to correspond to the way human nature *really* is and thus are unable fully to realize their humanity. Nor does he intend that ironists worry about whether they have inherited a language that fails to carve reality at its joints. Their thoroughgoing nominalism precludes this reading. An ironist's doubts primarily are not doubts about the *falsity* of her current final vocabulary. Rather, they are doubts about the *adequacy* of her current final vocabulary for her own projects of self-creation. So to say that she worries about becoming the wrong kind of human being as a result of inhabiting the wrong language game is to say that she is concerned that she is living her life on someone else's terms, with a self and world conception that leads her to miss out on novel and interesting possibilities for self-creation.[32]

Gutting offers a similar reading of Rorty on this point. He states:

> We are bound to wonder what could possibly be the source of the ironist's doubts. . . . Unless the ironist slips back into ethical objectivism, what sense is there to the worry that her final vocabulary is "wrong"? As final, it expresses what, all things considered, she really does value. The "worry" Rorty evokes makes sense only on the assumption of an ethical objectivism that he has firmly repudiated.
>
> The reaction of Rorty's ironist to the diversity of final vocabularies is, despite his misleading language, better construed as a matter of aesthetic fascination than of ethical worry. The ironist constantly seeks intellectual and aesthetic stimulation, the challenging of old vocabularies for describing ourselves and the formation of new descriptions that take account of more and more perspectives. The "worry" then is that the ironist's contingent perspective at a given time will cause her to miss something new and exciting, not that her perspective is wrong.[33]

There certainly is a strong aesthetic component to the ironist's quest for self-creation, as Gutting implies. Her intractable concerns are about missing out on novel and aesthetically pleasing forms of self-creation, not about her perspective's failing to capture objective criteria for human flourishing.

Yet it does not follow from this that an ironist's doubts are not at all ethical doubts. There remains a sense in which her doubts are ethical concerns.[34] Rorty sometimes refers to the ironist's self-creative struggle as a struggle for autonomy,[35] and as involving attention to a "duty to self."[36] He does not demur from the commonly held view that autonomy is an ethical good. Therefore, he takes the pursuit of autonomy to be an ethical project. Rorty also conceives of his ironist's struggle for self-creation as a struggle for self-realization and perfection. As he explains:

> The older Hegel became a name for such a vocabulary, and Kierkegaard and Nietzsche have become names for others. . . . We treat the names of such people as the names of the heroes of their own books. . . . We do not care whether these writers managed to live up to their own self-images. What we want to know is whether to adopt those images—to recreate ourselves, in whole or in part, in these people's image. We go about answering this question by experimenting with the vocabularies which these people concocted. We redescribe ourselves, our situation, our past, in those terms and compare the results with alternative redescriptions which use the vocabularies of alternative figures. We ironists hope, by this continual redescription, to make the best selves for ourselves that we can. . . . Ironists read literary critics, and take them as moral advisers, simply because such critics have an exceptionally large range of acquaintance. . . . They have read more books and are thus in a better position not to get trapped in the vocabulary of any single book.[37]

Here Rorty construes projects of self-creation as attempts at self-perfection. The good of self-perfection is not merely an aesthetic good. Formally speaking, it also is a moral good. Furthermore, in the same context Rorty adds that ironists read literary critics in order to gain insights for their efforts at self-creation. In this capacity, such critics serve as moral advisers. In another passage, Rorty refers to autonomy as a "criterion of private perfection."[38] He also explicitly identifies the pursuit of autonomy with "ethical considerations which arise from, for example, one's attachment to a particular person, or one's idiosyncratic attempt to create oneself anew."[39]

Consequently, Rorty's own understanding of his position is that his ironist's worries are aesthetic *and* ethical concerns.[40] We too take quests for autonomy and self-perfection to be ethical quests, at least in a formal sense. So, I do not think that we should reduce an ironist's doubts to just aesthetic worries, as Gutting suggests.[41] Nevertheless, this tweaking of Gutting's reading is minor. Even on Rorty's own view of his position, the main ethical component of an ironist's stance is not her quest for personal autonomy but her commitment to liberalism. Furthermore, as Rorty recognizes, there are obvious difficulties with the view that self-creation, as he construes it, is an ethical project. What about persons who believe that their own projects of self-creation have nothing to do with meeting ethical duties to others or to certain others? These persons might refuse to conceptualize their projects of self-creation in this way in an attempt to get out from under certain final vocabularies.

Clearly, projects of self-creation can be solipsistic and destructive of social goods. Even when self-creative projects are not antisocial, for many persons such projects are not easily reconcilable with the pursuit of other ethical goods. Rorty recognizes and even accentuates this problem of reconciling the good of self-creation with other goods that are more robustly ethical. In the context of introducing the positions that he advances in *Contingency*, he states, "This book tries to show how things look if we drop the demand for a theory which unifies the public and private, and are content to treat the demands of self-creation and of human solidarity as equally valid, yet forever incommensurable."[42] In a subsequent passage, he adds:

> Metaphysicians like Plato and Marx thought they could show that once philosophical theory had led us from appearance to reality we would be in a better position to be useful to our fellow human beings. They both hoped that the private-public split, the distinction between duty to self and duty to others, could be overcome. Marxism has been the envy of all later intellectual movements because it seemed, for a moment, to show how to synthesize self-creation and social responsibility, pagan heroism and Christian love, the detachment of the contemplative with the fervor of the revolutionary.
>
> On my account of ironist culture, such opposites can be combined in a life but not synthesized in a theory.[43]

These passages show that Rorty recognizes the difficulty of reconciling self-creation and other ethical goods, such as solidarity. The second passage contains an important additional point. In Rorty's view, some persons may be able to unify in their lives or in a practical way their struggle for self-creation and their social responsibilities. So, on Rorty's view, autonomy and solidarity will not be reconciled at the level of theory despite the best attempts of metaphysicians since Plato. But they may be practically reconcilable.

I take all of this to imply that an ironist's doubts about the adequacy of her final vocabulary for her pursuit of autonomy *are* ethical in a formal sense and *could be* ethical in more than a formal sense. To the extent that an ironist is able to harmonize in her life her pursuit of autonomy and her commitment to solidarity, to that extent her doubts about her final vocabulary become ethical doubts in more than a merely formal sense. In other words, if the autonomous person an ironist seeks to become is also a person who is committed to and promotes solidarity—if that is, in fact, how she pursues autonomy—then her worries about not being able to become autonomous are also worries about not being able to be committed to and promotive of solidarity. In that case, they clearly are ethical concerns in more than a formal sense.

But why does Rorty hold such a dim view of the prospects of reconciling goods associated with autonomy and social goods? Why is self-creation so difficult to square with solidarity? A full answer to this question would take us well beyond the purview of this chapter. We can attain a partial answer by exploring our final topics of this chapter: self-creation and redescription and irony and liberalism.

1.4   SELF-CREATION AND REDESCRIPTION

If someone were to ask Rorty what the main way is by which one comes to recognize the contingency of the final vocabulary she has inherited, or what primary tool an ironist utilizes in her attempts at self-creation, it is likely that Rorty would give the following answer. Encountering suggestive, provocative, and reorienting redescriptions of one's current final vocabulary is a main way in which one comes to see the contingency of that vocabulary; and the imaginative employment of redescription is the primary tool employed by ironists in their quests for autonomy. But what is redescription anyhow? Furthermore, why does getting clear on the nature of redescription help to illuminate the difficulty of reconciling self-creation and solidarity?

As I noted above, for Rorty, someone who employs redescription in the pursuit of self-creation is attempting to use a different final vocabulary than her current one to redescribe herself, her situation, and her past in a way that will help her see these things in a very different light. Someone who more passively succumbs to a redescription of her current perspective offered by another person gains a similar reorientation. In both cases, Rorty suggests, redescription is closely related to the formation of a new self in the sense that such a person comes to reject or revise certain beliefs, desires, and projects that had formed the core of her identity and acquires new identity-conferring beliefs, desires, and commitments.[44]

Consider, for instance, a married woman who has inherited an oppressive final vocabulary according to which the role of being a good wife carries with it the expectation that she submit to and even obey her husband. Suppose further that her husband exploits this conception of the social role of being a good wife by being abusive and demanding. Then she encounters other women, some of whom are married, who do not have this conception of wifehood and being female as part of their final vocabularies. These persons eventually strike her as much happier persons and as having much better marriages, if they are married. These experiences may lead her to question her understanding of being a good wife. She may also come to question the other features of her final vocabulary that lend credence to this notion, as she experiments with thinking of her life and social roles in other terms borrowed from the persons she encounters who have different final vocabularies.[45] It is not hard to imagine how her relationship to her husband might dramatically change as a result and how she may come to experience self-respect and expect respect from others in ways that had never occurred to her before she began to question her understanding of wifehood and what it is to be a woman. She then may become a different person with a different conception of the future self she aspires to be.

Admittedly this is a contrived and oversimplified example. Still, it helps to clarify what redescription is and how it may lead to substantial revisions in a person's self-conception. These revisions, in turn, help persons to become novel selves as they gain critical distance from stifling conceptions of social roles.

Rorty's discussion of Proust helps to clarify a bit more what he takes redescription to be and its relation to self-creation. Rorty admires Proust not only for his considerable literary ability and imagination, which Proust utilized in his own quest for autonomy, but also because Proust never lost sight of the contingency of all human descriptions, including his own. For these reasons, Proust stands out for Rorty as an exemplary ironist, a master of redescription in the service of self-creation. As Rorty explains:

> Proust, too, was interested in power, but not in finding somebody larger than himself to incarnate or to celebrate. All he wanted was to get out from under finite powers by making their finitude evident. He did not want to befriend power nor to be in a position to empower others, but simply to free himself from the descriptions of himself offered by the people he had met. He wanted not to be merely the person these other people thought they knew him to be, not to be frozen in the frame of a photograph shot from another person's perspective. . . . His method of

freeing himself from these people—of becoming autonomous—was to redescribe the people who had described him. He drew sketches of them from lots of different perspectives—and in particular from lots of different positions in time—and thus made clear that none of these people occupied a privileged standpoint. Proust became autonomous by explaining to himself why the others were not authorities, but simply fellow contingencies. . . .

At the end of his life and his novel, by showing what time had done to these other people, Proust showed what he had done with the time he had. He had written a book, and thus created a self—the author of that book—which these people could not have predicted or even envisaged. He had become as much of an authority on the people whom he knew as his younger self had feared they might be an authority on him. This feat enabled him to relinquish the very idea of authority, and with it the idea that there is a privileged perspective from which he, or anyone else, is to be described. . . .

Proust temporalized and finitized the authority figures he had met by seeing them as creatures of contingent circumstance. . . . He mastered contingency by recognizing it, and thus freed himself from the fear that the contingencies he had encountered were more than just contingencies. He turned other people from his judges into his fellow sufferers, and thus succeeded in creating the taste by which he judged himself.[46]

I find Rorty's description of Proust's employment of redescription suggestive and illuminating. In Rorty's reading of Proust, Proust utilized redescription mostly in his attempts to overcome the descriptions of himself offered by his friends and acquaintances. He wanted to be more and other than the sum total of what he was according to their descriptions of him. Proust found these descriptions limiting, oppressive, and stultifying. Through redescription he gained a kind of leverage over and against them that allowed him to create for himself a novel self.

As an analogue consider the common experiences of children in relation to their parents. Our parents provide most of the content of our initial self-understanding. As we become adults, we attempt to understand ourselves in other ways. Some persons reject in a wholesale way, others in a piecemeal fashion, the selves their parents take them to be and expect them to become. Not infrequently this process begins to occur when they encounter persons, in books, film, or in life, who in some way suggest to them a different self-conception. As a result they enlarge their thinking about who they are and could become. Perhaps these points are trite commonplaces of developmental psychology. Still, it is illuminating to take this way of becoming an individual to be a process of struggling to achieve autonomy through *redescription*.

Why this is so becomes clearer when we contrast redescription with other methods for promoting changes in self and world conceptions that foster autonomy. Rorty offers us one such contrast in the context of explicating a distinction between ironists and metaphysicians. He states:

> The metaphysician thinks that there is an overriding intellectual duty to present arguments for one's controversial views—arguments which will start from relatively uncontroversial premises. The ironist thinks that such arguments—logical arguments—are all very well in their way, and useful as expository devices, but in the end not much more than ways of getting people to change their practices without admitting they have done so. The ironist's preferred form of argument is dialectical in the sense that she takes the unit of persuasion to be a vocabulary rather than a proposition. Her method is redescription rather than inference. . . . An ironist hopes that by the time she has finished using old words in new senses, not to mention introducing brand-new words, people will no longer ask questions phrased in the old words.[47]

Rorty touches on several points here that clarify his notion of redescription. First, it is to be distinguished from logical argument, which proceeds on the basis of inference. Second, redescription has a deflationary effect, at least as Rortian ironists employ it. It is supposed to help us get over certain recurring problems that plague our old vocabularies not by solving these problems but by dissolving them as we take up new perspectives or new patterns of thought and speech. Third, that which is bandied about between interlocutors from contrasting perspectives is not a proposition, such as "God exists," for instance, but a vocabulary. I take Rorty to mean by this that redescription does its change-inducing work primarily at the level of final vocabularies. For instance, suppose redescription is involved in a crucial way in a person's conversion to atheism. As Rorty sees it, the role it plays in such a case is not to help one decide the logical coherence and plausibility of propositions for and against the existence of God. Rather, it is employed, in this case, to cast theism in a negative light and atheism in a superior and more attractive light. Of course, the question immediately arises: what makes one final vocabulary superior to or more attractive than another? Rorty's answer thus far seems to be that as long as both vocabularies are coherent, the one that promotes more novel and interesting forms of self-creation is superior. But then we might well wonder how this response could help, since what will count as novel and interesting is apt to be relative to each particular user of a final vocabulary. A person who is socialized in a strict and dull religious home might find an atheistic final vocabulary riveting when she encounters it. On the other hand, someone who is socialized into a sour and depressing form of atheism might find certain theistic final vocabularies inviting and inspiring when she encounters them. We might have hoped for more help than this in evaluating competing vocabularies.

Rorty recognizes and embraces to some extent these limitations. He states "although the thoroughgoing ironist can use the notion of a 'better description,' he has no criterion for the application of this term and so cannot use the notion of 'the right description.' "[48] One might wonder how a Rortian ironist can use the notion of a "wrong language game" or "wrong kind of human being" if she has no use for the idea of a "right description." On a charitable reading, however, the discrepancy here may only be apparent. Rorty can make use of a "better description" because "better" can consistently mean "more productive of novel and interesting forms of self-creation." But he cannot make use of a strong sense of "the right description" precisely because of the relativity across persons of what counts as novel and interesting. As Rorty puts this point in the same context, "what counts as resolution, perfection, and autonomy will always be a function of when one happens to die or go mad. But this relativity does not entail futility."[49]

Whether or not Rorty is right about this last claim, we now are in a position to understand more clearly why he thinks it is very difficult to reconcile the pursuit of self-creation with solidarity. Simply stated, there is no blueprint or script for self-creation that implies that one has to care about human solidarity in order to become fully realized or autonomous. For some persons these pursuits will coincide. There is no reason to think, however, in Rorty's view, that this happy convergence is anything but a quirk of a person's idiosyncratic background. Even a Platonist may concur with Rorty that the convergence of the quest for autonomy and commitment to solidarity, when it occurs in a human life, is a serendipitous bit of moral luck. Rorty's claim is more radical, though. He suggests that when these pursuits do converge, there is no reason, other than perhaps a practical one that is relative to a person's unique history, to think that this convergence is better than a lack of convergence or is something we ought to go to great lengths to impose on our lives. Whether a person's commitment to solidarity helps her become an autonomous person depends on the contingent circumstances of her own life.

Rorty is bothered by the thought that his position appears to endorse and promote cruelty. This problem arises for him in the following way. He rejects the idea that there is a normative account of human nature that makes it the case that human beings need to commit themselves to solidarity and not cruelty in order to lead interesting and autonomous lives. Furthermore, by Rorty's own admission, redescription, a main tool of the ironist in her struggle for self-creation, can be very cruel. As Rorty explains:

> Ironism . . . results from awareness of the power of redescription. But most people do not want to be redescribed. They want to be taken on their own terms—taken seriously just as they are and just as they talk. The ironist tells them that the language they speak is up for grabs by her and her kind. There is something potentially very cruel about that claim. For the best way to cause people long-lasting pain is to humiliate them by making the things that seemed most important to them look futile, obsolete, and powerless. Consider what happens when a child's precious possessions—the little things around which he weaves fantasies that make him a little different from all other children—are redescribed as "trash," and thrown away. Or consider what happens when these possessions are made to look ridiculous alongside the possessions of another, richer, child. . . . The redescribing ironist, by threatening one's final vocabulary, and thus one's ability to make sense of oneself in one's own terms rather than hers, suggests that one's self and one's world are futile, obsolete, *powerless*. Redescription often humiliates.[50]

By Rorty's own admission, then, redescription sometimes is very cruel. Yet it is a primary tool for the task of self-creation. This threatens to be a significant problem. If Rorty's position implied that cruel redescriptions are not apt to facilitate self-creation, then he would have a straightforward way out of this problem. He has no recourse to this sort of response, however. Consequently, it might appear that he has nothing to say to persons who commit themselves to projects of self-creation that involve cruelty.

Rorty offers two lines of response to this problem. The second line of response is much more involved than the first. I take it up in the next section. The first line of response can be summarized as follows. Redescription is not a specific or distinguishing mark of the ironist. It is "a generic trait of the intellectual."[51] Therefore, intellectuals in general have to deal with the problem of cruelty as they employ the tool of redescription. Ironists in particular arouse special resentment because they cannot consistently say that their redescriptions of others reveal their true selves or "the real nature of a common public world which the speaker and the interlocutor share."[52] So ironists, unlike other intellectuals, cannot promise those persons whose lives and commitments are redescribed that they thereby are empowered or put in touch with a deeper or greater reality. Rorty concludes that "what the ironist is being blamed for is not an inclination to humiliate but an inability to empower."[53]

When Rorty's position, in turn, is criticized on these grounds, he simply bites the bullet, so to speak. An ironist, unlike a metaphysician, cannot promise others that when they are redescribed possibly they are empowered, if the redescription corresponds to reality. Rorty does not think that this is a damning concession, however. He thinks that a metaphysician's promise to empower ultimately is empty. Also, he thinks that there is another basis for human solidarity that an ironist can accept and commend and that this alternative ground for solidarity is adequate. As he explains:

> The ironist thinks that the *only* redescriptions which serve liberal purposes are those which answer the question "What humiliates?" whereas the metaphysician also wants to answer the question "Why should I avoid humiliating?" The liberal metaphysician wants our *wish to be kind* to be bolstered by an argument, one which entails a self-redescription which will highlight a common human essence, an essence which is something more than our shared ability to suffer humiliation. The liberal ironist just wants our *chances of being kind*, of avoiding the humiliation of others, to be expanded by redescription. She thinks that recognition of a common susceptibility to humiliation is the *only* social bond that is needed. Whereas the metaphysician takes the morally relevant feature of the other human beings to be their relation to a larger shared power—rationality, God, truth, or history, for example—the ironist takes the morally relevant definition of a person, a moral subject, to be "something that can be humiliated." Her sense of human solidarity is based on a sense of a common danger, not on a common possession or a shared power.[54]

So Rorty argues that as long as an ironist shares a sense of danger and fear of humiliation with those she redescribes, she has reason to care about solidarity with them and avoid redescriptions that undermine it. A philosophical account that demonstrates in a non-circular way why we should not humiliate other persons is both unnecessary and not forthcoming, according to Rorty. Consequently, the fact that an ironist does not have recourse to such an account to motivate her commitment to solidarity with others does not indicate a damning or distinctive weakness in her position.

This last move still does not resolve the problem that there does not appear to be a reason for a Rortian ironist to care about human solidarity in circumstances where she can get along in her pursuit of autonomy while ignoring or even undermining solidarity. Even if human solidarity can be rooted in a perception of common danger, what is to stop an ironist from being as cruel as she wants to be in her redescriptions so long as these help her achieve autonomy and do not isolate her so much that she is unable to take advantage of the benefits of living among persons who share a stronger commitment to solidarity?

The lingering problem we have come up against here arises in part from attempting to locate an ethical component in Rortian irony mainly in the ethical value of autonomy, as Rorty understands it. One might think that Rorty has left himself in a position where he has little to say to reign in ironists who are fond of cruel redescriptions except to remind them that they too can be humiliated and that they also need the help of other persons in order to survive and flourish. Is this enough?

1.5　Irony and Liberalism

We are precisely at the juncture where Rorty introduces the more substantive ethical component of his account of irony. Ironists, as Rorty constructs and commends them, are not *mere* ironists. They are *liberal* ironists. The liberalism in their stance is supposed to provide the moral backbone that Rorty's account needs in order to be more responsive to the concerns raised above. The complexity of this component of Rorty's account, to which I alluded above, does not arise from Rorty's conception of liberalism. He follows Judith Shklar in construing liberalism roughly as the idea that "cruelty is the worst thing we do."[55] Rather, the complexity derives from Rorty's positing a "firm" distinction between the public and private in the final vocabulary, concerns, and life of his ironist.[56] What exactly does Rorty have in mind?

On a first pass, Rorty's introduction of a split between the private and public is to be understood as a division between redescription for private and for public purposes.[57] As Rorty explains:

> For my private purposes, I may redescribe you and everybody else in terms which have nothing to do with my attitude toward your actual or possible suffering. My private purposes, and the part of my final vocabulary which is not relevant to my public actions, are none of your business. But as I am a liberal, the part of my final vocabulary which is relevant to such actions requires me to become aware of all the various ways in which other human beings whom I might act upon can be

humiliated. So the liberal ironist needs as much imaginative acquaintance with alternative final vocabularies as possible, not just for her own edification, but in order to understand the actual and possible humiliation of the people who use these alternative final vocabularies.[58]

The private–public distinction therefore provides a way for Rorty to handle the potentially cruel redescriptions an ironist might offer. She is not to engage publicly in cruel redescriptions, since as a liberal she is committed to the idea that treating others cruelly is the worst thing she could do to them. In private, she can dissect and deconstruct the commitments and vocabularies of others as much as she wants, so long as this activity does not lead her to act cruelly. Furthermore, the ironist's penchant for imaginatively experimenting with other final vocabularies can serve her public commitment to liberalism insofar as it enables her to recognize more clearly the various ways in which others can be humiliated.

This last claim captures Rorty's thinking at one of the moments in which he tends toward the view that irony and liberalism are made for each other in certain respects. According to Nancy Fraser, this is the second of three distinct moments in Rorty's thinking regarding the distinction between public and private or the relation between liberalism and irony.[59] Fraser takes Rorty to move back and forth among perspectives where he characterizes the relation between irony and liberalism as: (a) antagonistic, (b) a relation between "natural partners," and (c) a "partition" relation, which seems to be Rorty's considered position.[60] The first category represents Rorty at his most pessimistic moments in his reflections on reconciling liberalism and ironism. The textual support Fraser cites as revealing this moment in Rorty's thought concerns his admission that ironists cannot be "progressive and dynamic" liberals since they "cannot offer the same sort of social hope as metaphysicians offer."[61] Rorty has in mind that ironists cannot promise that persons will become more autonomous as they become more committed to human solidarity. The second, "natural partners," moment in Rorty's thought is evident in the passage quoted above, according to which the ironist's inclination to experiment with alternative final vocabularies actually enhances her ability to recognize the various ways in which others can be humiliated. The third moment, the partition view, represents, according to Fraser, Rorty's coming to terms with the fact that he cannot bring himself to abandon either irony or liberalism even though they are largely incompatible. So, they simply have to coexist with each other without any sort of overall synthesis.[62]

Fraser's analysis helps to isolate certain tensions in Rorty's position regarding the relation between irony and liberalism. It is not difficult, however, to overstate these tensions and make too much of the differences among the perspectives in Rorty's thought that give rise to these tensions. Fraser provides little evidence for the claim that Rorty ever holds an entirely pessimistic attitude about the possibility of reconciling irony and liberalism, self-creation and solidarity. More important, the notion of reconciliation is ambiguous, as we have seen. It could refer either to theoretical or practical reconciliation. This ambiguity may explain away or significantly reduce the apparently strong tensions and double-mindedness in Rorty's account, to which Fraser alludes.

As we have seen, Rorty consistently rejects the idea that goods associated with autonomy and self-creation can be *theoretically* reconciled with the goods of solidarity. Furthermore, he consistently affirms the view that these goods may be reconciled *in a person's life*, if that person's idiosyncratic background predisposes the person to such reconciliation. That Rorty maintains both of these claims but focuses on one and then the other in his writings might explain why there appear to be moments when he is rather pessimistic about reconciling irony and liberalism and moments when he is quite optimistic about this. In the former moments, perhaps he has in view theoretical reconciliation. In the latter, he may have in mind the possibility that some persons, due to their peculiar histories, might not find it very difficult to reconcile their projects of self-creation and their commitment to human solidarity. In that case, Rorty's partition view is his *general* account of how ironists are to reconcile self-creation and solidarity, whatever their peculiar backgrounds happen to be. As a liberal, an ironist has to oppose cruelty and commit herself to solidarity, as she works out her own salvation or struggles to create herself as a new, autonomous self. Her liberalism refers to her public attitude of opposition to cruelty and commitment to solidarity. Her ironism refers to her abiding interest in self-creation, redescription, and the complex attitude she takes toward her own and other final vocabularies. If this interpretation is correct, an ironist has to privatize her ironic side to the extent that its public display would be cruel and undermining of human solidarity.

In his defense of Rorty, Gutting suggests a similar reading:

> Almost any action, no matter how apparently private, can and often does have social consequences. But Rorty's distinction between the private and public spheres need not deny this. Its point requires merely

that we be able, in practice, to separate actions that do not pose a serious threat to the freedom of others from those that do.[63]

This point is helpful as far as it goes. Rorty's private–public distinction also requires us, however, to be able to separate in practice actions that are cruel from those that are not, so that the former can be avoided as much as possible.[64] An action that might not pose a serious threat to another's freedom might be very cruel, nonetheless. A liberal ironist would not be a very committed liberal, if she routinely countenanced such actions.

Still, one might wonder why an ironist would be a committed liberal. If ironists face up to the contingency of human language and human selves, then to be consistent they have to face up to the contingency of their commitment to liberalism as well. Could a person be firmly committed to liberalism in such circumstances? One might think that such a person would constantly have to hold out the possibility of sheering off her liberal commitments in case she were to find a more interesting, autonomy-promoting vocabulary. Furthermore, even if she never finally rejects liberal principles, the fact that she holds them in this tentative way might appear to nullify the claim that she is *committed* to liberalism. When we view the tension between irony and liberalism from this angle, it suggests that Rorty's introduction of liberalism as a component in the final vocabulary of an ironist renders the ironist's position unstable.

Rorty anticipates this problem. His response turns on the claim that one can be fully committed to principles that one takes to be contingent. In fact, Rorty claims that this idea is a fundamental premise of *Contingency*.[65] As he explains, "a belief can still regulate action, can still be thought worth dying for, among people who are quite aware that this belief is caused by nothing deeper than contingent historical circumstance."[66] Rorty also approvingly refers to Joseph Schumpeter's idea that standing unflinchingly for one's convictions while acknowledging their relative validity "is what distinguishes a civilized man from a barbarian."[67] From Rorty's perspective, the notion of absolute validity is unhelpful, especially in sorting out significant differences among various ethical and political convictions. He thinks it would only have purchase if we were able to attain a standpoint "outside the particular historically conditioned and temporary vocabulary we are presently using."[68] Since we are unable to escape our own historicity in this respect, we have to settle for relative validity. But once we recognize this limitation, for Rorty, there is no longer any point to the alleged problem of a person's standing firmly for beliefs that she takes to have merely relative validity. As he states:

> We should learn to brush aside questions like "How do you *know* that freedom is the chief goal of social organization?" in the same way as we brush aside questions like "How do you *know* that Jones is worthy of your friendship?" . . . We should see allegiance to social institutions as no more matters for justification by reference to familiar, commonly accepted premises—but also as no more arbitrary—than choices of friends or heroes. Such choices are not made by reference to criteria. They cannot be preceded by presuppositionless critical reflection, conducted in no particular language and outside of any particular historical context.[69]

Notice how Rorty addresses the issue of an ironist's commitment to contingent convictions. I take Rorty's response to be that there are no beliefs, certainly no nontrivial ones, that are not contingent. So the problem is not an ironist's commitment to *liberalism* so much as it is her commitment to *any* ideals, since all her convictions are contingent. Once the problem is stated this way Rorty's response appears less evasive. In effect, he suggests that in a certain respect we simply *find* ourselves with the various allegiances we have to social institutions and the values that support them. We have to start where we are, with the convictions that we have.[70] So the question, why do we have convictions? or more specifically, how could ironists have basic moral convictions? is somewhat uninteresting to Rorty, at least as a question about the validity of these convictions and not their idiosyncratic origins.[71] He thinks we cannot get behind our convictions and discover a primordial choice, according to certain objective criteria, to have them. The same is true with respect to the more specific issue of how ironists manage to be liberals. As Rorty argues:

> We cannot assume that liberals ought to be able to rise above the contingencies of history and see the kind of individual freedom which the modern liberal state offers its citizens as just one more value. Nor can we assume that the rational thing to do is to place such freedom alongside other candidates . . . and then use "reason" to scrutinize these various candidates and discover which, if any, are "morally privileged." Only the assumption that there is some such standpoint to which we might rise gives sense to the question, "If one's convictions are only relatively valid, why stand for them unflinchingly?"[72]

Thus, Rorty's ironists have basic liberal commitments mainly because they find themselves with these commitments and they cannot escape the conclusion that it is good to have them.

If this reading is correct, it shows that Rorty has a thoughtful response to those who claim that ironists cannot be committed to liberalism because they perceive the contingency of their liberal convictions. Liberal ironists simply find themselves with their liberal convictions, presumably even after reflecting about why they should keep them. It is not as if they could ascend to an ahistorical perspective, moreover, in order to assess the validity of their beliefs. So what else can they do except stand for their convictions, if these beliefs seem right to them? The fact that their convictions are contingent and only relatively valid is no reason to abandon them. If it were, it would be a reason not to have any convictions at all. But that is not a possible human life.

This response raises a serious problem, however. Rorty does not intend to rule out the possibility of an ironist's being able to doubt and even to rid herself of some of the views socialized into her, even those convictions that are deeply ingrained. If Rorty's position did rule out these things, it would be incoherent. Furthermore, in Rorty's view, for a person to become autonomous it appears that she must substantially revise the final vocabulary that she inherits, whatever its content happens to be. It is not the *content* of her final vocabulary that makes her autonomous, after all. It is her getting out from under this inherited final vocabulary. But what if she inherits a liberal final vocabulary? Rorty has to say that she is able, if she is an ironist, to get out from under this vocabulary, at least to some extent. So, to the extent that she pursues autonomy through self-creation, it seems that she must substantially revise or set aside her inherited liberal convictions. To the extent that she remains committed to the liberal final vocabulary she has inherited, she fails to achieve autonomy. Oddly, it appears that, in Rorty's view, those who inherit a *liberal* final vocabulary are the only ones excluded from being full-fledged liberal ironists. That would imply that his main audience consists of those persons who are least able to aspire to the position that he advances. I will explore this difficulty and possible responses to it in chapter 3.

1.6 Conclusion

Irony, as Rorty construes it, is a complex attitude that one takes toward one's own final vocabulary and the final vocabularies of others. This attitude is characterized by antifoundationalism, respect for the explanatory and transformative power of redescription, a kind of light-mindedness, but also persistent doubts about the adequacy of one's final vocabulary for projects of self-creation. Furthermore, ironists not only recognize but also face up to the sheer contingency of human practices, beliefs, and desires, and human life in general.

For Rorty, recognizing and facing up to contingency greatly enhances one's chances for freedom, where freedom is understood as novel self-creation. Consequently, one main attraction of irony is that it promotes a good that many persons desire, the good of novel self-creation or autonomy.

The primary way in which we come to see the contingency of human final vocabularies is through redescription. Therefore, redescription promotes novel self-creation. But redescription can be cruel, as Rorty concedes. So what is to prevent an ironist from being very cruel to others in order to enhance her chances for self-creation? Rorty's answer is that a common sense of danger, in particular a common aversion to humiliation, binds together ironists and those persons whose most cherished beliefs, desires, and practices ironists seek to redescribe. For Rorty, this bond implies a commitment to liberalism. For a commitment to liberalism, as he construes it, is a commitment to avoid cruelty as "the worst thing we do." So Rorty's ironists are *liberal* ironists because they have an aversion to cruelty that is as basic as their desire for novel self-creation. This aversion leads them, in turn, to relegate cruel redescriptions to their own private quests for autonomy. In that way, even though an ironist's pursuit of self-creation does not necessarily involve her in the promotion of human solidarity, according to Rorty, it does not have to involve her in cruelty, as long as she observes a private–public split in her employment of redescription. In Rorty's view, unless a person's unique personal history predisposes her to unify her quest for autonomy and promotion of human solidarity, she will have to settle for this sort of compromise, if she values both goods.

There is much that is attractive about Rorty's liberal irony. The tolerance, sense of finitude, openness, and light-mindedness of liberal ironists make them well suited for life in a pluralistic, liberal democracy. Furthermore, there is something quite powerful and appealing about redescription, which Rorty manages to capture, most clearly perhaps in his illuminating discussion of Proust. Rorty's success in this area owes to his appreciation for the good of novel self-creation, an enthusiasm that he conveys with subtlety.

I have tried to display clearly and sympathetically the nuances and eccentricities of Rorty's position while also addressing some of the potential difficulties with it. Not a few of these difficulties are merely apparent difficulties, as we have observed. Reading Rorty somewhat closely and patiently allows us to dispatch with these surface-level problems. Other difficulties, however, are more difficult to handle. We need a subtler analysis of Rorty's position in order to determine whether they are intractable problems.

For starters, there is the problem that persons who have inherited a liberal vocabulary appear to be the least promising candidates for liberal irony, insofar as they need to get out from under their inherited liberalism in order to pursue novel self-creation. At the same time, they are supposed to remain committed liberals. It is not clear that this project is coherent. If it is not, then the vast majority of persons that compose Rorty's audience cannot coherently adopt his position. This problem seems ultimately to derive from Rorty's defining autonomy as getting out from under an inherited vocabulary without any regard to the *content* of that vocabulary. Even if this problem generated by Rorty's way of appropriating Nietzsche can be resolved, moreover, another one looms in the same vicinity. Some philosophers argue that Rorty attempts to combine in his ironist two attitudes that simply are incompatible: facing up to contingency and being committed to moral ideals—whether this commitment is to liberalism or some other set of ideals. I have offered a preliminary defense of Rorty's position on this point. But there is much more to say from the critic's perspective and from Rorty's. I clarify and explore these difficulties related to Rorty's views on irony, autonomy, and moral commitment in chapter 3.

Rorty's frequently strident antirealism and his complete rejection of objectivity constitute another potential problem in his position. These features surface in Rorty's persistent invective against metaphysics and metaphysicians and are part of his facing up to contingency program for contemporary philosophy. Some philosophers think that these aspects of Rorty's account render it incoherent, inconsistent, or relativistic (or some combination thereof).[73] Indeed, these antirealist and antiepistemological features of Rorty's position now are notorious in contemporary philosophy. I want to explore, however, features of Rorty's position that have been neglected on account of preoccupation with his antirealist program. Nevertheless, I recognize the prominence of this agenda in Rorty's overall position and the importance of assessing its merits. So, in the first section of chapter 3, I address some of the issues related to Rorty's views on truth and objectivity, albeit very briefly.

Finally, Rorty's claim that ironists recognize that "anything can be made to look good or bad by being redescribed" has generated much controversy. Some philosophers argue that this feature of liberal irony reveals its deep moral laxity. They and others are dubious as well about Rorty's attempt to privatize redescriptions that are cruel. I now turn to these controversial features of Rorty's account of redescription and the criticisms that have been leveled against them.

CHAPTER 2

The Ethics of Rortian Redescription

Rorty's claim that anything can be made to look good or bad by being redescribed is at the center of a number of prominent criticisms of his account of liberal irony. Rorty's critics point to this feature of his position as a clear marker of his nonchalant attitude toward morality. I think that not a little of this moral outrage is unwarranted because it turns on inattentive and dismissive interpretations of Rorty's position. These readings are avoidable and do not capture what he intends. So in this chapter I attempt to clarify the precise meaning of Rorty's claim and explain why the criticisms raised against Rorty, which center around this claim, miss their mark. I argue that, when it is properly construed, the claim that anything can be made to look good or bad by being redescribed does not express a flippant attitude toward morality. Rather, for Rorty, it is related to the possibility of self-creation through redescription, the promotion of tolerance and imaginative identification with others, and the morality of conflict.

One of the criticisms leveled against Rorty is that his exaggerated appreciation for the power of redescription belies a lack of concern for truthfulness. In recent clarifications and modifications of his proposed private–public distinction, Rorty emphatically denies this charge and endorses truthfulness as a central virtue in liberal societies. This implies that liberal ironists, if they are to count as good liberals, will need to be committed not only to opposition to cruelty but also to truthfulness. This implication is in some tension with the impression that Rorty gives in *Contingency* that the redescriptions ironists use privately for self-creation have no relation to their obligations to others other than whatever relation is suggested by their opposition to cruelty. An ironist's commitment to truthfulness places additional important constraints on her employment of redescription that Rorty has yet to acknowledge. So while I do not concur with some common criticisms of Rorty's account of redescription, which construe it as morally lax and even outrageous in some respects, I do think that Rorty needs to sort out more the implications of his avowed commitment to truthfulness for his account of redescription. In the latter part of this chapter, I try to justify this claim. My analysis of the relation between truthfulness and redescription leads me to suggest that Rorty should drop altogether the metaphor of *place* from his positing of a private–public split in the lives of his ironists. Instead he should adopt the alternative notion of "responsibilities to self" and "responsibilities to others," which he sometimes uses, as a permanent replacement for this metaphor. This idea of dual responsibilities better captures Rorty's considered views about his private–public split.

2.1 SELF-CREATION, REDESCRIPTION, AND RORTY'S "ANYTHING CLAIM"

Liberal ironists fundamentally desire to be novel selves. So they want to relate autonomously to their inherited vocabularies. For Rorty, this implies that they will be engaged in projects of getting out from under these vocabularies. What exactly is required for achieving this goal is an interesting and somewhat vexing question for Rorty. I address it in the next chapter. Here I begin with the observation that, in the hands of an ironist, redescription is the engine of self-creation. When persons employ it proficiently, they are better able to shed inherited vocabularies and pursue autonomy, as Rorty understands it. One reason for this, according to Rorty, is that good redescriptions help to reveal the sheer contingency of our concepts and perspectives. Once a person recognizes the contingency of her inherited final vocabulary and other final vocabularies, she is more inclined to experiment with different descriptions or conceptions of herself and others and alternative ways of life. If a person's inherited final vocabulary cannot be made to look bad to her, however, or other final vocabularies cannot be made to look good or better to her, it is unlikely that she will attempt to revise the vocabulary that she has inherited, no matter what she believes about its supposed contingency. Consequently, for Rorty, to pursue autonomy through the employment of redescription minimally requires either that one be able to countenance redescriptions of one's inherited vocabulary that make it look bad or descriptions of alternative vocabularies that make these vocabularies look better.

Rorty does not isolate this minimal condition for the pursuit of autonomy and distinguish it carefully from a broader, more controversial claim about ironists and redescription, that is, that ironists recognize that anything, including any vocabulary, can be made to look good or bad by being redescribed. Perhaps that is why some of his critics have misconstrued the precise meaning and significance of this claim.

For simplicity's sake, I will refer to this claim as Rorty's "anything claim" (AC). AC is somewhat ambiguous. One might think that the point of it is that *any person* could view *anything* as good or bad in the presence of a sufficiently positive and sympathetic or negative and unsympathetic redescription of the thing in question. An alternative reading takes the scope of this claim to be limited merely to *any ironist*. I will refer to these possible interpretations of AC as the strong and weak versions of it, respectively.

Michele M. Moody-Adams, a sharp critic of Rorty, alludes to this ambiguity in AC when she states:

> At times the ironist's thesis seems to be principally about the uses of redescription: human beings, Rorty contends, have at their disposal certain "instruments"—including philosophy and poetry—that "can be turned to any and every purpose." This is an uncontroversial observation, whatever one might make of Rorty's insistence, principally against Plato, that philosophy is used as such an "instrument" just as often as poetry. . . .
>
> On occasion, however, the ironist thesis appears to be something quite different from a claim about the uses of redescription. Sometimes that thesis appears to be an empirical psychological claim about how redescriptions affect those who contemplate them. The ironist, in fact, is *defined* in part as someone so "impressed" by other people's final vocabularies that he doubts the merits of his own. Yet construed as an empirical claim—an inductive projection about how things will "look" to any human being—the thesis is undermined by readily available evidence. Few victims of human wrongdoing would be "impressed" by favorable descriptions of that suffering. To return to Rorty's example, for most surviving victims of Hitler or Stalin the notion that to *them* "anything" might be made to "look good" would be sheer anathema.[1]

Moody-Adams argues here that the strong version of AC, which Rorty appears to endorse on occasion, in her view, clearly is false. Human beings obviously have limits in regard to what they can view as good and what they can view as bad, no matter what redescriptions they encounter. The weak version, furthermore, implies that ironists are incredibly insensitive to victims, especially those who have suffered horrific evils. Their unusual susceptibility to redescription is indicative of a deep moral flaw in their characters. For instance, while they ought to be decidedly repulsed by the bloodthirsty regimes of Hitler and

Stalin, instead, Moody-Adams argues, by dint of their irony they are able to be wowed by sympathetic redescriptions of them. On this reading, a Rortian ironist is a prime target for propaganda.

We can immediately dispatch the strong version of AC. Rorty nowhere implies or even subtly intimates that anything can be made to look good or bad *to any human being*, particularly any victim, by being redescribed. As I explain below, he concurs with Moody-Adams that this claim is psychologically absurd.

In regard to the weak version of AC, the first thing to note is that it is not a logical implication of Rorty's defining an ironist as someone who is impressed by other people's vocabularies. What is implied by this feature of Rorty's account is that his ironists are impressed by some and perhaps many other final vocabularies. However, liberal ironists too are human beings with commitments. So there will be limits to what they can countenance as good, on the one hand, and bad, on the other. Thus we have reason to doubt both the strong and weak readings of AC.

Nevertheless, Moody-Adams's reading helps to clarify a crucial ambiguity in AC. This ambiguity concerns this question: *to whom exactly* can anything be made to look good or bad by being redescribed? If Rorty's answer is not "to ironists" but is merely "to someone somewhere at some time," then why does he treat AC as if it were an important insight rather than a banal truism? On the other hand, if Rorty does indeed intend to suggest that he and other liberal ironists can view just anything as good or just anything as bad, when under the spell of a sufficiently compelling redescription, then he is placing a severe requirement on himself and other liberal ironists. At this preliminary stage, the options do not look good for Rorty. It appears that AC reduces either to a trivial platitude or a claim with morally reprehensible and psychologically absurd implications.

Before I address this issue in defense of Rorty, I want to develop briefly an analogous line of criticism of AC from Jean Bethke Elshtain, since Rorty's considered views on this point emerge in response to Elshtain. To support her claim that AC is "genuinely troubling— ethically and politically,"[2] Elshtain relays Albert Camus' story of a German officer who, having taken a woman and her three sons as hostages, allows the mother to designate one of her sons as the one whose life will be spared, after the mother has begged for mercy. The woman chooses her eldest son on the grounds that he has a family that depends on him. Elshtain then remarks:

> How might this story be redescribed in order to make it "look good?"
> Rorty, remember, insists on this possibility. I will put this point in

stronger terms: He *requires* this possibility in order to sustain his larger argument about the utter contingency and arbitrariness of our characterizations. So it is something that "just happened" that Europe acquired a habit of using other words, words that promote "don't be cruel." Camus describes a moment of genuine terror. He means to evoke our horror and revulsion. He means to do this to alert us to how dangerous the world is and how necessary it is to sustain an ethical-political stance that limits the damage.

Were I to suggest that Camus' story is but one way of describing something that could be as easily described in an alternative way designed to make it look good, I would make myself loathsome; I would become a ravager.[3]

Like Moody-Adams, Elshtain's understanding of AC leads her to raise moral objections to it. She also alludes to a horrific evil to make her point. The crux of Elshtain's complaint against Rorty seems clear enough: to say that Camus' soldier's behavior could be redescribed in such a way that it appears good is to evince a profound moral blindness. Or worse, for someone like Rorty, who should know better, to say such a thing is silly and irresponsible at best, reprehensible at worst. Yet, according to Elshtain, Rorty's position commits him to saying this because it is part of his facing-up-to-contingency project. Furthermore, unlike Moody-Adams's critique, Elshtain's criticisms do not seem to turn crucially on either the strong or weak reading of AC. For Elshtain, the mere fact that liberal ironists believe that horrific evils, for instance, can be redescribed so that they look good is anathema.

What is so objectionable about the liberal ironist's position? I detect three distinct criticisms in Elshtain's remarks, which are not easy to disentangle. The first criticism is aimed at a view that underlies AC, on Elshtain's reading of it, namely, that our most basic moral judgments and sentiments ultimately are arbitrary.[4] Elshtain intimates that there is something psychologically dubious about the view that we could simultaneously (a) believe that our sense of moral repulsion and outrage in the presence of certain actions and events ultimately is arbitrary and (b) be morally repulsed and outraged by these actions and events just the same. She also suggests that if we did manage to view our deepest moral sentiments and convictions this way, in a sense we would betray them.

Second, Elshtain takes issue with the related idea that one could *easily* describe horrific evils in alternative ways that make them appear good. Apparently Elshtain takes Rorty to hold that the contingency of our most basic moral commitments and sentiments is closely related to their malleability, which is evidenced by the ease with which compelling, alternative descriptions of horrific evils can be generated. The relations among these ideas of contingency, malleability, and ease of redescription are not entirely clear, however. My hunch is that Elshtain takes Rorty to reason as follows: the horrific evil Camus describes must be able to be redescribed in such a way that it appears good, *since* our moral commitments and sentiments ultimately are arbitrary and contingent. For if human beings in general were unable to redescribe certain horrific evils in such a way that they appear good, this fact would imply that there is something necessary, or noncontingent and nonarbitrary, about the particular moral commitments and sentiments that prevent us from being susceptible to alternative redescriptions of horrific evils.

Elshtain's third criticism, as intimated above, is that simply to suggest that horrific evils could be redescribed in such a way as to make them appear good is somehow to make oneself "loathsome." This objection differs from the first and second objections for the following reasons. The objection is not merely that constructing a compelling sympathetic redescription of horrific evils is *not easy* and to think that it is easy is to make oneself loathsome. After all, if this captured the entire force of the objection, then Rorty could simply grant that such redescriptions are not easy but are possible for imaginative persons, nonetheless. Rorty could consistently maintain this position regardless of what he thinks about the putative arbitrariness and contingency of our most basic moral convictions. Even in Rorty's view a belief or entire vocabulary can be thoroughly contingent and still be extremely difficult, if not impossible, to set aside. The contingency of a description of some horrific evil *as* a horrific evil, or of the vocabulary within which this description is embedded, does not imply that a compelling, alternative redescription of that evil is easy to construct. It does seem to imply, however, that an alternative description or redescription of that evil is possible. That point itself seems to bother Elshtain quite a bit.

So how does Rorty respond to these objections? Also, how does his response clarify the "to whom?" question in regard to AC to which Moody-Adams leads us? Interestingly, Rorty takes Elshtain to hold that anything can be made to look good or bad *to Rorty* and other ironists, by implication. Rorty seizes the opportunity in his response to point out that this is a misconstrual of AC. He states:

> Saying, as I do, that you can make anything look good (not, obviously, to Elshtain or me—but certainly to yourself and a few select fellow spirits) is just to seize upon the grain of truth in Socrates' claim that

nobody knowingly does evil. Everybody (usually just before doing evil, but if not, then shortly afterward) tries to whip up a story according to which he or she did the right thing, and usually succeeds.[5]

Rorty clearly repudiates here the idea that anything can be made to look good or bad *to him*. So his endorsement of AC does not imply that he and other ironists are able to view anything as good or bad. Rather, he intends partly to convey the idea that persons generally are quite capable of coming up with good explanations for their actions, no matter how evil those actions may appear to be to others. Indeed, Rorty counters Elshtain's claim that to suggest that the actions of the German officer could be redescribed in such a way as to make them appear good is to make oneself loathsome. He not only makes this suggestion. He also constructs his own redescription of the officer's actions. Here is his redescription:

> Suppose that the German officer in question had been, before the war and while a student, a member of one of those little circles of Nietzsche fans—circles that specialized in vaguely sadomasochistic, homoerotic male bonding—which were dotted about the German universities in the 1930s. He and his friends prided themselves on their ability to rise above slave morality. They strove to outdo each other in scorn for the weak, in *Entschlossenheit* and a concomitant contempt for everything stemming from Platonism and Christianity. Home on leave, the officer tells his friends the story of how he broke a Greek mother's heart. He tells it as an episode in the saga of German will gradually cleansing Europe, enforcing its distinction between the pure and noble races and the ignoble and despicable ones. His friends, hearing his story, are envious of the robustness of his moral stance; they secretly wonder if they themselves might not, at the last moment, have succumbed to weakness and sentimentality, might not have heard their own mother's sobs when the Greek mother was faced with her choice. They swear to themselves that, when they return to their posts, they will imitate the good example their friend has set.[6]

Of course, the point of this redescription is not that Rorty himself finds it compelling. Rather, he is trying to show that, contra Elshtain, one need not become loathsome or abandon a moral point of view in order to countenance the possibility that the German officer's actions can be redescribed in such a way that they appear exemplary *to someone*, particularly the German officer himself and his friends. It is not necessary to believe that our most basic moral convictions ultimately are arbitrary and contingent, moreover, to concur with Rorty on this point.

In fact, Rorty does not respond at all to Elshtain's passing critical reference to Europe's "just happening" to acquire the habit of using the words "don't be cruel." I suspect that he does not respond to Elshtain on this point because he considers this issue a *red herring* with regard to assessing AC.[7] Rorty might well believe that anything can be made to look good or bad (*to someone*) by being redescribed and that even our most basic moral commitments and the vocabularies in which they are embedded ultimately are arbitrary and contingent. He also might believe the former because he believes the latter or vice versa. Nevertheless, one could agree with Rorty about AC and yet not believe that our moral convictions are arbitrary and contingent. Or one could believe that our moral convictions ultimately are arbitrary and contingent and yet not subscribe to AC. (Not to mention that one might also embrace contingency but reject arbitrariness.) So we can assess AC without having to settle questions about the ultimate arbitrariness and contingency of moral convictions and the broader vocabularies from which they derive. That is why Rorty simply ignores the arbitrariness issue in his defense of AC.

With regard to Elshtain's second criticism, it is possible that Rorty's redescription of the German officer's actions also is supposed to show that one can suggest that it is easy to redescribe a horrific evil in a way that makes it appear good, without thereby becoming loathsome. The most convincing way to make this suggestion is to provide such a redescription oneself with relative ease while occupying a moral point of view. That is what Rorty manages to do. So, either Rorty's redescription itself stands as a plausible response to Elshtain's second criticism or, as I argued above, Rorty can simply concede that alternative redescriptions of horrific evils are not easy but are possible for imaginative persons. In either case, Rorty has available to him a satisfactory response to this particular criticism.

Now we are in a position to clarify AC. What Rorty and other ironists believe about redescription is this: anything can be made to look good or bad *to someone somewhere* by being redescribed. On a first pass, this claim seems to be extremely trivial. We might also regret that it is true, if it is true. Why would Rorty and other ironists celebrate it as an important insight?

Consider what follows if we reject AC, as Rorty intends it. In that case, we commit ourselves to the view that there is at least one phenomenon that either cannot be made to look good to any person or cannot be made to look bad to any person (who seriously reflects on the phenomenon in question). Rorty thinks that if we adopt this view we will be very tempted to adopt another belief in its train, namely, that *all* or *most* things that strike us as bad cannot be made to look good to anyone and *all* or *most* things that appear good to us cannot be made to look bad. In other words, once we grant that there is at least one phenomenon that cannot be made to look good to anyone, it is a short step from this belief to the view that most things we call evil could not be viewed any other way. We will be tempted as well to think that most things we deem good could not be taken to be bad. But this attitude is apt to make us intolerant, inflexible, dogmatic, and unable imaginatively to identify with others who are very different from us. In addition, it is very dangerous when it becomes the stance of a polis. It is the stuff that fascism is made of, so to speak. Therefore, the rejection of AC is an invitation to a very unhealthy attitude toward our current characterizations or descriptions and those of others.[8]

What would we make of competing descriptions anyhow under these circumstances? If we believe that most things we consider evil could not be viewed any other way, then persons who *seem* to hold alternative descriptions according to which such things are good either (a) are not being truthful with us or (b) are crazy—their actions are unintelligible. Consider again Camus's example of the German officer. Elshtain thinks we are loathsome if we believe that the officer's actions could be made to look good. Rorty responds by giving a redescription according to which the German officer's actions are intelligible because the officer is pursuing what we take to be a horrific evil under the category "good thing to do." Rorty thinks that endorsing AC is linked to being able to make sense of the officer's behavior because he associates disbelief in AC with the view that our current descriptions exhaust the possible ways in which various phenomena can seriously be described.

If we concur with Rorty here, it follows that belief in AC helps to preserve what Robert Adams has called "the morality of conflict." As Adams puts this point, "The possibility of virtues being manifested in the service of the wrong cause is crucial for the morality of conflict. Conflict is dehumanized when we lose the sense that our enemies can be admirable in opposing us, even though we think them wrong."[9] One way that we maintain the sense that our enemies can be admirable is by recognizing that even though certain of their beliefs, desires, and actions may be morally repugnant to us, it is possible for those same things to appear morally right to them. Those who endorse AC, as Rorty construes it, are more likely to come to this recognition.

At the conclusion of his response to Elshtain, Rorty sums up this defense of AC as follows "It is not the smallest advantage of such an ethics that it helps a child realize that, had Lady Luck given him or her the wrong parents in the wrong country at the wrong time, he or she might have been that German officer. Making such ironies vivid is, it seems to me, important for the inculcation of tolerance and sensitivity."[10] The idea expressed here is that recognizing that anything can be made to look good or bad by being redescribed helps us see just how contingent our own beliefs are and, as a result, may lead us to be more tolerant toward those who hold very different, perhaps even repulsive, beliefs. To put the point starkly, Rorty has in mind that we could have been Nazis and we might have executed mothers and their sons, if we had undergone similar patterns of socialization. It is in many respects a matter of sheer luck that we are not Nazis ourselves or tempted to adopt such attitudes. Moreover, other persons could view us in precisely the same light that we now view Nazis. Rorty's hope is that once we understand this, we will be less likely to demonize and be intolerant toward others.

This response emphasizes the possible morally advantageous implications of AC. I do not think that it captures, however, the primary intent of Rorty's endorsement of AC. Rorty simply is pointing out that not only is AC not troubling politically and ethically, as Elshtain avers, but also it has genuine and perhaps unanticipated benefits for political and ethical life. Rorty's main interest in AC, though, has to do with its relation to self-creation. In his view, we may very well diminish our chances for novel self-creation if we reject it. We will not be inclined to examine our current vocabulary in any wholesale way if we believe that our current descriptions could not be unseated by competing descriptions. The rejection of AC tempts us to this belief. In that case, we will not attempt to get out from under our current vocabulary, even if it is not our own in any important sense. We also will be unlikely to revise it in less wholesale ways. Persons who are locked into their current beliefs, desires, and projects in this way are not likely to be or become novel selves.

If these lines of defense are on the right track, then AC is neither trivial nor regrettable. But one might argue in response that persons such as Rorty who embrace AC display outrageous insensitivity to those who *suffer* horrific and lesser evils, even if they are more tolerant than others toward the *perpetrators* of such evils. After all, if one is going to be guilty of being insensitive or intolerant, it is far better to err on the side of being insensitive or intolerant to victimizers than on the side of being insensitive or intolerant to their victims. Rorty and other defenders of AC might appear to abandon a moral point of view in an important respect. For they seem to side with or excuse, to some extent, victimizers by accepting that such persons might be justified from their own perspective and might therefore merit only measured condemnation.

Moody-Adams offers this sort of response to Rorty's position. She argues:

> Refusing to treat the victimizer's perspective as defensible is an important expression of resistance to the victimizer's purposes. . . . A victim's refusal to try to adopt the victimizer's point of view, recall, is for the ironist a "vulgar" mistake. But many feminist theorists are concerned about the distressing consequences of failures to voice *precisely* this sort of refusal. Consider the regularity with which female victims of rape or sexual harassment, for instance, wonder what they might have done to "deserve" or "provoke" the rape or the harassment. Such reflection unwittingly perpetuates practices that encourage the victim to blame herself—but by means of reflection that require her to adopt the point of view of the person who committed the harm. Appeals to notions like provocation and desert, in fact, require the victim to treat the victimizer's perspective as the *correct* point of view on that harm. . . . Yet though an ironist might be "impressed" by a vocabulary in which women cannot be described as human beings, few feminists would be—nor would they be troubled by that fact.[11]

Here again a reading of Rorty's position is the occasion for serious moral outrage. There is no doubt that the attitudes Moody-Adams condemns are worthy of her and our condemnation. The question, though, is whether Rorty and other liberal ironists can fairly be said to have these attitudes by dint of their ironism.

I discern three distinct criticisms in Moody-Adams's remarks. First, she claims that Rorty's position somehow implies that victims should not refuse to adopt "the victimizer's point of view." There are two components to this criticism. Apparently the victimizer's perspective, for Rorty, is to be treated as "defensible." Since the victimizer's perspective is defensible in some respect, moreover, victims make a "vulgar" mistake when they refuse to adopt it. Her second main criticism is that since Rorty's position calls for a kind of sympathetic identification with victimizers, it thereby places subtle pressure on victims to endorse the victimizer's perspective as the "correct" point of view on the harms that they have suffered. Another distinct criticism is Moody-Adams's passing remark that ironists, by definition, are "impressed" by sexist and degrading vocabularies. This objection is a variation on the theme that Rorty's position promotes sympathetic identification with victimizers and other evil persons.

Rorty can avoid all these criticisms. For starters, why think that, on Rorty's account, a victimizer's perspective is "defensible" and a victim's refusal to consider it is a "vulgar mistake"? Moody-Adams probably has in mind Rorty's contention that although feminists often have to "speak with the universalist vulgar, they might profit from thinking with the pragmatists."[12] Rorty intends that feminists might better achieve their purposes by avoiding in their theorizing concepts such as "human being" that are loaded with essentialist connotations. Rorty does not, however, use the term "vulgar" to describe victims or their perspectives in the sense that Moody-Adams suggests. Perhaps Moody-Adams's charge could be made to apply to Rorty, however, if indeed he thinks victimizers have a defensible perspective that victims ought to consider. So, I will examine that claim before passing a final verdict on Moody-Adams's contention that Rorty accuses victims of making a vulgar mistake because they refuse to countenance sympathetic redescriptions of victimizers.

The idea that, for Rorty, victimizers have a defensible perspective is motivated by a somewhat severe interpretation of Rorty's claim that anything can be made to look good or bad by being redescribed. Immediately following the passage in which Moody-Adams advances this criticism, she criticizes Rorty's thesis about redescription on the grounds that it trades on subtly blurring the distinction between a sympathetic redescription of a practice and an internal perspective that leads to approval of it.

As Moody-Adams puts this point:

> Imagine a sincere observer from a monogamous family who contemplates a sympathetic redescription of the polygamous family structure. This observer will see that polygamous families promote many values that she takes to be important—perhaps even that they effectively promote values that the monogamous family is intended to promote, but doesn't. But she will probably also see that polygamy promotes values that she doesn't share—and this may well prevent her from converting understanding, perhaps even tolerance and possibly respect, into personal approval. Her inability to make this evaluative leap is important: even the sincere contemplation of a sympathetic redescription of a practice may fail to produce what H. L. A. Hart has called the "internal perspective" on the practice. . . .
>
> The ironist thesis about redescription thus conflates the process of considering a redescription with the quite different process of developing an internal perspective on the practice that has been redescribed. Some people may be better able than others to make the leap that converts understanding into approval; they probably make the best ironists. But

that evaluative leap is not essential to understanding, or to learning to tolerate and even respect unfamiliar practices. One can accept the contingency of one's own projects and plans—and sometimes the defensibility of others—without rooting such acceptance in irony.[13]

Moody-Adams rightly wants to embrace the ethical benefits of openness to sympathetic redescriptions of others without the untoward consequences that come with full approval of just any sort of practice. She intimates that, whether it is for the sake of expanding our sympathies for others or for novel self-creation, ironists subtly succumb to a position that amounts to the promotion of imaginative identification with victimizers (and unconscionable blame for victims). The problem with this criticism is not the proposed distinction between a sympathetic redescription of a practice and an internal perspective, which carries with it approval of the practice. Rather, it is that Rorty is quite aware of this distinction and his position does not imply that he or any other liberal ironist can or should ascend (or descend) to an internal perspective on just any practice. Rorty does not even hold that ironists need to be able to describe sympathetically any practice they encounter. Yet Moody-Adams concludes that by virtue of their experimentation with redescription ironists come to approve of the practices of victimizers.

In order to give this criticism its best shot, consider the fact that Rorty does imply, after all, that to endorse AC is to seize upon the grain of truth in Socrates' notion that no one knowingly does evil. So in a certain respect it is true that, for Rorty, victimizers have a "defensible" perspective insofar as they usually can "whip up" a story according to which their victims deserve the treatment they receive. But this rejoinder derives its plausibility from a crucial ambiguity in the word "defensible." It turns on thinking that Rorty implies that victimizers have a defensible position *both* in their own eyes *and* in the eyes of ironists. The victimizers have their own reasons for their actions, their own goods that they pursue. Ironists see the victimizer's reasons as well and from an insider's perspective, according to Moody-Adams. Ironists even are *impressed* by them, presumably because ironists are able to see anything as good. That is why, on Moody-Adams's reading, ironists *blame* victims for refusing to consider the perspectives of those who victimize them.

However, Rorty does not hold that ironists, by definition, are able to see anything as good or bad or that they are impressed by *all* other final vocabularies, including sexist and degrading ones. Some ironists might be impressed with such vocabularies, and might be able to identify closely with victimizers, if they are very lukewarm liberals; others will not. There is no reason on Rorty's account, however, to think that ironists, on account of their ironism, are able and are likely to identify with victimizers, unless their own idiosyncratic backgrounds predispose them to such an attitude. Furthermore, when Rorty invokes the grain of truth in Socrates' "virtue is knowledge" thesis, he does not intend that if a person can make sense of his own actions, then his actions are defensible to ironists as well, no matter how evil those actions may appear to be. His actions may be defensible to himself and his friends. But this hardly implies that Rorty and other ironists will find them defensible, unless by "defensible" Moody-Adams means "intelligible" or "not indicative of insanity but able to be understood by others."

It is clear, however, that this is not what Moody-Adams intends by "defensible." This sense of defensible is far too thin and flimsy to account for the attitudes that ironists are said by Moody-Adams to exhibit toward victims and victimizers on the basis of finding the latter's perspective defensible. Someone who believes merely that victimizers are sane persons who pursue the good as they see it would hardly blame victims, on the one hand, for failing to identify with those who victimize them and, on the other hand, offer support for victimizers as persons with impressive perspectives that, when properly appreciated, show that victims deserve the treatment they receive. Yet the "not insane" sense of "defensible" is the only sense in which it may be true that ironists generally find the perspectives of victimizers defensible. I conclude, then, that the charge that Rorty's position somehow justifies the actions of victimizers rests on a serious misreading. Rorty's ironism in no way compels him to embrace the perspective of victimizers as defensible in the thicker sense that is objectionable.

Still Moody-Adams has a point when she notes that recognizing the contingency of one's own concerns and projects and a corresponding tolerance for and imaginative identification with others do not have to be grounded in irony. These attitudes and perspectives could have a number of different genealogies across all persons. But why would Rorty deny this? To say that AC is related to the cultivation of these goods is not to say that only AC is. Nor is it to say that endorsing AC is the best or quickest route to these goods. What Moody-Adams wants to argue, however, is that there are better ways to achieve these goods, routes other than irony to these goods, that do not carry with them the dangers that attend AC.

On closer examination, however, it is not clear just what these dangers are. After all, the account of irony that Rorty has to defend is not an account of uncontrolled, withering, flippancy-inducing irony but is liberal irony. In his exchange with Elshtain, Rorty merely wants to show that AC is not the depraved idea that she, Moody-Adams, and others take it to be. If my defense of Rorty is on the right track, we can also say that a main reason to affirm AC is to repudiate emphatically the likely implications of its denial. If anything can be made to look good or bad by being redescribed, then no description must inevitably and necessarily catch on with all persons who encounter it. There will always be another possible way to describe whatever is in view. This upshot, in turn, has implications both in the direction of promoting tolerance and in regard to future possibilities for novel self-creation. A monolithic and Orwellian future in which all human beings share the same final vocabulary and set of descriptions is not a world in which tolerance is needed. It also is not a world in which there could be truly novel selves. So while there are other routes to contingency, tolerance, and moral imagination, it is not clear that Rorty's is a dangerous, morally questionable, or strangely circuitous one.

Rorty also can avoid the charge that he implies that victims make a "vulgar mistake" when they refuse to adopt a victimizer's point of view. As I noted above, this criticism appears to rest on an uncharitable interpretation of Rorty's advice to feminists to avoid the "universalist vulgar." In an exchange with Thomas McCarthy, which Moody-Adams herself cites, Rorty clearly rejects the idea that victims should adopt the perspectives of victimizers. He argues:

> The urge to redescribe, cultivated by reading novels, is different from the urge to demonstrate, cultivated by reading metaphysics. . . .
> Does this mean that the wisdom of the novel encompasses a sense of how Hitler might be seen as in the right and Jews in the wrong? Yes, I am afraid that it does. Someday somebody will write a novel about Hitler that will, momentarily, make its readers feel that the poor man was much misunderstood. . . . Someday somebody will write a novel about Stalin as Good Old Uncle Joe. I hope nobody writes either very soon, because reading such a novel seems too much for the remaining victims of either murderer to have to bear. But such novels will someday be written. If we are to be faithful to the wisdom of the novel, they *must* be written.[14]

Like Moody-Adams, I find Rorty's remarks here about the "wisdom of the novel" both perplexing and distracting. Somehow the "wisdom" of the novel requires, according to Rorty, that some novelists experiment radically with redescription of even the most horrific evils. We should not allow these remarks to be so distracting, however, that we lose sight of Rorty's other remarks. Whatever the wisdom of the novel amounts to, for Rorty, clearly it does not underwrite the view that victims make a vulgar mistake when they fail to countenance sympathetic redescriptions of those who victimize them. On the contrary, Rorty explicitly hopes that no one will write a compelling and sympathetic novel about Hitler or Stalin in the lifetimes of his victims. Rorty might even consider someone's writing such a novel now or in the near future a "vulgar mistake." Regardless, it is evident that Rorty would not fault Hitler's victims and Stalin's victims for failing to read such a novel. He refers to Hitler and Stalin as murderers. So, if this charge were accurate, then Rorty himself would be guilty of a vulgar mistake by his own lights.

The idea that Rorty implies that victims are required to treat the victimizer's perspective as "the correct point of view" on the harm they suffer is even more difficult to account for than the previous criticism. For Rorty not only rejects the notion that victims should consider sympathetic redescriptions of those who victimize them; he also has no truck with the notion of a "correct" description that trumps all other descriptions. This is not to say that Rorty thinks that all descriptions are equally compelling. He embraces liberalism and its fundamental rejection of cruelty. He does not think that the notion of a correct description, as Moody-Adams intends it, however, is very useful.[15] But Rorty's eccentric and controversial views on truth are largely irrelevant here, at any rate. So I will set aside the problems that arise for this interpretation of Rorty on account of his well-attested disinterest in the notion of a correct description.

Finally, we can quickly dispatch with the objection that Rortian ironists, by virtue of their commitment to AC, are impressed by "vocabularies in which women cannot be described as human beings." This criticism rests on the inaccurate supposition that, for Rorty, anything can be made to look good to ironists. Otherwise, there is no reason to think that they will find sexist and degrading final vocabularies impressive. No doubt ironists, in order to count as ironists, need to be impressed with some alternative final vocabularies. However, this claim does not license the charge that they are impressed by sexist and degrading final vocabularies. Indeed, liberal ironists are much more likely to identify their attempts at self-creation with the task of escaping sexist and degrading vocabularies, since it is very likely that they inherited such vocabularies. Rorty himself, for instance, is not impressed by such vocabularies and attempts to escape them.

I conclude that when we examine carefully the main criticisms of AC, advanced most notably by Moody-Adams and Elshtain, none of them turns out to be a decisive objection to it. Each objection raised against this claim ultimately depends on a misinterpretation of it and its implications. Or, as in the case of Elshtain's concern about Rorty's alleged belief that our moral convictions ultimately are arbitrary, the objection is irrelevant to an assessment of AC. I hasten to add, however, that this conclusion does not imply that Rorty's overall account of redescription is unobjectionable.

2.2   REDESCRIPTION AND THE VIRTUE OF TRUTHFULNESS

Another important cluster of criticisms of Rorty's view of redescription and, in particular, his claim that anything can be made to look good or bad by being redescribed, has congealed around the claim that Rorty's position undermines the virtue of truthfulness, which is vital to the survival and flourishing of liberal communities. For example, Richard Bernstein states:

> My main point is to challenge Rorty's claim that he has given a more attractive redescription of liberalism. On the contrary, Rorty actually *describes* one of the most dangerous and virulent tendencies in liberalism—the conviction that anything can be made to look good by redescription. For this is just the mentality that possessed our political leaders during the Vietnam war and the sordid Watergate affair. What happens to liberal democracy when those who have the power to do so believe that they can make anything look good by redescription and have the power to enforce their vocabulary?[16]

Bernstein suggests that there is a relation between the conviction that anything can be made to look good (or bad) by being redescribed and duplicity, especially public duplicity for the promotion of one's narrow self-interests.

Now while it may be true that in order to deceive others through the manipulation of appearances, one has to believe that appearances are malleable—otherwise one's actions are unintelligible—it also is quite unfair to identify, as Bernstein does, the perspective of ironists who endorse AC with the mentality of immoral politicians who perpetrate public deceptions, such as those that occurred during the Vietnam war and Watergate. The problem to which Bernstein refers is not, as he suggests, the conviction that anything can be made to look good or bad by being redescribed. Rather, it is blatant lack of concern for truthfulness. But there is no reason to think that Rorty's conviction that anything can be made to look good or bad by being redescribed gives rise to lack of concern for truthfulness, if one interprets Rorty's position as he intends it. Dishonest persons who concur with Rorty about the malleability of descriptions may thereby be emboldened to attempt grand deceptions. But if they are, what they need is respect for truthfulness and respect for others; they do not need to be instructed that descriptions are not as malleable as they think.

Suppose a person who shares Bernstein's view is given the task of helping to reform someone who was involved in the Watergate scandal. If she were able to convince the Watergate crook that descriptions are not as malleable as he thinks, that is, if she convinced him that AC is false, what would she have achieved? Suppose the Watergate crook is released on parole. He has learned the lesson that he cannot make just anything look good to others. So what does he do? If he still is a dishonest person, he simply is not as brazen and foolhardy a deceiver as he used to be. If he is a dull ex-Watergate crook, he might not reform his behavior much at all. If, *per accidens*, he is reformed, we might feel very fortunate that his coming to disbelieve that anything can be made to look good has somehow led him to reconsider his lack of concern for truthfulness. But we should not in that case identify the deceitful mentality he used to have with an ironist's belief in the malleability of descriptions. Truthful and deceitful persons alike could have this belief.

Perhaps Rorty should caution us that believing that anything can be made to look good or bad by being redescribed is dangerous for persons who independently have no regard for truthfulness. But, of course, many *true* beliefs are dangerous for persons who have no regard for truthfulness or who have other significant character flaws. A fearful person, for instance, might avoid the dentist because she correctly believes that the dental work she needs is very painful. Such a person does not need to be instructed that, after all, dental work is not painful; she needs courage. The same sort of thing holds true for the Watergate crook. I conclude that Bernstein's criticism of Rorty is a nonstarter.

More recently, Alasdair MacIntyre has presented another version of the sort of critique that Bernstein raises against Rorty's position. In *Dependent Rational Animals*, MacIntyre addresses the role of irony in ethical life. His treatment of irony is embedded in a broader discussion concerning how we become morally accountable to others, especially vulnerable and dependent others, by learning to assume their point of view and to articulate it for them, if necessary. MacIntyre argues that one important virtue for relating to others this way is truthfulness. He then enumerates three types of offense against truthfulness. The first two offenses are not related to irony. The third type of offense, as MacIntyre explains, "has to do with our relationship to the shared language in which we speak with others, when making ourselves accountable to them."[17] He identifies the type of offense he has in mind as irony. Furthermore, the account of irony he mentions explicitly is Rorty's.[18]

Why does MacIntyre think that irony, as Rorty construes it, is an offense against truthfulness? Here is what he has to say in response to this question:

> A first consideration to note is that the vocabulary in which I make intelligible and justify or fail to justify my actions, beliefs, and life within a network of relationships of giving and receiving is never merely *mine*. It is always *ours*, a set of shared expressions put to shared uses, uses embedded in a wide range of common practices of receiving and giving, in a common form of life. When I am called to account as a practical reasoner in this shared evaluative language, what I am invited to consider is whether what is said about me is or is not true and justified in the light of our shared standards of truth and justification. I fail in responding to this invitation, not only if I were to lie, but also if I were to become evasive, if, for example, in such a context I were to remark that "anything can be made to look good or bad by being redescribed." For in the shared vocabulary of the common life of such a society, I may only justly claim that my action should be redescribed, by showing that it has been in some relevant respect misdescribed.[19]

Some of MacIntyre's remarks here are aimed at Rorty's appropriation of Nietzsche. I will examine these claims in the next chapter. For my purposes here, notice that MacIntyre envisions Rortian ironists using AC as a tool for evading accountability to other persons, especially persons who generally speak the same moral vocabulary as liberal ironists. MacIntyre's comments are vague between intending that (a) ironists will simply say to others in certain situations in which they are called to account for their actions that anything can be made to look good or bad by being redescribed or (b) ironists will offer a specific redescription of their actions that makes them appear to be good but not in the terms of the evaluative vocabulary shared by ironists and their interlocutors. We do not have to choose between these readings. Presumably if an ironist were pressed for more specifics after initially invoking AC in response to a challenge to justify her actions, she then might quickly "whip up" a specific redescription according to which her actions appear good. If an ironist responds in this manner instead of attempting to account for her actions using the evaluative terms she shares with her interlocutors, then, according to MacIntyre, she is being untruthful and evasive. But why think that an ironist's endorsement of AC will lead her to behave this way?

Behind MacIntyre's criticism is the same suspicion that Bernstein has about AC: believing that anything can be made to look good somehow inclines a person to duplicity and evasiveness.[20] This sort of reasoning is somewhat akin to blaming a person for believing "most of the time persons get away with drunk driving" on account of the fact that this belief is dangerous for persons to have, especially alcoholics. If an alcoholic believes that she probably can get away with drunk driving, then she may be emboldened to drive while she is drunk. But her problem in this case is not her belief that drunk driving mostly goes undetected (assuming that it does). Rather, it is either (a) her lack of sufficient concern for others and herself, who are endangered by her drunk driving, (b) her erroneous beliefs about her ability to drive safely while she is drunk, or (c) both a and b. The belief, "most of the time persons get away with drunk driving," should be assessed on its own merits without regard for the potentially harmful effects that might occur when alcoholics hold it. The same holds true for "anything can be made to look good or bad by being redescribed." This is a claim about the malleability of human descriptions and our ability to make our actions and those of others intelligible. The fact that an untruthful or irresponsible person might do more harm to others and herself if she holds this belief does not at all imply that it is dubious or intrinsically harmful. Besides, if we take this kind of approach to assessing the merits of a belief, which beliefs that we have will pass this test? Not very many will, if any.

I think we can safely conclude that Bernstein and MacIntyre fail to show that AC or belief in AC undercuts truthfulness. They subtly conflate an ironist's belief in AC either with the vice of deceitfulness or evasiveness. But these things ought to be sharply distinguished. Indeed, Rorty seeks in his ironist to combine belief in AC and commitment to truthfulness. He bristles at the charge that he devalues truthfulness. Consider, for instance, his remarks in response to James Conant, who suggests that Rorty's position encourages hostility to truthfulness.[21] Rorty rejoins:

> Much of Conant's criticisms of me, as well as many other philosophers' criticisms of pragmatism, run together truthfulness and truth. Pragmatists are often said not to recognize the political and moral importance of truth-telling.
> I do not think this charge is even remotely plausible. Truthfulness, in the relevant sense, is saying publicly what you believe, even when it is disadvantageous to do so. This is a moral virtue whose exercise is punished by totalitarian societies. This virtue has nothing to do with

any controversy between Realists and non-Realists, both of whom pay it equal honor.[22]

Although Rorty's exchange with Conant concerns his views about truth and not AC, still this passage clarifies Rorty's views about truthfulness. Perhaps it is worth pointing out first that Rorty, of course, does not intend to undermine the virtue of truthfulness. Rorty's response also clarifies what he takes truthfulness to be and thus what, on his view, counts as an offense against it. According to Rorty, to be truthful is to be honest about one's beliefs in public even when doing so is costly. Consequently, by Rorty's own lights, his position offends against the virtue of truthfulness only in case he somehow licenses duplicity about one's beliefs in public.

On a first pass, this clarification appears to help Rorty. For, as I noted in the previous chapter, he offers a private–public split for his ironists and he identifies the public side of that split with commitment to liberalism. This implies that liberal ironists are not to invoke AC in order to evade their moral obligations to other persons, which they accept as part of their liberalism. Playfulness with redescription, especially when it involves cruelty or other vices that undercut liberal values, is to be kept private, on Rorty's account. Since it is not difficult to argue that truthfulness is important for the sustenance of liberal societies, it follows that redescriptions that undermine truthfulness are not to be advanced in the public sphere. That is why Rorty embraces truthfulness in his response to Conant, which jibes with his views in *Contingency*. So, coupled with his understanding of truthfulness, Rorty's private–public distinction provides a way for him to respond to critics who allege that he does not take truthfulness seriously. Consistent liberal ironists, Rorty might argue, will not use the notion that anything can be made to look good or bad as a tool for evasiveness and duplicity in the various communities to which they belong. The public use of this notion is restricted to its utility in expanding tolerance for and more humane relations with others. With regard to truth telling, then, to the extent that ironists exemplify the ideals of liberal irony, publicly they will not be distinguishable from other citizens who value truthfulness.[23]

2.3 Truthfulness and the Private–Public Split

The various objections to Rorty's position that I have considered miss their mark as criticisms of AC. Yet they may lead us in a roundabout way to a subtle difficulty in the way that Rorty construes his private–public split. This proposed split in the final vocabulary, concerns, and life of a liberal ironist has been widely criticized.[24] As I suggested in the previous chapter, many of these criticisms rest on readings of Rorty's position that exaggerate what is required for ironists to maintain such a split. I want to focus here on a potential difficulty with Rorty's twofold claim in *Contingency* that we are to understand the split (a) as a division between redescription for private and for public purposes and (b) as providing a sanction in the private sphere for redescriptions of any sort—cruel or kind, liberal or illiberal—so long as these redescriptions do not lead to cruelty to others. Rorty's way of putting this last point is as follows:

> For my private purposes, I may redescribe you and everybody else in terms which have nothing to do with my attitude toward your actual or possible suffering. My private purposes, and the part of my final vocabulary which is not relevant to my public actions, are none of your business.[25]

Rorty accentuates here the separateness of private life and the important differences between public and private norms that govern our employment of redescription. The norms in view are related to avoidance of cruelty and freedom from interference—particularly freedom from moral busybodies in private life. Since Rorty also endorses the virtue of truthfulness, however, are other norms that govern public and private redescriptions in play, which are not mentioned here? Also, would recognizing these other norms significantly alter the way we think about the private sphere and its relation to the public sphere?

I think that to be consistent, Rorty must concede that there are other norms that govern private and public redescriptions, namely, those related to truthfulness. I also think that the way Rorty describes his private–public split needs to be modified to some extent in order to reconcile his account of this split with these norms.

Rorty believes that to be truthful is to say publicly what you believe, even in difficult situations. I assume that *what* we believe does not change when we move back and forth between public and private spheres in the sense that we do not have one set of beliefs for public life and another for private life. So when Rorty says that truthful persons say publicly what they believe, I take it that we do not need to qualify in any way the phrase "what they believe." [For emphasis, we might add that truthful persons say publicly what they *really* believe.] Otherwise Rorty's construal of truthfulness would be almost entirely vacuous. If we could be truthful just by stating publicly what we believe *in public* but may not or do not believe *in private*, then truthfulness would be consistent with rank hypocrisy and the sort of political dissembling that Bernstein rightly finds so deplorable. Presumably that is why Rorty does not qualify the phrase "what you believe" when he sketches his understanding of truthfulness.

This seemingly trite point calls our attention to the fact that a person is not being truthful if she misrepresents in public what she (simply) believes. But why not just say that a person is untruthful if she misrepresents what she believes, whether she misrepresents what she believes in private or in public? Why does it matter here *where* a person misrepresents her beliefs?

On a first pass, it appears that Rorty's answer to this question is that it is no one's business whether a person misrepresents her beliefs in private as long as she does not injure anyone if she does so. On this reading, the reason Rorty adds the qualifier that being truthful is saying *publicly* what you believe is that, as a liberal, he is only concerned with truthfulness in public. He might prefer that persons be truthful in private as well. But to inscribe this idea into his account of truthfulness would be to go beyond liberal principles. Rorty thinks that such a move is unnecessary. So Rorty offers us an unambiguously liberal conception of truthfulness, which is unsurprising but still significant.

Does Rorty really think, however, that a person can plausibly be said to be truthful if she is dishonest in her private life, as long as she manages to say publicly what she believes? Is a person who dissembles to his friends and family but says what he believes at work and in local Parent Teacher Association (PTA) meetings a truthful person? If Rorty's answer is "yes, and that captures all I need to say about truthfulness," then his account of truthfulness is so minimalist that it hardly deserves to be called a liberal account of this virtue. For we do not consider persons who are dishonest to their friends and family truthful persons, even if for some reason they happen consistently to say what they believe in public settings. Furthermore, liberals now recognize—at least those with whom Rorty identifies—that family life and friendships are not apolitical and thus, are not partitioned off as "nobody's business." For such liberals and many other persons, including many nonliberals, truthfulness matters a great deal not only in obviously public settings but also in some areas of personal life. Does Rorty intend to suggest otherwise?

Nancy Fraser suggests that he does. In a seminal essay on Rorty's private–public split, as he advocates it in *Contingency*, she argues:

> The social movements of the last hundred or so years have taught us to see the power-laden and therefore political character of interactions

which classical liberalism considered private. Workers' movements, for example, especially as clarified by Marxist theory, have taught us that the economic is political. Likewise, women's movements, as illuminated by feminist theory, have taught us that the domestic and the personal are political. . . . Yet Rorty's partition position requires us to bury these insights, to turn our backs on the last hundred years of social history. It requires us, in addition, to privatize theory. Feminists, especially, will want to resist this last requirement, lest we see our theory go the way of our housework.[26]

Of course, Fraser has much larger issues in view than truthfulness in personal life. She thinks that Rorty's private–public split takes us back to a naïve view of the private sphere, which fails to recognize the deeply political aspects of domestic and personal life.

However, Rorty emphatically rejects this reading of his private–public split. In an interview almost a decade after the publication of *Contingency*, he clarifies his position as follows:

> The original misinterpretation came from Nancy Fraser, who said "Rorty didn't realize the personal is the political." I think she and I were at cross purposes. I was thinking of one sense of private, something like Whitehead's definition of religion: "what you do with your solitude." Fraser was thinking of the private as the kitchen or bedroom, as opposed to the marketplace and the office. There was no relevance to what I was saying.[27]

So Rorty concurs with Fraser that in certain important respects domestic and personal life is not to be relegated to a domain that is entirely no one else's business. What clearly is no one else's business, according to Rorty, roughly is "what you do with your solitude."

Thus when Rorty argues that for his private purposes he can redescribe other persons in ways that have nothing to do with his attitude toward their suffering, he intends to convey at least that the norms that govern redescription in public life and some aspects of personal life do not apply to our use of redescription in our moments of solitude. In that case, it is not accurate to say that, for Rorty, a person can be dishonest in her relations with her family and friends and yet be a truthful person as long as she publicly says what she believes. For Rorty clearly believes that certain aspects of personal life are not private in the relevant sense, that is, governed by different norms that are much more widely divergent and may be much looser than and beyond the reach of public norms.

It turns out to be somewhat tedious to determine exactly what is involved, for Rorty, in saying publicly what you believe. The difficulty derives from trying to pin down more precisely what counts as public and what counts as private. If we take "private" to refer merely to "what one does with one's solitude," then Rorty's understanding of truthfulness is rather uncontroversial. But then it is somewhat curious that he defines truthfulness as saying what you publicly believe since, on this reading, just about any social context counts as a public domain. So to whom would one be stating one's beliefs when one is in private? The answer is, only those persons, if there are any, who are part of one's solitary life. But it is a bit of a stretch to think that in his exchange with Conant, Rorty inserts the qualifier "publicly" simply to clarify that truthfulness does not also require saying in moments of solitude (i.e., in private) what you believe. After all, for many persons moments of solitude are not infrequently given to sorting out their beliefs. Such moments often are times of candor with oneself and loved ones.

On the other hand, if we take saying "publicly" what you believe not to include saying what you believe in domestic and personal life in general, then we are back to the problem that Rorty's view of truthfulness is far too minimalist. As Fraser suggests, it also harks back to a kind of liberalism that many liberals now repudiate, a kind that Rorty himself explicitly disowns. If our relations in domestic and personal life are as power laden as Fraser suggests, truthfulness matters quite a bit in these areas of life. I find it hard to believe that Rorty would disagree.

To gain greater clarity about Rorty's view of truthfulness, we first need a clearer understanding of his private–public distinction. Perhaps setting aside the whole metaphor of place or social location is useful for clarifying this distinction. In other words, it may be helpful to reconstrue Rorty's private–public split without reference to private and public spheres or domains. In a recent exchange with Daniel Conway, Rorty himself suggests an alternative way of getting at his private–public distinction, one that recalls another way that he describes it in *Contingency*. He states:

> I must have been very misleading in what I wrote about this distinction in *Contingency, Irony, and Solidarity*. For Conway is right that those passages have rubbed a great many people the wrong way. . . . All I wanted was a firm distinction between responsibilities to oneself and responsibilities to others.[28]

Here Rorty licenses the substitutions "responsibilities to oneself" for "responsibilities incurred in private life" and "responsibilities to others" for "responsibilities incurred in public life." The main thought behind this alternative description of his private–public split is that persons should be left alone to pursue self-creation in their own highly idiosyncratic ways as long as their personal projects do not violate their obligations to others.

Other recent remarks of Rorty's about his private–public distinction confirm and elaborate this reading. He notes:

> I didn't say everybody had a public/private split, but some people do. There is a spectrum here. Some people have no public consciousness. This is the case of the sociopath; he simply doesn't think that there are any moral subjects out there. There are also a lot of other solitaries: hermetic poets who don't care if they have an audience. At the other extreme, there are people who have a minimal inner life. Their happiness consists entirely of being the soccer coach, or being the pater familias, or being chair of the Rotary Club. My private/public distinction wasn't an explanation of what every human life is like. I was, instead, urging that there was nothing wrong with letting people divide their lives along the private/public line. We don't have a moral responsibility to bring the two together. It was a negative point, not a positive recommendation about how everybody should behave.[29]

Here Rorty indicates that his private–public split is just a device for accentuating the idea that persons do not have a moral obligation to create themselves precisely through fulfilling their moral obligations to others. We have the freedom to pursue our own peculiar interests and projects in our private lives as long as we do not violate our basic obligations to others (not to be cruel to them and so on). The other point that Rorty makes here is that persons do not have a moral obligation to pursue novel self-creation apart from their fulfilling of civic and familial duties and other obligations they have to others. We can be as bourgeois or bohemian as we want to be while we attend to our duties to others.

Now we are in a position to grasp more clearly Rorty's understanding of truthfulness. It is evident that truthfulness falls under the category "responsibilities to others." Not that we should not be truthful to ourselves, but whether you are truthful with yourself is not Rorty's concern. Presumably it is not Rorty's concern because he does not think that it is crucial to the flourishing of liberal communities. But saying what you believe to others is crucial. I think Rorty's considered view of truthfulness is just this. In other words, saying *publicly* what you believe amounts to saying *to others* what you believe. I concede that this reading may not capture exactly what Rorty has in mind in his response to Conant. However, this reading puts Rorty's position in its best light and reflects his considered views on his private–public distinction.

But now what is the difference between redescription for private purposes and redescription for public purposes? The difference in principle at least is that private redescriptions, if one dabbles in them, are aimed at novel self-creation. Public redescriptions, however, aim primarily at the promotion of solidarity and are guided by stricter norms. For some persons, these aims will complement each other or will even be fused into one unified project. This is not a requirement of Rorty's position, however. His point is negative: as long as a person meets her obligations to others, it is no one's business how she chooses to create for herself a novel self. There need not be any consistency at all between the redescriptions she uses for the sake of novel self-creation and those she employs to promote solidarity. These redescriptions have different purposes, and we are not obliged to bring them together into an overall unity.

Is this position consistent, however, with Rorty's advocacy of the virtue of truthfulness? Rorty states that for the purposes of self-creation he may redescribe a person however he chooses. But a person who is committed to truthfulness should not have quite this attitude. If, for the sake of self-creation, I redescribe a person in ways that are antithetical to the description that I offer of her on other occasions for different purposes, and I believe this redescription, then I am not being truthful on those other occasions. For on those other occasions I am not saying *to others* what I believe, if I do, in fact, believe the redescription I use for my project of self-creation and it is antithetical to the descriptions that I offer of the person otherwise.

Rorty gives the impression that it really does not matter at all how he or anyone else redescribes other persons for the purposes of self-creation, as long as his redescriptions do not promote the sort of cruelty and injury to others that liberal communities legitimately seek to prevent. These redescriptions do not need to foster solidarity or have anything to do with this good. The problem that arises here is not that Rorty seeks to protect individuals who employ redescriptions in their pursuit of self-creation from moral busybodies who are bothered or offended by their redescriptions or who want them to promote moral goods. Rather, it is that once Rorty endorses truthfulness, he has to accept that there are additional norms that govern our use of redescription. These norms imply that redescriptions that are used in one's pursuit of self-creation, if one believes them, have consequences for one's other descriptions and redescriptions—those that are offered to others in one's interactions with them. These other descriptions and redescriptions need to be consistent with the redescriptions that one uses for self-creation, in order for one to be truthful.[30]

We can drop for the moment all the cumbersome qualifiers and put the central point this way. In one's interactions with others, in order to be truthful one needs to say what one believes even when this is very inconvenient. So when we employ redescription, whether we employ it in pursuit of novel self-creation or for some other reason, in cases where we subscribe to the redescriptions that we use, our statements to others then need to be consistent with these redescriptions.

I have deliberately described the relation that needs to obtain between our statements to others and the redescriptions that we believe vaguely as a relation of consistency. The reason is that truthfulness does not require full disclosure to others or emptying the contents of one's mind on a subject. Two statements or descriptions can be consistent with each other and be in some tension or have no obvious relation on the surface.

Imagine a PTA meeting, for instance, during which an ironist clashes with a fundamentalist parent over the teaching of sex education in the public schools in their community. Suppose that the two parents are civil, respectful, and courteous to each other. Each parent is called upon to explain and defend her views and to explain why she does not agree with the opposing view. The ironist prefaces her explanation of her views as follows: the parent whose views I oppose holds a reasonable position; still I do not think it should be the basis of public educational policy about sex education.

If the ironist parent is being truthful, then she really believes that the fundamentalist parent's position is reasonable. But this belief is consistent with also believing many other things about the fundamentalist parent and her views that she might not say at the PTA meeting in order to be civil, kind, and tolerant. These other beliefs might be captured in redescriptions she uses in other settings that have nothing to do with her duties as a parent and interested citizen. Perhaps she was socialized into the very perspective that the fundamentalist parent endorses and is trying to get out from under it because she finds it stultifying and uninformed. She might then find it useful after the meeting to redescribe this perspective rather negatively to her friends or perhaps to herself while taking a walk after the meeting in order to unwind. Suppose her redescription goes something like this: that person is poorly educated and her views are naïve and inane. She believes this redescription and simply refrains from using it at the PTA meeting for the sake of civility and kindness. What, then, should we make of her very different comments at the meeting?

Certainly there are some senses of "reasonable" that are inconsistent with "uninformed," "stultifying," "naïve" and "inane." For instance, if the ironist parent thinks that a reasonable view is a view that is well-informed, then it is difficult to see how her private redescription of the fundamentalist parent's views is consistent with her remarks at the meeting. In that case, I think we have to say that the ironist parent is not being truthful at the meeting.[31] However, there are some, if not many, senses of "reasonable" that are consistent with the ironist parent's negative redescription of the fundamentalist parent's views. For instance, suppose the ironist parent is a Rawlsian. She thinks that the fundamentalist parent's perspective on sex education is reasonable in the sense that it derives from a broader comprehensive view that (a) expresses an intelligible view of the world, (b) isolates certain values as centrally important and gives guidance as to how to balance these values when they conflict, and (c) draws from a tradition and so is not based on a fad.[32] Yet for all that she still could consistently believe that the fundamentalist parent's views are uninformed, stultifying, naïve, and inane. In that case, her redescription is consistent with her remarks at the meeting. So she is not violating her obligation to be truthful even if she could be much more candid and forthcoming in her remarks than she is.

One last thing to notice about this example is that the ironist parent has moral reasons for not being more candid and forthcoming. So it is not as if she fails to be completely candid because she is concerned just enough about her moral obligations to be consistent but is not any more concerned about them. Even the remarks that she makes take some courage. It is not convenient or pleasant to expound one's views on such a topic in such a setting and also to have to oppose another person at the same time.[33] We should keep these points in mind, lest we suspect that this view of truthfulness tends to moral laxity.

I began this section with the suggestion that there is a subtle problem in the way that Rorty describes his private–public split. The genealogy of the problem goes back to Rorty's failure to recognize that an ironist's commitment to truthfulness has implications for the way she employs redescription. An ironist cannot be committed to truthfulness and be entirely cavalier about a redescription just because it is one that she employs for self-creation, if she also subscribes to this redescription. Once I latch on to a redescription as an accurate characterization of someone or something, no matter what purposes it serves in my life, my descriptions to others of this person or thing need to be consistent with this redescription, if they are to be truthful. Now a person may redescribe others unseriously or just for the sake of play however she chooses, as long as she is not cruel to them. This sort of redescription may be part of her pursuit of self-creation. But it is simply not true that all the redescriptions we use for purposes of self-creation are ones that we do not take seriously or believe. So it is important to note that those redescriptions believed by us have implications for our relations with others, if we are committed to truthfulness. When we say what we believe to others our words need to be consistent with our beliefs and those redescriptions that reflect our beliefs (in the relevant sense). I doubt that anyone can pin down very precisely what this relation of consistency involves. Nonetheless, we generally acknowledge that there is such a relation and that truthfulness requires it.

We also now recognize that domestic and personal life is shot through with goods that are not narrowly private. So Rorty needs to acknowledge unambiguously that truthfulness matters in domestic and personal life. The clarifications and modifications he has offered in regard to his original sketch of his private–public distinction give him the conceptual space to do this, in my view.

The problem in Rorty's account that I have highlighted here is not a silver bullet that fells liberal irony. But it is significant, nonetheless. For truthfulness, as Rorty himself recognizes, is a crucial virtue for the flourishing of liberal communities. So it is important to be clear about what a commitment to truthfulness entails. Perhaps if Rorty were to be more forthcoming about this feature of his position, critics like Bernstein, Conant, and MacIntyre would be less inclined to suspect that Rorty's position is morally lax.

Rorty's simply dropping the language of private and public in favor of responsibilities to self and responsibilities to others might promote this end as well. But it would be a helpful move anyhow because it fits better with Rorty's concession to Fraser that the domestic and personal are not private in important respects. There is no place that we go where, if we meet another person there, we have no moral obligations to that person. But there is a limit to what others can expect of us. We ought to be able to pursue self-creation without interference from others, if we have met our obligations to them. That is a main burden of Rorty's private–public distinction. It is not intended to drive a wedge between public life, on the one hand, and domestic and personal life, on the other. I think the idea of a dual set of responsibilities better captures Rorty's intent, when this idea is sufficiently qualified.

2.4 CONCLUSION

This chapter began with a critical analysis of Rorty's claim that anything can be made to look good or bad by being redescribed. Since the time that Rorty advanced this claim in *Contingency* over a decade ago, he has been severely criticized for it. Commentators have claimed that Rorty's position indicates a flippant attitude toward morality; that one would have to be loathsome to endorse it in the face of horrific evils; that to endorse it is to side with victimizers over against victims; that it undermines truthfulness, in addition to other charges. I hope to have demonstrated in the first two sections of this chapter that these criticisms rest on misreadings of Rorty's position, which are sometimes severe. Part of the confusion derives from the lack of careful attention to this question: for Rorty, *to whom* can anything be made to look good or bad by being redescribed? Ironists like Rorty believe that anything can be made to look good or bad by being redescribed. But this belief does not imply that anything can be made to look good or bad *to ironists*. The distinction between these claims is crucial. The claim that anything can be made to look good or bad by being redescribed is not a pivot point that enables ironists to evade their moral responsibilities to others when it is convenient for them to do so. Rather, for Rorty, it is a belief that is closely related both to the pursuit of autonomy, as it is related to the possibility of substantial revisions in one's current final vocabulary, and the development of tolerance and moral imagination.

In the last part of this chapter, I argued that there is a problem in Rorty's account that traces back to his failure to acknowledge the implications that a commitment to truthfulness has for an ironist's use of redescription. It is not the case that an ironist's redescriptions for purposes of self-creation have no relation at all to her obligations to others except that she should avoid cruelty to others when she uses them. An ironist's commitment to truthfulness implies that what she says to others needs to be consistent with the redescriptions that she believes regardless of the purposes of those redescriptions. Furthermore, this requirement derives from Rorty's own remarks about truthfulness and his considered view of his private–public split. So, it is not an external imposition of a nonliberal view of truthfulness.

Finally, Rorty also should drop the metaphor of private and public spheres and replace it with his "responsibilities to self" and "responsibilities to others" metaphor. This move might ward off readings such as Fraser's by clarifying in Rorty's account the scope of moral goods that are related to the basic good of solidarity, such as avoidance of cruelty and truthfulness. The idea of a split between these sets of responsibilities still has utility for Rorty. It helps him emphasize that projects of self-creation need not also be projects that promote solidarity. On the other hand, these projects do not have to be distinguishable from projects that promote solidarity, either, as Rorty clarifies in "Against Bosses."

CHAPTER 3

Autonomy and Moral
Commitment in Liberal Irony:
Problems and Proposals

As I noted in the first chapter, Rorty construes autonomy as getting out from under inherited vocabularies, whatever the content of these vocabularies happens to be. For Rorty, no vocabulary is essentially or naturally conducive to self-creation. An ironist's pursuit of self-creation, moreover, seems to succeed to the extent that she is able to construct her own terms for understanding and evaluating herself and others. This way of construing autonomy no doubt owes much more to Nietzsche than Kant, if it is Kantian in any sense.

Rorty also builds into his overall account of irony a basic commitment to liberalism about which he and other liberal ironists are "frankly ethnocentric."[1] Liberal ironists such as Rorty simply find themselves with liberal convictions that seem right to them and cling to these beliefs even though a noncircular argument is not available to demonstrate that these beliefs are morally superior to illiberal convictions.

Taken singly, these positions have some merit. It is implausible to think that we can climb out of our own minds and social practices to a God's-eye point of view from which to demonstrate the absolute validity of our convictions. Becoming autonomous, moreover, does have something to do with taking a critical stance toward inherited vocabularies. When we juxtapose these ideas, as Rorty understands them, however, a significant conundrum emerges. It appears that those persons who inherit or are initially socialized into a liberal final vocabulary are not at all likely candidates for liberal irony. In order to pursue autonomy, as Rorty construes it, such persons need to get out from under the liberal vocabulary that they inherited. In order to be good liberals, however, they need to embrace this vocabulary. Yet such persons compose the vast majority of Rorty's audience, and he himself is such a person.

It is clear from my analysis in the previous chapter, moreover, that Rorty's private–public distinction is much too porous to provide a way out of this problem. As Rorty has continued to expand and revise the account of liberal irony that he first advanced in *Contingency*, he has tended to embrace a much looser distinction between the private and public. Consequently, a resolution of this problem has to be located somewhere else in Rorty's account, if is a resolution is to be found.

Some critics of liberal irony have alluded to this problem in a roundabout way by focusing on problems that are said to arise from a liberal ironist's inability to be ironic about liberalism. For instance, Simon Critchley states:

> My critical question here is simple: if Rorty defines liberalism in terms of a claim about the need to minimize cruelty, reduce humiliation, or be responsive to suffering, then what is the status of this claim? More particularly, can this claim be relativized? And more sharply, is cruelty something about which liberals can be ironic? I think not.[2]

For Critchley, a Rortian ironist's commitment to liberalism undermines her claim also to be an ironist. But the reason a so-called liberal ironist fails to be an ironist, according to Critchley, is simply that she has an earnest commitment to liberalism, not that she fails to get out from under her inherited (liberal) vocabulary. Furthermore, Critchley focuses mainly on what he takes to be the untoward social and political consequences that follow. For instance, as he sees it, liberal ironists fail to offer or even countenance radical critiques of liberal societies. In his view, this is not the stance of an ironist. Critchley does not focus on an ironist's difficulty in achieving autonomy.

Critchley's criticism suggests that there may be other difficulties related to an ironist's commitment to liberalism lurking in Rorty's account. For starters, some critics claim that a Rortian ironist cannot be serious about any self-description, since she takes every self-description to be contingent. But that raises perplexities about what sort of attitude ironists take toward their own ironic stance. Furthermore, suppose, as Rorty avers, that his ironists can be fully committed to ideals and still be ironists. Critchley prompts us to wonder why they are committed to liberalism and not something more basic and less parochial. Also, some philosophers argue that a Rortian ironist's commitment to her ideals is irrational, even if it is psychologically possible.

In this chapter, I clarify and carefully examine these and other closely related difficulties with Rorty's account of liberal irony. I also propose several possible responses in defense of Rorty, which range from mild tweaks to more involved revisions of his position. I argue that there is nothing incoherent or implausible about being committed to ideals that one perceives to be contingent. Nevertheless, some of Rorty's remarks about novel self-creation, if taken in isolation from qualifications he makes in his appropriation of Nietzsche, generate moral and conceptual problems for his overall account of liberal irony.[3] When we take into account Rorty's qualifications, however, these problems lose much, if not all, of their force. At least they no longer can be pursued as internal criticisms of liberal irony.

3.1   Contingency, Truth, and Commitment

Can persons be committed to ideals that they perceive to be contingent? If they cannot, then Rorty's position is fatally flawed from the outset. Every ideal is couched in a vocabulary and every vocabulary, according to Rorty, is contingent. Consequently, there are no ideals that are not contingent in the eyes of a Rortian ironist. So, if the perceived contingency of an ideal precludes commitment to it, then Rortian ironists cannot be committed to any ideals.

The question posed here should not be confused with another question: can a person's commitment to ideals that she takes to be contingent be rational? When we question whether an ironist can have the convictions that Rorty says that she has, it is important to distinguish between: (a) questions concerning the psychological possibility of her commitments and (b) questions concerning the rationality of her commitments. These are not at all the same thing. Persons can hold beliefs that are irrational. In such cases, the beliefs in question obviously are psychologically possible but are logically inconsistent or irrational in some other respect.

Another question that arises here concerns whether a person can be committed to ideals that she thinks are not rationally justified. Certainly persons can be committed to beliefs that just are irrational. But can a person clearly recognize the irrationality of a belief and still maintain it? Of course, the answer to this question is a trivial "yes," if we construe rational justification in a strong enough way. For instance, if a person believes that only indubitable beliefs have rational justification, then she will have to conclude that many of her beliefs are not rationally justified. But a person can recognize clearly that many of her beliefs are dubitable and still be firmly committed to them, if she believes that dubitable beliefs are not necessarily false. By her own standards, she would not be rationally justified in holding these beliefs. But for all that she might still hold them. By rational justification, I have in mind, however, something much more ordinary, such as having some good reason, as one sees it, for the belief that one holds.

Obviously a person who clearly perceives that a belief lacks rational justification in this sense cannot rationally hold such a belief. A person cannot rationally believe, for instance, that Elvis is alive, if at the same time she also clearly perceives that her belief that Elvis is alive is patently irrational. Could she yet simply find herself with the persistent belief that Elvis is alive, nonetheless? In other words, is it psychologically possible to hold a belief and also clearly recognize that one does not have at least some good reason, as one sees it, for holding this belief?

I think we want to say that under normal circumstances the answer to this question is "no." Persons with an obsession might have this problem. But a person whose mental faculties are functioning properly will not. If a person concedes that she has no reason at all to believe that Elvis is alive and some reason to believe that he is dead and then says that she nonetheless believes that he is alive, then she is not leveling with us or perhaps with herself. She must have some reason for thinking that Elvis is alive, if she believes this. Perhaps she just does not want to tell us what her reason is for fear of being ridiculed. She thinks this reason that she fails to give, which perhaps is only inchoate in her mind, is a good one in some respect. But she recognizes that others might think it is absurd. This state of affairs is not at all the same as one in which she thinks that she has no reason for believing that Elvis is alive and some reason to believe that he is dead, even if it is consistent with her suspecting or worrying that her Elvis belief might be absurd or appear that way to others. So I tentatively conclude that under normal circumstances a person cannot hold a belief that she clearly recognizes she has absolutely no reason to hold and some reason not to hold, much less rationally hold such a belief.

Some of Rorty's critics invite us to think that he disagrees with this conclusion. They give the impression that Rorty's position has the implication that persons can rationally subscribe to and even die for beliefs that they firmly and clearly believe are no truer than contrary beliefs, which they reject. For instance, in a review of *Contingency*, Lloyd Gerson states:

> In reply to the obvious objection that one still has to live and so believe some things, the Sceptics' reply (and Rorty's) is that we will believe whatever we will believe as a result of the historical circumstances in

which we find ourselves. Although such beliefs are no more true than any others, including their opposites, "they can still regulate action, can still be thought worth dying for, among people who are quite aware that [they are] caused by nothing deeper than contingent historical circumstances." The claim that people die defending ill founded beliefs is unremarkable; the claim that they die defending beliefs they know to be ill founded is remarkably silly.[4]

Here Gerson moves from a Rortian ironist's recognizing that she is a product of her age in profound respects to the idea that she also believes that her views are "no more true than any others, including their opposites." Then he notes that, in Rorty's view, such persons still may die for their beliefs even while they recognize that they most likely would have had very different beliefs if they had lived in a different place and at a different time. Gerson subsequently chides Rorty for holding a "remarkably silly" position. This position, as Gerson construes it, amounts to supposing that persons die for beliefs they recognize as ill founded.

Gerson thinks that Rorty's ironists recognize that, by their own lights, their liberal convictions have nothing more going for them, epistemically speaking, than extremely illiberal beliefs. Ironists recognize that their convictions are no truer than illiberal convictions, which they reject. That would seem to be an obvious reason why their liberal convictions are ill founded for them. Gerson also takes Rorty to hold that it still is psychologically possible for his ironists to hold firmly and even die for their liberal convictions despite this insight into the ill founded nature of their beliefs. Assuming that Rorty does not intend to inscribe irrationality or an epistemic vice into his ironists, moreover, it follows as well that Rorty not only has it that his ironists can sustain their liberal beliefs under these conditions but that these beliefs can be rationally justified. This certainly stretches credulity.

I think that Gerson's critique is based on an interpretation of Rorty's position that Rorty can avoid. I begin with what Gerson gets right. Rorty does believe that we are creatures of our time and place in a profound sense. Or roughly as he puts it, our beliefs, desires, and lives are riddled with contingency. Rorty also holds that our recognition of contingency need not lead us to give up our most deeply held convictions.

Thus far, I see nothing objectionable about Rorty's position, and perhaps neither does Gerson. We commit a kind of genetic fallacy when we assume that if a belief has contingent origins or is caused by contingent circumstances, it cannot be worth dying for. The genealogy of a belief is not a reliable indicator of its validity or of the value that the belief should have for the person who holds it. For instance, for all we know, a parent's belief that her child's flourishing has supreme value may be caused by radically contingent circumstances. Still a parent might make great sacrifices or even give her life for her child because she has this belief. Yet who would blame her or find her behavior irrational on account of the fact that she is motivated by a belief that is contingent?

So then why does Gerson accuse Rorty of having a "remarkably silly" position? He has Rorty moving from the contingency of a belief to the idea that it is "no more true than its opposite." When it is "no more true than its opposite," it has nothing more going for it in the way of reason than its opposite, according to Rorty, as Gerson understands his position. In that case, liberal convictions have nothing more going for them in the way of reason than extremely illiberal convictions, which ironists reject. Yet ironists who recognize all this manage to be so committed to their groundless liberal convictions that they are willing to die defending them.

If this is Rorty's view, then he should abandon it. The contingency of a belief does not imply that the belief is no truer than a contrary belief. Furthermore, as I argued above, it is implausible to think that a person can hold a belief that she clearly thinks she has no good reason to hold and some reason not to hold, much less a belief that is no truer, as she sees it, than a view she rejects. As Bernard Williams explains:

> Beliefs aim at truth. . . . When somebody believes something, then he believes something which can be assessed as true or false, and his belief, in terms of the content of what he believes, is true or false. If a man recognises that what he has been believing is false, he thereby abandons the belief he had. And this leads us to the second feature under this heading: to believe that p is to believe that p is true. To believe that so and so is one and the same as to believe that that thing is true.[5]

Williams intends to clarify our thinking about our commonsense understanding of belief. To believe something is the same as to believe that it is true or that it is the case. Consciously and deliberately to reject a belief is just to take it to be false or not to be the case. So, if a person rejects illiberal views, for instance, she thinks that it is not the case that they are true. If she also believes that liberal principles are no truer than illiberal convictions, then it would appear that she is committed to the belief that liberal principles are not true, either. A person in this predicament who dies fighting against enemies of political liberalism and defending her liberal principles is irrational by dint of her holding deeply inconsistent views. It is doubtful, though, that she can even be in this terribly incoherent mental state, under normal circumstances. If Rorty thinks that she can be and can be rationally justified at the same time, then his position is deeply puzzling and problematic, as Gerson argues.

However, Rorty does not hold this view. He emphatically rejects the idea that a person can hold, much less die for or believe with justification, a belief that she takes to be logically inconsistent with her other beliefs. As he explains:

> We cannot, no matter how hard we try, continue to hold a belief which we have tried, and conspicuously failed, to weave together with our other beliefs into a justificatory web. No matter how much I want to believe an unjustifiable belief, I cannot will myself into doing so. The best I can do is distract my own attention from the question of why I hold certain beliefs. For most matters of common concern, however, my community will insist that I attend to this question.[6]

Here Rorty argues that a person cannot continue to hold a belief that she comes to recognize is incorrigibly inconsistent with her other beliefs. He does not intend, moreover, simply that such a person could not rationally continue to hold such a belief. Rather, he intends that it is not psychologically possible to hold such a belief under these precise circumstances. In a certain respect, Rorty's remarks are stated just the way a person who is wary of truth talk would put Williams's remarks about belief.

One might think that Rorty's view is implausible because it implies that all our beliefs are rationally justified. If we have a belief that is not rationally justified, as Rorty construes this, then we cannot will ourselves into continuing to hold this belief. But his view does not have this implication. Rorty leaves open the possibility that a person could unwittingly have a belief that is inconsistent with her other beliefs and, thus, is not rationally justified. When he remarks that we cannot will ourselves into believing unjustifiable beliefs, he does not intend that somehow we never latch on to unjustifiable beliefs. He has in mind that we cannot intentionally believe something that we unambiguously take to be irredeemably inconsistent with our other beliefs. That is why Rorty concludes with the observation that by focusing our attention away from this sort of belief we might eventually be able to hold it, if perhaps we forget or overlook the fact that it is inconsistent with our other beliefs. But then others may call our attention back to the inconsistency, which will lead us, most likely, to lose the belief.

This clarification of Rorty's position implies that Gerson's criticism misses its mark. For Gerson's objection turns crucially on the idea that, on Rorty's account, a person can (and can rationally) die defending a belief that she takes to be ill founded, as *she* understands "ill founded." What is dubious, according to Gerson, is the idea that a person can (and can rationally) die defending a belief that she knows to be ill founded, not that is ill founded by Gerson's lights or that she suspects could be ill founded or knows that others believe is ill founded.

Perhaps I have moved too quickly here, however. I have assumed that "ill founded," for Rorty, refers to "logically inconsistent with one's other beliefs." Clearly this is one sense of "ill founded" in Rorty's account. I think it is also the primary sense and the one that Rorty really cares about. Gerson, however, has in view another sense of "ill founded." He suggests that we take "no more true than any other belief, including its opposite" as the rough equivalent of "ill founded." Since he thinks Rorty does inscribe into his ironist the view that her beliefs are ill founded in this sense, he concludes that Rorty endorses the dubious view that ironists can (and can rationally) defend to the death their convictions while believing that these convictions are no more true than other beliefs that are completely contrary to them. In that case, Gerson might rejoin, it is irrelevant what Rorty says in other contexts about being unable to will oneself into beliefs that one takes to be incurably inconsistent with one's other beliefs.

I concede to Gerson that there are passages in *Contingency* that appear to support this sense of "ill founded." I also concur with him that there is something incoherent about dying for a belief about which one has this attitude. It would be highly irrational to die fighting fascists while also lucidly believing that their convictions are as true as one's own, if this is even psychologically possible.

However, we do not have to construe Rorty's position this way. As noted in the previous chapter, Rorty does not believe that Stalin's views, for instance, are as true as liberal views. What he believes is that we cannot offer compelling noncircular arguments against Stalin's sympathizers, arguments given from a neutral standpoint that do not already beg questions against them and that they would have to accept, if only they were rational. Of course, neither can Stalin's sympathizers turn the tables and do this for us. As far as I can tell, this is the only relevant sense in which, for Rorty, our beliefs and the beliefs of Stalin's sympathizers are equally ill founded. Rorty does not conclude from this concession to our finitude and contingency, though, that his liberal views are ill founded in any sense that lends credence to Gerson's objection. Instead, he offers reasons to be a liberal and not a Stalinist, which he recognizes are bound to beg questions against Stalinists but are compelling to him and many others, nonetheless. As Alan Malachowski explains:

> Far from trying to smuggle certain liberal values into political discourse under the cloak of philosophically impartial rhetoric, Rorty *openly* defends such values. Not only that, he openly defends an *ethnocentric defence* of liberalism.
>
> This should come as no surprise. For Rorty's distrust of traditional notions of "philosophical neutrality" means that he has to keep his feet firmly on local ground not just when choosing a political position, but also when defending that choice. If there is no far-off philosophical place that provides refuge from "time and chance," Rorty must start his political deliberations from where he is. Notice, however, that a non-relativistic element of normativity enters the picture here. It is *not* that Rorty thinks or wants us to think:
>
> 1. There is no philosophically neutral ground
> 2. Therefore I *might as well* start from where I am (wherever that happens to be).
>
> For there is a suppressed premise in this quick argument that Rorty strongly disputes:
>
> (R) No ground is better than any other ground for purposes of inspiring political deliberation.
>
> This relativistic premise is, itself, supposed to follow from (1). Rorty disputes it because he believes he has particular pragmatic reasons for preferring to stake his political claims on the local ground of American liberalism. These "reasons" serve two purposes: they block the inference from (1) to (R), the relativistic premise that appears to license (2), and they also introduce "normativity" by showing why Rorty *ought* to "start from where he is."[7]

Notice that the suppressed premise that Malachowski isolates and dispatches is almost precisely the position that Gerson attributes to Rorty. "No ground is better than any other ground" is very similar to "no belief is any truer than any other belief, including its opposite." Malachowski helps us see that Rorty thinks he has good reasons for being a liberal even if these reasons cannot be grounded in a philosophically neutral vocabulary.

Furthermore, the sense of finitude and epistemic humility in Rorty's account that surface in his doubts about our ability to ground our convictions in compelling, noncircular premises is far too thin a reed to bear the weight of Gerson's criticism. Surely we can die defending beliefs that we firmly believe while recognizing that we cannot demonstrate their validity from a philosophically neutral perspective, and be rational while doing so. Only an extreme notion of rationality rules out this possibility. Rorty would argue that any such notion fails to come to terms with our finitude and our long history of failed attempts to climb outside of our own minds and see the world from a God's-eye point of view.

Perhaps Gerson's criticism of Rorty's position just comes down ultimately to what he takes to be the paradoxical implications of Rorty's disavowal of correspondence theories of truth. Is this enough to justify his criticism? At least Gerson owes us more argument for his position, if it comes down to this.

Suppose Gerson thinks that Rorty's controversial views on truth commit him to the incoherent view that he endorses liberalism while also believing that liberal principles are "no more true" than blatantly illiberal principles, which he rejects. It is now clear that Gerson cannot maintain that Rorty holds that liberal principles have no more going for them than illiberal principles. Still Gerson might think that Rorty's views on truth commit him to a perspective on his own liberalism and illiberal principles that ultimately is incoherent. Can Gerson rest his case just on Rorty's controversial views on truth?

Despite Rorty's occasional lapses into denials of correspondence, as I understand his considered position he disavows correspondence theories of truth only in the sense that he thinks they are not useful since we cannot show in any unproblematic way that correspondence obtains or make full sense of the notion of correspondence.[8] Also, he wants to avoid the unhelpful idea, as he sees it, of mental representation. It seems a circuitous route from these positions to the charge that Rorty commits himself to the view that the beliefs he defends are "no more true than their opposites" and are ill founded by his own lights in the sense of "ill founded" that Gerson's criticism trades on. As far as I can tell, a charitable reading of Rorty on this point yields merely the view that he does not know that he has correspondence to reality on the side of his beliefs. But this is not the same as denying that he has correspondence to reality on his side or affirming that his view and opposite views both have it on their side or even that they both fail to have it on their side. Rorty may have it open to him, moreover, to take an even milder view about correspondence. As Merold Westphal explains, "[A person] might hold that correspondence is the meaning of truth and that, in the absence of our ability to achieve this lofty goal, conversational consensus is the best approximation we have to go on."[9]

Suppose a liberal ironist takes this position on account of her sense of finitude and recognition of contingency. Unless we construe conversational consensus in an extreme way, where it requires near universal agreement, she could rationally hold her liberal convictions and even die for them, even if she refrains from drawing any conclusions at all about whether they achieve correspondence to reality. For now there is much conversational consensus about the good of liberalism. It is plausible to think that this consensus makes liberal convictions well grounded or at least certainly not ill founded in any relevant sense.

Another reason to give Rorty the benefit of the doubt here is that he himself now concedes that he needs to speak less paradoxically about truth, lest he invite more criticisms like Gerson's. In a recent exchange with Simon Thompson, he states:

> I quite agree with Simon Thompson that I should have been more careful to distinguish between truth and justification, and to remark that one notion is absolute and the other relative. I have done this fairly consistently in the last decade or so, but there are some unfortunate passages in my earlier writings in which I run truth and justification together (something William James also did sometimes, though not in his better moments). . . .
> Sometimes, even in recent years, I have spoken in incautious ways. When, for example, I said in 1993, in "Putnam and the Relativist Menace," that "the rightness or wrongness of what we say is just for a time and place," I was taking it for granted that my readers would interpret "rightness" as a matter of conformity to current justificatory practice. But of course those who think of truth as correspondence to reality often construe "the rightness of what we say" as "fitting unchangeable reality," and so my remark was easy to misinterpret as saying something wildly paradoxical. I hope that I am gradually learning to be less aphoristic and less susceptible to accusations of paradox-mongering.[10]

In this passage, Rorty admits that in the past he has left himself open to accusations of "paradox-mongering," such as those leveled by Gerson, on account of his conflating truth and justification. But he also unambiguously takes a position on truth that, as far as I can tell, removes any suggestion that he believes that his convictions are no truer than any other beliefs, including their opposites. So we can finally put to rest Gerson's criticism.

Rorty would help himself by taking an additional step away from his past remarks about truth. He should also affirm a kind of *humdrum* realism, as Gutting puts it, about the everyday world in which we live.[11] When I said above that a liberal ironist might refrain from drawing any conclusions at all about whether her convictions achieve correspondence to reality, I did not intend, of course, that a liberal ironist might not have any beliefs. However, suppose that to have a belief just is to believe that something is true or is the case, as Williams plausibly argues. Is to believe something, then, just to believe that it corresponds to reality? If so, then a liberal ironist could not fail to believe that her convictions correspond to reality, if she has any beliefs at all. But this is to conflate *humdrum* realism and *metaphysical* realism, or belief in truth and belief in truth as correspondence. However, since Rorty rejects metaphysical realism (or Realism, as he sometimes labels it) he needs in his account at least some rough alternative to it to make sense of his own beliefs and those of his ironists, in view of Williams's analysis of belief.

Some philosophers think that there is a kind of humdrum realism already present in Rorty's position.[12] Others emphasize that it is open to Rorty to articulate such a position and that he would strengthen his position by doing so. Gutting articulates a clear, subtle, and sensible path for Rorty to take on this issue. He states:

> We are, from the beginning, in cognitive contact with objects independent of us, not only knowing that there is such a world, but also knowing many specific things about it. However, this baseline knowledge of the world is simply a matter of knowing certain commonplaces, not of having any theoretical account of this knowledge—in terms, for example, of representations. Rorty may still be right that there is no prospect for our arriving at a substantive theoretical account of our knowledge.
>
> In fact, I think he is right. Although we always start inquiry and reflection from baseline, humdrum truths, these are, of course, only privileged de facto. There is no reason in principle why they could not be criticized—analyzed, questioned, justified, or even eventually rejected. Such criticism is the business of philosophy. Philosophers have successfully criticized baseline truths about science, morality, religion, and politics. However, a couple of millennia of frustration should have taught us that there is no fruitful (or even coherent) way of criticizing baseline truths about truth itself. We can and must

subscribe to all the commonplaces: we know truths, many truths are about the world, such truths tell us the way the world is, and so on. But whenever we try to get a critical perspective on these truths about truth, we wind up with dubious assumptions, misleading pictures, incoherent formulations. This view is not itself the conclusion of a philosophical perspective on truth, but merely a prudential judgment based on the historical record.

Accepting this sort of humdrum, philosophically unloaded sense of truth allows us to avoid the pitfalls of many of Rorty's formulations, which run aground by trying to avoid talk of our knowing truths about the world. Without a forthright acceptance of humdrum realism, Rorty is tempted to replace truth with group consensus and hesitates to say that philosophical views opposed to his are wrong, maintaining only that he offers preferable "alternative descriptions." Such equivocations leave him open to charges of incoherent relativism and skepticism. But these difficulties dissolve once we accept humdrum realism.[13]

Gutting clarifies how we can take account of what matters most to Rorty in his polemic against correspondence theories of truth and representation while overlooking the potential paradox-mongering that now concerns Rorty himself. In order for Rorty to support (a) his claim that we have dim prospects for a theoretical account of human knowledge and (b) the subsequent, prudential judgment that further attempts to arrive at such an account are fruitless, he need not deny the commonplaces we affirm that form the core of our commonsense view of the world.[14]

By no means do I intend to suggest that these considerations adequately address the various controversies that surround Rorty's views on truth and objectivity. However, what they do show is that Rorty's position is more resourceful than Gerson allows. We cannot fairly deduce a "remarkably silly" position on commitment from Rorty's views about contingency, truth, and rational justification, if we give Rorty his due.

Nevertheless, the reading of Rorty that I have offered here suggests that Gerson is right to locate in Rorty's position some striking similarities to Pyrrhonian scepticism. As David Hiley observes:

> In much the way that Hume's critique of false philosophy's attempt to achieve autonomy from the world of appearance brought us back to the beliefs and customs of common life, the end of philosophy on Rorty's view brings us back to notions of inquiry, truth, and social criticism as . . . subject to all the fallibility and contingency of our circumstances and conditions. . . . It is this that connects Rorty to the tradition

of opposition to philosophy that I have traced to the Pyrrhonian skeptics.[15]

Hiley's reading of Rorty parallels Gutting's. Both find in Rorty's position not a wildly counter-intuitive relativism but a thoroughgoing sense of fallibility and contingency.

This sort of perspective is consistent with commitment, even rational commitment, to convictions that seem right to one. After all, what is one to do once one recognizes one's finitude and contingency and the profound impact of socialization? All we can ask of each other is that we do our best to reflect critically on our beliefs in view of contrary positions and the internal relations our beliefs have to each other. Then we should stand for what seems true and right to us, as best as we can tell, but always with a profound sense of fallibility and tolerance.[16] If any of this seems inconsistent with rational commitment, then we need to reexamine our concept of rationality and make sure that it is reconcilable with our humanity. Of course, Rorty's position is much more complicated and controversial than these remarks suggest. Still, these remarks capture, I think, what matters to Rorty.

It would be hasty to conclude from this analysis, however, that Rortian ironists can be (and also be rationally) committed to ideals that they perceive to be contingent, with all that this recognition implies for them. The reason is that some critics of liberal irony have argued that irony itself precludes commitment. They object to Rorty's position on the grounds that an ironist cannot be an ironist and be committed to moral ideals at the same time. They argue that either the irony has to go or the commitment. Either way, liberal irony cannot be maintained. It is inherently unstable.

3.2   CONTINGENCY, IRONY, AND COMMITMENT

Recently Anthony Rudd has forcefully stated this objection as follows.

> For Rorty, there is nothing that we fundamentally are; no sense in which a particular "basic vocabulary" is true to my essence, as opposed to seeming attractive to me as a result of my upbringing, my contingent desires or my whims. This means that, as he says, the ironist can never take any self-description which he gives himself entirely seriously. For he always retains a certain aloofness from all such descriptions; even the one which he is currently adopting is only provisional. . . . As soon as the ironist says, with real seriousness, "Here I stand, I can do no other," he has necessarily ceased to be an ironist.[17]

Anticipating Rorty's injection of a commitment to liberalism into his overall account of irony as a response, Rudd continues:

> It seems that Rorty's ironist either makes an arbitrary choice to adopt liberal values (though he could equally well have chosen to adopt illiberal ones) or, as Rorty sometimes seems to suggest, he simply adopts those values because they are the dominant values of our culture, and we cannot really step outside them. Either way, he seems to abandon his ironism. In the first case, if he has adopted any values that he does take with real seriousness, and to which he is more than provisionally committed, he has clearly abandoned the ironic stance. Unless of course, one points out the absurdity of supposing that someone can be seriously bound by a choice which he consciously realises to be wholly arbitrary; in which case the commitment goes, and he lapses back into irony. In the second case, he has to admit that he cannot re-describe himself except within the narrow compass of ideas acceptable to "Enlightened" Western liberals, in which case he has abandoned the irresponsibility of the ironist for that of the social conformist.[18]

Rudd's analysis yields several important objections to Rorty's position. He argues first that a Rortian ironist cannot take seriously any self-description. This implies that serious commitment is incompatible with irony, as Rorty construes it. The rest of Rudd's critical analysis depends on this idea. The moment an ironist takes a stand for liberalism or some other set of moral principles, according to Rudd, she no longer is an ironist.[19] In the second quotation, Rudd unintentionally but helpfully suggests a subdivision of the problem of moral commitment for ironists into (a) the problem of commitment for ironists who choose to become liberals or convert to a liberal vocabulary and (b) the problem of commitment for ironists who have inherited a liberal vocabulary. These problems are not identical, even if they are closely related. For the first sort of ironist, the choice to become a liberal ironist could not fail to be arbitrary, according to Rudd. In that case, these ironists will not be able to take their commitment to liberalism very seriously, since they just as easily could have been fascists or religious fundamentalists. If they do manage to take this commitment seriously, then they arbitrarily become committed social conformists, which is incompatible with an ironic stance. Ironists who have inherited a liberal final vocabulary, on the other hand, face the familiar problem, to which I alluded above, that there is at least one feature of their inherited vocabulary or one inherited self-description—being a liberal—which they cannot get out from under or redescribe. Consequently, they are not ironists but are mere conformists or, to use Rorty's language, ethnocentrists.

In Rorty's defense, he does not claim, in the sense that Rudd's criticism turns on, that liberal ironists cannot take any self-description seriously. The light-mindedness that characterizes ironists in their more reflective and philosophical moments should not be conflated with an inability to stand unflinchingly for one's convictions. Furthermore, while it is true that Rorty sometimes disparages "moral seriousness," some philosophers misconstrue what he has in mind when he does this. They fail to separate Rorty's invective against certain ways of philosophizing from criticisms of moral commitment itself.

For instance, in a recent exchange with Simon Critchley, Rorty states, "I think that if you can manage to act decently you can take moral seriousness or leave it alone. That is another reason why I see no problem about the psychological impossibility of liberal ironism."[20] On a first pass, these remarks seem to confirm Rudd's interpretation. They might also seem disingenuous when they are juxtaposed with Rorty's response to Elshtain. As noted in the previous chapter, in his row with Elshtain, Rorty strongly condemns Hitler and Stalin while invoking his own moral sentiments as a committed liberal who also is an ironist. So, one might ask, is Rorty dissembling in response to Critchley or perhaps in response to Elshtain?

We do not have to opt for either alternative. If we take into account the wider context of Rorty's remarks in his exchange with Critchley, it becomes clear that by "moral seriousness" Rorty intends the kind of seriousness exemplified by a moral philosopher or meta-ethicist who searches for a supreme ethical principle to ground particular moral sentiments. As Rorty explains in the same context:

> Unlike Critchley, I don't think we need a "supreme ethical principle," any more than we need to ask whether we have a pre-reflective and pre-sentient set of responses to others' pains. I do not see the point of delving down to the roots of the difference between people who care about others' suffering and those who don't. For all I know, the difference is all acculturation, or all a matter of the environment of the first few days of infancy, or all in the genes. Maybe it's acculturation in some people and genes in others. . . .
>
> I hesitate to lug out the ultimate weapon so soon, but Critchley's attitudes strike me as—yes, you guessed it—*metaphysical*. . . . Metaphysicians think that there is a Right Context, where things are seen as they truly are, without reference to anybody's purposes. So they look for ultimate sources of this, and indefeasible presuppositions of that. Critchley keeps suggesting that moral seriousness requires us to conduct such a search.[21]

Whatever we make of Rorty's disparaging remarks about metaphysics and metaphysicians, when he dismisses moral seriousness in his exchange with Critchley, he does not intend to dismiss moral commitment. Rather, he rejects attempts of philosophers to find a supreme ethical principle and related projects of locating something in human nature (as such) that provides a universal foundation for our various moral sentiments. A detailed analysis of *Contingency* yields a similar conclusion.

Rudd might rejoin, however, that, despite Rorty's stated intentions, his account of irony still cannot be reconciled with moral commitment. After all, Rudd does not have to base his criticisms on Rorty's disparaging remarks about certain meta-ethical projects. So what more can be said in Rorty's defense?

In the first place, there is nothing incoherent about the idea that one can be firmly committed to ideals that one takes to be contingent. So Rudd makes an illicit move when he concludes that an ironist's commitment to her liberal ideals will be provisional and lukewarm because she takes these ideals to be contingent. Rorty's original and subsequent sketches of a liberal ironist, moreover, do not imply that commitment as such is incompatible with an ironic stance, as Rorty defines such a stance. Rorty defines an ironist as someone who has radical and continuing doubts about her vocabulary because she is impressed by the vocabularies of others she has encountered, and she realizes that she cannot provide a noncircular demonstration of the superiority of her vocabulary. If she philosophizes about her situation, moreover, she does not conclude that her vocabulary is "closer to reality" than others.[22] When we unpack what Rorty intends by these claims, it is clear that a person can meet these conditions and still be firmly and rationally committed to ideals.

Consider first an ironist's radical and continuing doubts about her vocabulary. These are doubts about the adequacy of her vocabulary for her quest for autonomy. It is not difficult to see how lingering and deeply felt doubts of this sort can coexist with commitment to moral ideals. Indeed, one can easily imagine an ironist worrying that her ideals, which she finds herself unable to abandon, may inhibit her attempt to become a novel self. This sort of inner turmoil is not unfamiliar. Nor is it something that counts against the rationality of an ironist's commitments.

Suppose, however, that my reading is mistaken. Suppose Rorty's ironist lapses into a metaphysical realist's mindset and so her doubts are doubts about whether her vocabulary corresponds to reality.[23] In that case, it still is possible for such a person to be committed to moral ideals at the same time. It is even possible to be rationally committed to one's ideals in these circumstances.

For instance, consider a white Southerner in the reconstructionist era who has come to embrace the view that slavery is an immoral institution. She might have this conviction because at one time she came to identify strongly with certain slaves. She might also doubt that her view is more defensible than the views of her pro-slavery, racist fellow citizens. She might be impressed by the certainty with which they hold their convictions and by the consistency of their views. She might doubt that she could ever get rid of her misgivings altogether through a reasoned argument. If she were to philosophize a lot more about her situation, she might even doubt that her anti-slavery views are any closer to corresponding to reality than the racist views of her friends. She could come to have this doubt not because she incoherently does not believe her own beliefs and disbelieve contrary beliefs, but on account of doubts about her ability to show in a non-question–begging way that correspondence to reality is on her side or because of other doubts she has about the idea of correspondence. It is possible that racism is so deeply ingrained in her that she is not able to have any more confidence than this sort of weak confidence in her antislavery views.

What then could be the basis of her commitment to the ideal of dismantling slavery? It might be nothing more than the strong sympathies that she has for slaves, which she cannot deny. Commitment, even rational commitment, is compatible with a significant amount of cognitive dissonance about that to which one is committed.

Still, as we observed above, for Rorty, for the newborn abolitionist even to become an abolitionist she has to be able to weave abolitionist beliefs into her set of beliefs. But a person can do this and achieve a modicum of consistency across her beliefs, to the extent she is clear about them, and still have the sort of doubts that Rorty's ironists have. A person could give the benefit of the doubt to her pro-slavery fellow citizens, try her best to convince herself that she must be misguided about her newfound abolitionism, and still find herself convinced that she cannot deny her sympathies. I think she then would have to believe that pro-slavery persons hold cruel views. At least she would have to suspect that they are misguided. But these beliefs are consistent with her having continuing doubts about her own position and with her being impressed with pro-slavery views in other respects.

However, could such a newborn but conflicted abolitionist be rational in holding firmly to her convictions? Of course, it depends on what we have in mind by "rational." But if the question is, "could our newborn abolitionist be logically consistent while holding firmly to her convictions?" I think the answer is "yes." Why not? Logical consistency tolerates a good deal of tension. If the question is, "could our newborn abolitionist be exemplary in fulfilling her epistemic duties while holding firmly to her convictions?" the answer still is "yes." She could do her very best to scrutinize critically her newfound convictions and give the pro-slavery advocates as fair a shot as she can at redescribing her sympathies for slaves, and she still might turn out a resolute abolitionist.

Consequently, whether we construe a liberal ironist's doubts as doubts about the truth of her vocabulary or as doubts about the adequacy of it for her project of novel self-creation, such doubts are neither incompatible with moral commitment nor with rational moral commitment. This holds true, moreover, even if ironists realize that they cannot rid themselves of their doubts through arguments phrased in their current vocabularies. So my preliminary conclusion is that one can meet the conditions for being an ironist, as Rorty construes them, and still be (and rationally be) committed to moral ideals.[24]

I turn now to the second half of Rudd's case against Rorty, that is, his specific charge that an ironist who chooses to adopt liberal values either (a) makes an arbitrary choice to be a social conformist or (b) uncritically and heteronomously succumbs to the dominant and narrow values of her society, neither of which is compatible with an ironic stance. It is somewhat odd that Rudd offers the first horn of this dilemma as a viable reading of Rorty. Rudd recognizes that Rorty sometimes seems to suggest an alternative view, namely, the second horn of the dilemma that Rudd poses. As an exegetical claim, I find this remark slightly misleading. In *Contingency* and since its publication, Rorty has consistently and repeatedly endorsed some version of ethnocentrism along with a strong view of the impact of socialization on human beings. I will set aside this exegetical quibble with Rudd, however, so that we may focus on what is most instructive in his remarks.

It is helpful to take the dilemma that Rudd foists onto Rortian ironists as a suggestion, albeit unintended, to consider their problem with commitment as in fact two distinct problems that have different causes. The arbitrariness problem arises for Rortian ironists who adopt liberalism as an alternative to the vocabulary that they inherited.[25] That is why this problem receives so little attention from Rorty. Since he himself inherited a liberal vocabulary, he is not as attuned as he otherwise would be to this potential problem. Presumably the problem centers round this question: given that all values are contingent and equally unable finally to be vindicated through noncircular argument, why be a liberal ironist rather than some other morally committed ironist or simply an ironist with no moral commitments? The social conformity problem arises for Rortian ironists who have inherited a liberal vocabulary and choose to retain it even as ironists. This problem arises from the apparent incompatibility of social conformism and irony.

These problems are distinct and both are significant. So I address the arbitrariness problem in detail in the next section. Then I treat the social conformity problem in a subsequent section.

3.3 THE PROBLEM OF ARBITRARINESS

Rudd implies that ironists who adopt liberal values because they are the dominant and inescapable values of their culture do not make an arbitrary choice to adopt such values. Whereas, ironists who could equally well choose illiberal values do make an arbitrary choice. The difference between these cases is not that in the former case values that have noncircular justification are adopted. Rather, it is that in the former case the ironist has a reason to adopt or continue to hold liberal values, whereas in the latter case she has no reason. She could just as well flip a coin or roll dice to determine whether to be a liberal, a religious fundamentalist, or a fascist. But why does Rudd think that an ironist's adoption of liberal values is arbitrary in this way, if not ethnocentric?

The clearest case in which a problem of arbitrariness might emerge is a case in which an ironist opts for a liberal vocabulary as an alternative to an illiberal vocabulary that she inherited or came to adopt in some other way. In such a case, one might wonder why an ironist would commit herself to a form of liberalism, since as an ironist she believes that all values and vocabularies are contingent, and she does not think that liberals have demonstrative arguments for the superiority of their values. If she did not inherit a liberal vocabulary and she is an ironist, why would she limit her range of possibilities by committing to liberalism? Does not this move seem arbitrary, as Rudd argues?

There are at least three likely answers that Rorty might offer in response to this question. First, ironists might encounter or be subjected to extreme cruelty and be led to adopt liberalism in response. Second, since ironists value self-creation, they might reason that liberal societies afford the best opportunities for self-creation. As a result, in order to bring more consistency to their set of values, they might become liberals. Third, because self-creation involves getting out from under inherited vocabularies, for Rortian ironists, adopting a liberal vocabulary is *a* way to begin to become a novel self, if one inherited an illiberal vocabulary. For Rorty, it seems that the extent to which one fashions a distinctive and idiosyncratic kind of vocabulary for oneself is the extent to which one achieves novelty as a self. Thus, a first move in the direction of novel selfhood for a person who has inherited a nonliberal vocabulary could be cobbling together pieces of an established liberal vocabulary and combining them in novel ways.

Rudd anticipates the first two responses. I begin with his rejoinder to the second response above. Rudd replies:

> Rorty does not . . . make things quite so easy for himself, as he accepts Judith Shklar's rather odd definition of liberalism as the belief that "cruelty is the worst thing that we do." What, though, is the connection between an abhorrence of cruelty and a commitment to a life of ironic self-description?[26]

In other words, Rudd wonders why an ironist who values self-creation would become an advocate of liberal values since, for Rorty, there is no natural connection between these values and a life of ironic self-description in the pursuit of self-creation.

If Rudd is looking for some sort of metaphysically necessary connection between abhorrence of cruelty and a commitment to self-creation through ironic redescription, surely he will not find one, and neither will Rorty. However, these pursuits can be connected in a life and, short of that, they can coexist. Rorty does not have to say that every ironist who converts to liberalism from an illiberal vocabulary does so because she finds in her life a connection between abhorrence of cruelty and self-creation. But this can be one reason for some ironists in this kind of situation to convert to liberalism. Furthermore, a society that is fundamentally opposed to cruelty might also be more likely to offer more opportunities for self-creation, especially if policies that needlessly hinder self-creation are commonly taken to be cruel policies. So, if an ironist believes that this sort of relation between liberal values and novel self-creation holds in her current circumstances or that she might better promote the having of policies that are conducive to self-creation, if she promotes liberal values, then she might convert to liberalism in this case as well.

Furthermore, Rorty can construe his understanding of liberalism so that his commitment to it clearly implies a basic commitment to the value of self-creation within the boundaries of an even more basic abhorrence of cruelty. It would not be difficult for Rorty to argue that taking away a person's opportunity to pursue self-creation in harmless ways is very cruel. Thus, Rorty could argue that liberalism, as he defines it, already contains within it a basic commitment to the value of self-creation, even if self-creation is not the most ultimate value of liberalism, that is, even if it is trumped by a more basic abhorrence of cruelty.

One gets the impression from Rudd, however, that this issue—the way that Rorty defines liberalism—is not the main problem. Rudd might quickly concede these points. His reply to the first possible response from Rorty above, that an ironist might become a liberal due to a life-changing experience of cruelty, gets to the heart of the debate between him and Rorty. Rudd counters:

> A hatred of and concern to lessen cruelty would seem to place limits on the self-descriptions that one can adopt . . . the opposition to cruelty is something that seems to demand to be taken seriously. I cannot regard my moral abhorrence of cruelty as simply one more ironic pose which I may adopt or drop at will if it becomes tiresome. Indeed, a vivid sense of the suffering of others is exactly the sort of strong impression that may shake an ironist out of his ironism, and convince him that there are some commitments which he must take with absolute seriousness.[27]

Rudd reiterates here his assertion that if a person is an ironist, she cannot be a morally committed person. I have argued above that this is not an accurate assessment of Rortian irony. Yet, as we now see, Rudd's critical analysis of Rorty's position depends almost entirely on this assumption. The main issue between Rudd and Rorty is not arbitrariness. An ironist might well be converted to liberalism as an additional commitment by the very sort of experience to which Rudd refers. Rudd's real difficulty is reconciling this kind of commitment with irony. It is not the supposed arbitrariness of this commitment. He recognizes reasons that ironists might have for converting to liberalism. For Rudd, however, this sort of conversion could not fail to be a movement *from* an ironic stance *to* a liberal one. It is impossible to be an ironist and a morally committed person at the same time, in Rudd's view of irony.

How then do we account for Rudd's charge of arbitrariness? In a recent essay in which Rudd defends Kierkegaard against MacIntyre's charge that *Either/Or* presents moral agency as an arbitrary choice, Rudd argues:

> One can, on a whim, choose to *act* in a way that conforms to ethical rules. But to *be* ethical is to have internalised those rules, to have

developed virtuous dispositions. In which case the actions which are prompted by those dispositions will not be whimsical or arbitrary. Could one choose to adopt such dispositions themselves on a whim? To do so would involve committing oneself to continue to work at the development of such dispositions over time.... But a genuinely arbitrary choice is one which, by its nature, can always be reversed by another arbitrary choice; it cannot, therefore, involve making a long-term commitment.[28]

We now have the middle term that, for Rudd, connects irony and arbitrariness. In his analysis of Rortian irony, Rudd takes irony as such to be incompatible with commitment. In this more recent quotation, Rudd takes ethical choice apart from long-term commitment to be arbitrary. Since ironists cannot make commitments of this sort, on Rudd's view, their choices must be arbitrary. When they choose to become liberals, it is just for a time—so long as being a liberal is interesting, as Rudd sees it. If their choice is not just for a time, then they no longer are ironists. Therefore, an ironist's choice of liberalism could not fail to be either arbitrary or an abandonment of irony, in Rudd's view.

Consequently, when we get to the bottom of Rudd's critical analysis of Rorty's position, we find that the real difficulty he has with Rorty is that Rorty tries to combine irony and moral commitment in a complex position or stance. Rudd simply begins his critical assessment of Rorty's position with an *a priori* assumption about the nature of irony, namely, that it is incompatible with serious, long-term commitment. It is not surprising, then, that Rorty's position turns out to be deeply problematic, in Rudd's view, and that the problems ultimately derive from Rorty's attempted fusion of liberalism and irony.

Perhaps Rudd proceeds in this way because his analysis of Rorty's position serves a larger purpose in his essay. He wants to show that Kierkegaard's critique of romantic views of irony, which turns on the charge that this sort of irony is morally irresponsible and socially destructive, applies as well, with little translation, to Rorty's account of irony. But Rortian irony is not at all the same thing as romantic irony, which Kierkegaard characterizes as "infinite absolute negativity."[29] In this case, the differences are decisive. Rortian irony, even without its liberal component, is not and never was the sort of pure irony or "infinite negative power that dissolves all positive belief or commitment"[30] that Kierkegaard critiques. Rorty's antifoundationalism and recognition of contingency, which Rudd highlights, do not entail that an ironist find her identity solely in her imaginative and critical powers of dissociation. Rorty wants to help us to overcome contingency by facing up to it, not through imaginative flight from it.[31] The closest Rorty comes to endorsing the sort of pure irony that Kierkegaard critiques is in his Nietzschean account of self-creation. I now turn to this controversial feature of Rorty's account and the second horn of Rudd's dilemma.

3.4 Irony, Autonomy, and Liberalism

I have suggested that we take the second horn of Rudd's dilemma as a problem for Rortian ironists who have inherited a liberal vocabulary. At the beginning of this chapter, I also suggested that the problem that arises for this sort of ironist is related to her pursuit of autonomy or novel self-creation. According to Rorty, an ironist needs to get out from under inherited vocabularies in order to become a novel or autonomous self. But what if she has inherited a liberal vocabulary? How can she be both a liberal and an ironist? It seems that she has to set aside her quest for autonomy, in which case she can be an ironist only in a minimal sense.[32] Or she has to get out from under her inherited liberalism, which disqualifies her from being a committed liberal. Rudd gets at this problem by suggesting that someone who cannot redescribe herself without reference to her (inherited) liberal identity is, in fact, a social conformist and certainly is no ironist.

Here Rudd leads us to what at first glance seems a more formidable problem in Rorty's account. Before I consider ways that Rorty might avoid this problem, I consider it in a bit more detail and try to disclose its initial force.

Rorty construes autonomy without regard for the specific content of the final vocabulary that is said to be conducive to autonomy. On a first pass, an autonomy-enhancing vocabulary for a Rortian ironist is just a vocabulary that is different from the vocabulary that she inherited. Of course, this vocabulary will not be and could not be created *ex nihilo*. The novelty it might come to have derives from two sources: (a) the mere fact that it is different and (b) the new and different ways in which the vocabulary that is adopted is employed—new uses for old terms, new terms with new uses, and so on. Rorty does not claim that liberalism is a vocabulary that is naturally or essentially superior to other vocabularies in the second way in which a vocabulary can be conducive to novelty. Furthermore, the first way in which a vocabulary can be novel seems to function as a necessary condition for the pursuit of autonomy in Rorty's account, since he equates novel self-creation with getting out from under inherited vocabularies. The implication of this reading is that an ironist who has inherited a liberal vocabulary initiates her quest for autonomy by rejecting liberalism and experimenting with nonliberal vocabularies.

Rorty cannot evade this problem by invoking his private–public distinction. As I argued in the previous chapter, this distinction still has an important role in his account but has softened almost to the point of dissolution in his publications since *Contingency*, especially in response to feminist critiques of it. What little is left that unproblematically counts as private leaves insufficient room for anything more than extremely modest attempts at self-creation for persons who have to get out from under liberalism in order to become novel selves.

Furthermore, Rorty's concessions in regard to his private–public split in "Against Bosses" reveal a blind spot in his position, if he retains a full-fledged Nietzschean view of self-creation (as he interprets Nietzsche). He says that many persons do not need a private–public split. He also clarifies that his private–public distinction just is a negative point to affirm that it is not necessary to construct one's identity around social and civic life in a liberal democracy. But the vast majority of persons in his audience have inherited a liberal vocabulary. Does it not follow then that these persons need to experiment with illiberal vocabularies, if they are to become novel selves? If so, then to the contrary of Rorty's suggestion in "Against Bosses," it follows that most persons in his audience need a firm private–public distinction that works, if they are to pursue autonomy, as Rorty construes it, while remaining committed to liberalism. It also follows that as liberalism becomes more widely disseminated and embraced, there arises a greater need for more persons to adopt a firm private–public split. As persons who have inherited a liberal vocabulary become more civic-minded and socially engaged, their need expands for a firmer and more expansive private–public split so that they will have more solitary space for experimentation with illiberal vocabularies, if they are also in pursuit of Nietzschean autonomy. So, it seems that, in Rorty's view, as a liberal ironist who has inherited a liberal vocabulary becomes a better liberal, that is, more engaged in public pursuits that promote liberal values, she finds it more difficult to become an autonomous person.

These implications are odd and counterintuitive to say the least. It is one thing to embrace the fragmentation of value, as Rorty does, and the permissibility of a private–public split. It is quite another to advance a view of autonomy that makes commitment to liberal ideals almost inevitably heteronomous for persons who inherit a liberal vocabulary just because that vocabulary is inherited.

Other problems may arise as well for Rorty on account of his way of appropriating Nietzsche. As John Owens explains:

> Rorty does not seem to raise what could be considered an obvious question here—whether the urge to overcome the vocabularies of others might itself be an inherited contingency. . . . The Enlightenment and its aftermath after all imposed a powerful rhetoric of overcoming mere contingency on the West. If the urge to overcome is itself an inherited contingency, there is no reason why it should not be overcome in its turn.[33]
>
> Why can I not acknowledge my own contingency in a straightforward inherited language? Why do I need to create my own?[34]
>
> Why is it not possible to accept contingency while remaining with someone else's vocabulary (for example the vocabulary of Freud)? Why should acceptance of contingency necessarily lead to poetry? Rorty's answer seems to rely on a rhetoric of dubious alternatives, implying that there is no middle ground between Plato and Nietzsche. . . . However, surely there are other possibilities besides the metaphysician and the strong poet—for example, a familiar language which is neither metaphysical nor idiosyncratic?[35]

Rorty has to say that the urge to overcome the vocabularies of others is at least a contingent urge, if not an inherited one as well. If it is inherited as well, then it too must be overcome somehow, if one is to pursue autonomy as Nietzschean overcoming of inherited vocabularies. Exactly what is involved, though, in getting out from under the view that one needs to get out from under inherited vocabularies in order to become autonomous? What other way can one do this except by setting aside, for the purposes of self-creation, the view that one needs to get out from under an inherited vocabulary, since this view itself is inherited? In that case, Rorty's account yields the following paradox: becoming autonomous requires that one get out from under an inherited vocabulary, unless one inherited a vocabulary according to which becoming autonomous requires getting out from under inherited vocabularies. Otherwise one is acting in accord with an inherited view about autonomy or heteronomously when one sets aside other inherited views in order to pursue autonomy *as* getting out from under inherited vocabularies.

How might Rorty avoid these problems and counterintuitive implications? Rorty could opt for a more ethnocentric view of autonomy in order to reconcile his account of autonomy with his commitment to liberalism. In fact, I think that there is a weaker but less problematic version of autonomy somewhat implicit in Rorty's account that can be seized on here. I consider now this weaker position and discuss whether it delivers Rorty from the problems sketched above.

Rorty embraces liberalism as an unavoidable starting point for his own moral, social, and political reflection. Since autonomy partly is a moral notion, it makes sense for Rorty to embrace a more liberal view of it rather than a full-fledged Nietzschean view. Such a move is more consistent with Rorty's overall account.

What would a more liberal view of autonomy be? How would it be different from a Nietzschean view (as Rorty appropriates Nietzsche)? It would begin with the idea that autonomy that is purchased at the expense of cruelty to others is not worth having or pursuing, a position that Rorty already endorses very explicitly. It also would reject mere social conformity as incompatible with autonomy. These moves, taken together, imply that the kind of autonomous life that liberals seek is somewhere between a life of uncritical social conformity and a life of independence and self-governance that is purchased at the expense of cruelty to others. Very broadly speaking, then, from a liberal perspective, an autonomous life can roughly be construed as a life of independence and self-governance that is also characterized by tolerance and abhorrence of cruelty. Of course, there are many philosophical accounts of autonomy from liberal standpoints to which one could recur in order to fill out this kind of position, not least of which are Kant's and Rawls's accounts.[36] For my purposes here, the decisive feature of these accounts is that they do not require Nietzschean overcoming of inherited vocabularies.

Now, I concede that the broad, alternative account of autonomy that I have sketched thus far leaves out something that is important to Rorty. For not only does it set aside the requirement that we shed inherited vocabularies, it also leaves out the closely related idea, for Rorty, that freedom is bound up with the recognition of contingency.[37] Rorty construes freedom this way because he believes that recognizing the contingency of vocabularies and self-descriptions helps one gain critical distance from them, especially one's own, so that one can begin the process of achieving autonomy.

Rorty does believe, however, that extremely illiberal ways of life, for instance, are not good ways to live, even if he does not base this view on the idea that these ways of life fail to conform to some ahistorical human telos. Furthermore, although he recognizes that he might have been a fascist himself, had he been socialized differently, and that he does not have a noncircular argument for the superiority of liberal values, still he is committed to these values and their implications, which he inherited. He also is engaged in a project of novel self-creation.

Consequently, he should and we can clearly disentangle the idea that freedom is related to the recognition of contingency from the idea that autonomy must involve shedding inherited vocabularies.

There is an interesting section in *Contingency* that implies that Rorty is quite open to this suggestion. Indeed, the problems and counterintuitive implications that I highlighted above largely disappear when we give prominence to this passage. In the midst of his discussion of the contingency of selfhood, Rorty approves of Nietzsche's idea that we construe self-knowledge as self-creation. However, he then *rejects* what he takes to be Nietzsche's rather extreme way of understanding this idea. Rorty first construes Nietzsche's position as follows:

> To fail as a poet—and thus, for Nietzsche, to fail as a human being—is to accept somebody else's description of oneself, to execute a previously prepared program, to write, at most, elegant variations on previously written poems. So the only way to trace home the causes of one's being as one is would be to tell a story about one's causes in a new language.[38]

Here Rorty sketches the Nietzschean view of self-creation that some philosophers take him to adopt without revision for himself. To fail as a human being is to fail to become a novel self. To fail to become a novel self is to fail to come up with one's own terms for understanding one's life and the lives of others. The idea that sloughing off inherited vocabularies is necessary for novel self-creation is prominent in this position.

Rorty uses his reading of Freud to combat the excesses that he finds in this view and to democratize Nietzschean self-creation. Rorty thinks that Freud shows us that "every human life is the working out of a sophisticated idiosyncratic fantasy."[39] He rebukes Nietzsche for losing sight of the frailty and finitude of human beings. Then he weakens Nietzsche's stringent conditions for autonomy. As Rorty explains:

> But if we avoid Nietzsche's inverted Platonism—his suggestion that a life of self-creation can be as complete and as autonomous as Plato thought a life of contemplation might be—then we shall be content to think of any human life as the always incomplete, yet sometimes heroic, reweaving of such a web. We shall see the conscious need of the strong poet to *demonstrate* that he is not a copy or replica as merely a special form of an unconscious need everyone has: the need to come to terms with the blind impress which chance has given him, to make a self for himself by redescribing that impress in terms, which are, if only marginally, his own.[40]

This passage significantly downplays the Nietzschean elements in Rorty's account of self-creation. It indicates to us that self-creation is closely related to self-knowledge, for Rorty, in the sense that coming to recognize the various contingencies that have happened to come together to constitute one's life is a way not only of owning them but facing up to them or recognizing them for what they are. Facing up to such contingencies, though difficult and sometimes very painful, can be very liberating.

Redescription comes in here, for Rorty, partly because he has in mind that when a person comes to recognize a constituent of her inherited identity as contingent, she then sees it or describes it in a different light. In that case, it may lose the tight grip that it has on her.

There is a significant difference between a person who reflects critically on who she is; where her various peculiar habits, beliefs, and desires come from; and who she might become in the future, as she comes to terms with the self that she largely has inherited; and a person who fails to undertake this sort of critical reflection. Rorty suggests that we can describe the difference between such persons roughly this way: the critically reflective person is much farther down the path of novel self-creation. She has more autonomy, for as she recognizes the web of contingencies that she is, in a profound respect she gains a perspective on herself and others that is liberating just by virtue of the fact that she gains some critical distance from her inherited identity and is able to see it in a different light. This perspective also enhances her chances for novel self-creation in the future. Indeed, such a person comes to recognize clearly a project that is implicated in all her more specific pursuits of self-creation: the project of coming to terms with her inherited identity.

The reason I say that, for Rorty, a person such as this is *farther* down the path of novel self-creation is that Rorty's reading of Freud leads him to believe that all of us are attempting, to a greater or lesser extent and consciously or unconsciously, to come to terms with "the blind impress which chance has given us." Whatever one thinks of Rorty's appropriation of Freud, the crucial point here is that it leads him to democratize Nietzschean self-creation. It is not only strong poets who are involved in self-creative projects. So also are Cub Scout leaders, televangelists, and analytic philosophers, to list just a few kinds of persons who might otherwise have seemed barred from novel self-creation, as Rorty understands it.

Now it is clearer why, in "Against Bosses," Rorty says that many persons do not need private–public splits. It is not that he thinks that relatively few persons are or should be engaged in self-creative projects. Rather, he thinks that the pursuit of self-creation need not take the form of Nietzschean overcoming of inherited vocabularies. For those few persons for whom it does take this form, if they inherited liberalism as part of their final vocabulary, then they have to observe a firm private–public split in their lives in the sense that they must keep their shedding of liberalism relegated to their own solitude. It must not ebb over into their relations with others in such a way that they flout their basic obligations to others. But even Nietzschean strong poets, Rorty suggests, will be able merely to construct terms for redescribing their lives that are only marginally their own.

These clarifications of Rorty's account of self-creation significantly alter the impression that he simply reiterates Nietzsche's position, as he understands it. Rather, Rorty weakens the requirements of self-creation and then argues that to some extent we all are involved in creating for ourselves idiosyncratic selves through coming to terms with our inherited identities. Furthermore, these clarifications help to reveal symmetry between *Contingency* and "Against Bosses," not a failure in the latter to recognize and come to terms with problematic implications of the former.

Then what sets apart ironists from other persons? Ironists are very deliberately and consciously engaged in projects of self-creation. Nonironists may be as well, of course. But ironists are by definition. Also, they are keen observers of contingency. Their recognition of contingency, moreover, leads them to hold an antifoundationalist attitude. So while liberals and other persons might still ground their various commitments in complex, metaphysical pictures of the world, ironists embrace their commitments without philosophical foundations of this sort. None of this implies that an ironist cannot be or rationally be a committed liberal while she retains her ironism.

But what about Owens's concern that the very idea that we need to get out from under inherited vocabularies in order to become autonomous is itself part of an inherited vocabulary? Once Rorty weakens Nietzsche's conditions for self-creation, the problems brought to our attention by Owens lose much of their force. Owens himself somewhat concedes this point. He states:

> As if aware of the vulnerability of his position, Rorty heavily qualifies his demand for a new vocabulary as a condition for acknowledging contingency.[41] . . . Rorty points out that new metaphors depend on older speech for their force, and cannot avoid being "marginal and parasitic." . . . With this, Rorty's requirement starts to look more like a new use of an old vocabulary, rather than a completely new one.[42]

So Owens concedes that Rorty ratchets down the need for a new vocabulary in quests for self-creation. Still I think we can go farther than Owens implies in qualifying Rorty's position. For as long as we emphasize the idea of using vocabularies in new ways, we fail to take full account of the way in which Rorty utilizes Freud to democratize self-creation. For Rorty, we need not literally use vocabularies in new ways to pursue self-creation. This is one rather poetic way of creating oneself. Perhaps it also is one that Rorty especially admires. But it is not the only way that we can create ourselves, as "Against Bosses" makes clear.

But why not abandon preoccupation with inherited vocabularies in the first place and redescribe it as a fixation bequeathed to us by the Enlightenment? The reason why a person needs to examine her inherited vocabulary is that it has so much significance for her as it profoundly impacts her life in ways she can only begin to understand. The reason why recognition of the contingency of an inherited vocabulary is important to Rorty is that such recognition is apt to loosen greatly the grip that an inherited vocabulary has on a person. A person then can own or continue to identify with this vocabulary. Or she may repudiate it and spend the rest of her life trying to overcome the profound influence that it exerts on her. In either case, it remains important to reflect critically on one's inherited vocabulary and to come to recognize it for what it is—an inherited contingency. This is Rorty's basic pattern for overcoming inherited vocabularies, that is, for relating to them autonomously.

Of course it is true that the idea that we should critically examine our inherited vocabularies is part of the legacy of the Enlightenment. This fact, in turn, suggests perhaps that we should consider carefully the claim that we ought to examine our inherited vocabularies. But there is nothing incoherent about this state of affairs. We might just take it to imply that, as children of the Enlightenment, we should be on guard against excessive self-examination or hyper-suspiciousness of our inherited ideals.

Rorty also can acknowledge Owens's point that we can accept contingency while remaining in someone else's vocabulary. After all, Rorty himself largely remains in the vocabularies of others, including, for example, the vocabularies of Freud, Nietzsche, Hegel, Mill, Darwin, and Donald Davidson, as he creates himself as an author. He acknowledges, moreover, that even our best attempts at novelty in our vocabularies are not very successful. The idea that Rorty cannot adequately accommodate Owens's insights turns on a reading that locates in Rorty's position too simple a reiteration of Nietzsche's account of self-creation. This reading of Rorty fails to take into account a decisive passage in *Contingency* that shows how we can and should avoid it.

What about Rudd's specific charge that Rortian ironists are mere social conformists and not ironists, if they cannot set aside their inherited liberalism? I think it is difficult for this objection to be sustained. Rortian ironists subject their inherited liberalism to critical scrutiny. Furthermore, they recognize it as an inherited contingency, not as a necessary commitment for all rational persons. They stick with their liberal commitments for the sort of pragmatic reasons to which Malachowski alludes. None of these reasons amounts to saying, as Rudd suggests, I am committed to liberal values because they are the dominant values of my culture. This would be a very peculiar way for an ironist to explain why she is committed to liberalism. Perhaps Rudd thinks that a Rortian ironist would give this kind of response because he reads such a response into Rorty's ethnocentrism. However, for Rorty, to be ethnocentric is to be committed to those values that seem right to one, even though one recognizes that (a) socialization has predisposed one to adopt such values, (b) these values are contingent, and (c) there is ultimately no noncircular way to demonstrate their superiority.[43] It is not to adopt values just because they are the dominant values of one's society, which *is* mere social conformity. Consequently, if Rorty is asked why he is committed to liberal values, the most straightforward reply that he could give is that he is committed to them because they seem better than illiberal values—he finds himself with liberal values and without any compelling reason to abandon them. The only other reason that I discern for Rudd to think that this kind of stance is incompatible with irony is his conflation of Rortian irony with romantic irony. These brands of irony are not the same in the relevant sense. I conclude that Rorty can avoid Rudd's dilemma that his ironists either opt arbitrarily for liberalism or abandon their ironic stance by lapsing into crass social conformity. When we examine Rorty's position carefully, it becomes clear that this dilemma is a false dilemma for liberal ironists. They need not grasp either horn of it.

3.5   MacIntyre on Rortian Autonomy

Rorty is the sort of iconoclastic writer who sometimes is criticized seemingly from all sides. Rudd finds mere social conformity in Rorty's account. Whereas, MacIntyre alleges that Rorty's ironists are radical individualists who undermine the liberal communities to which they belong. In this section, I explain and assess this criticism of Rorty's account of self-creation.

As I indicated in the previous chapter, MacIntyre objects not only to Rorty's notion that anything can be made to look good or bad by being redescribed but also to Rorty's account of self-creation. MacIntyre argues that all evaluative vocabularies have social origins since they are based on "shared expressions put to shared uses" that are "embedded in a wide range of common practices of receiving and giving, in a common form of life."[44] Consequently, if an ironist employs evaluative concepts, as any ironist must and Rortian ironists do, these will not be novel concepts or old ones put to novel uses, if they retain their evaluative meaning. In that case, an ironist's moral commitments seem to represent a formidable obstacle in her pursuit of autonomy through novel self-creation. MacIntyre thinks that indeed they are an obstacle. He also argues that it is a serious mistake for an ironist to think that she could, as he puts it, "find a vantage point quite outside those relationships and commitments" that have made her what she now is.[45]

Two distinct criticisms emerge from these considerations. First, it is not possible for ironists to construct entirely novel vocabularies, at least to the extent that ironists retain moral concepts in their vocabularies. This criticism brings us back to the now familiar idea that the most an ironist can do in this regard is patch together pieces of existing vocabularies and put them to new and different uses. However, MacIntyre adds that the evaluative part of this new patchwork will not be novel even in this modest respect. Interestingly, Rorty's own position seems to indicate that MacIntyre's assessment is accurate. Rorty simply borrows his concept of liberalism from Judith Shklar, who in turn developed it from existing liberal sentiments and practices.

MacIntyre's second criticism is that since communal bonds undergird and give rise to evaluative vocabularies, attempts to overcome these vocabularies could not fail to involve ironists in disengagement from shared judgments and from "the social relationships which presuppose the use of [these vocabularies] in making those judgments."[46] So he suggests that even the attempt to pursue novel self-creation in the way that Rortian ironists do is destructive of social bonds. Since these social bonds provide the glue that holds together the liberal communities to which Rortian ironists belong, they are guilty of undercutting the stability of their own communities.

I think that both of these criticisms miss their mark. Rorty concedes that ironists manage at most to come up with vocabularies that are only marginally their own. There is no imperative in Rorty's position, moreover, that they even attempt this. If MacIntyre's criticisms have any relevance to Rorty's position, they apply at most to persons Rorty refers to as "strong poets" or "Romantic intellectuals," persons whose quest for poetic novelty puts them at odds with public ideals.[47] We now see, however, that it is a mistake to think that Rorty holds these persons up as models for all of us in the relevant sense as we pursue self-creation. These persons must observe a firm private–public split, according to Rorty. So, in effect, Rorty somewhat concurs with MacIntyre in the sense that Rorty thinks that even strong poets will have to limit their pursuit of sheer novelty to aspects of their vocabularies that are distinct from our most basic shared judgments, the judgments that make possible our lives together. Of course, for Rorty, these shared judgments will not be as expansive as they are for MacIntyre. But if MacIntyre's critique of Rorty's account of irony then reduces to a critique of liberalism itself, at that point we have moved to an entirely different issue. Although this issue is very important, it is not within the purview of my project to address it.

On the basis of the criticisms noted above and those discussed in the previous chapter, MacIntyre concludes that Rortian irony is irredeemably flawed.[48] Oddly, though, he brings his critical analysis of Rortian irony to a close with a terse dismissal of irony *per se*.[49] Even if one were to concur with MacIntyre's criticisms of liberal irony, however, it would not follow that irony is to be rejected altogether, as MacIntyre dismisses it. That implication would follow only if the following dilemma holds: either we embrace Rortian irony or we reject irony entirely. But that is a false dilemma because there are other accounts of irony to consider, no matter what we make of Rorty's position.

Another false dilemma also lurks in MacIntyre's position. Because he only considers Rortian irony, he comes to the view that we have to choose between irony and moral commitment, since he concludes that Rortian irony ultimately requires disengagement from social bonds that hold together liberal communities. But that is another either/or that depends on taking Rortian irony to be synonymous with irony itself; and, of course, it also depends on taking Rortian irony to be incompatible with moral commitment. While the latter claim has some initial plausibility but is very difficult to sustain, the former claim is simply false, or perhaps better, a very hasty generalization.

Consequently, even if MacIntyre's criticisms of Rorty's position were plausible, it would not follow that we should reject irony altogether. MacIntyre reaches this conclusion by invoking two false dilemmas: (a) either we embrace Rortian irony or reject irony outright or (b) either we opt for irony or moral commitment. If one accepts this formulation of our options with respect to irony and moral commitment, irony is likely to be dispatched rather quickly, especially on account of the second dilemma. It would be extremely short-sighted to accept MacIntyre's presentation of the options that are open to us in this area, however, since his critique of Rorty's position is problematic and there are other accounts of irony to consider.

3.6 Conclusion

I have argued in this chapter that in general persons can be (and be rationally) committed to ideals that they perceive to be contingent. More specifically, Rortian ironists, contra Rudd, have no problem with commitment as such. We likely would need to assume some kind of foundationalist view of moral commitment in order to locate a serious problem with the fusion of irony and moral commitment in this area. But why do that?

However, even if Rorty's view of irony does not generate this sort of problem for his ironists, the view of novel self-creation that Rorty includes in his position does create serious problems for those ironists who have inherited liberal values, unless we take a more modest view of it. How are ironists who have inherited a liberal vocabulary supposed to overcome or shed this vocabulary while remaining committed to liberalism? The very idea that autonomy requires getting out from under inherited vocabularies itself is part of an inherited vocabulary for not a few would-be ironists. How are they to overcome this inherited contingency, if not simply by setting it aside? If they can do this, however, why cannot other ironists do the same? I think that they can and that Rorty acknowledges as much when he rejects what he takes to be Nietzsche's "inverted Platonism" and uses Freud to democratize self-creation. Then it begins to look as if overcoming inherited vocabularies, for most persons, may have little or nothing to do with shedding them. Rather, it has more to do with critically evaluating them, recognizing their contingency, and coming to terms with the identity one has inherited through them. Rorty should welcome this implication because it brings more internal consistency to his overall position, since it helps to reconcile self-creation and commitment to (inherited) liberalism. However, if Rorty lapses back into a less qualified Nietzschean account of self-creation, then he opens his position to the criticisms advanced by Owens and MacIntyre. These objections get at conceptual and moral problems with the idea that self-creation requires completely abandoning inherited vocabularies in favor of entirely novel ones.

Rorty can avoid these criticisms and many others that have been leveled at his position. But even if we grant them, they do not justify an outright rejection of irony, unless we simply equate Rortian irony with irony as such, as MacIntyre does. There is no compelling reason to do this. Whatever we make of Rorty's position, it is open to us to consider alternative accounts of irony and moral commitment.

Although I have tried to show that Rorty's position is not nearly as problematic as many of his critics suggest, I concede that it does have certain difficulties. In the previous chapter, I argued that Rorty should be more forthright about the implications of his commitment to truthfulness and abandon his metaphor of place in his private–public distinction. In this chapter, I suggested that Rorty unambiguously embrace a kind of humdrum realism in order to avoid the "paradox-mongering" that sometimes plagues his work in infelicitous passages. Also, Rorty needs to adhere closely to his proposed modifications of Nietzschean self-creation in order to avoid serious conundrums in his overall position. Admittedly, all these criticisms are piecemeal and internal. There is no silver bullet lurking in them, as far as I can tell.

Still we might hope for more in an account of irony and moral commitment. We might look for an account of irony that is not so preoccupied with undoing the philosophical excesses of the Enlightenment. A liberal ironist, moreover, may be too narrow a model in certain respects for a life that combines irony and moral commitment. Finally, supposing that Rorty manages to show how irony can promote autonomy, tolerance, civility, and epistemic humility, still one might think that it has other important functions in personal and ethical life that Rorty overlooks or downplays.

There are reasons then to consider an alternative to Rorty's position, even if it is not as problematic as many philosophers think. I turn now to Søren Kierkegaard's account of irony and moral commitment in order to examine its viability as an alternative view.

CHAPTER 4

Kierkegaard on the Problems
of Pure Irony

I have argued in the previous chapters that Richard Rorty's account of liberal irony is insightful, suggestive, and not nearly as morally objectionable as some of Rorty's harshest critics have argued. Still it faces certain difficulties and is hampered by Rorty's preoccupation with overcoming metaphysics and epistemology. It would be rash, however, to dismiss irony out of hand, as MacIntyre does, because of concerns with Rorty's view of irony. Rather, these problems give us reason, if we needed it, to consider alternative accounts of irony and its relation to moral commitment. The alternative account that I begin to consider and sketch in this chapter and extend and modify in the next two chapters is that of Søren Kierkegaard.

It is safe to say that Kierkegaard was preoccupied with irony and its relation to ethical life. His first substantial work, *The Concept of Irony, with Continual Reference to Socrates*, which also was his thesis,[1] explicitly reflects this interest, as does what is arguably his most important pseudonymous work, *Concluding Unscientific Postscript*. This interest in irony also shows up in a subtler way in many of Kierkegaard's writings. For instance, in his first pseudonymous work, *Either/Or*, Kierkegaard sketches a character, "A," who takes up and exemplifies irony as a comprehensive, existential stance. Then, under the guise of Judge William, a person who represents an ethical viewpoint, Kierkegaard offers an extended critique of this stance. Furthermore, mastered irony, a concept that Kierkegaard sketches in the brief, but highly suggestive, concluding section of his thesis, arguably is, as Robert Perkins argues, "the keystone of Kierkegaard's pseudonymous authorship."[2] It is a key interpretive concept that illuminates many philosophical themes in Kierkegaard's pseudonymous works, perhaps even Kierkegaard's very use of pseudonyms, and, moreover, Kierkegaard commends mastered irony to his readers.[3]

In this chapter, I discuss Kierkegaard's original account of irony, as he presents it in his thesis. I attempt to clarify how Kierkegaard conceives of irony as a comprehensive stance and how, as such, it is a stance of "infinite absolute negativity," as Kierkegaard puts it, following Hegel.[4] I also explain why Kierkegaard thinks that irony, as a comprehensive stance, is unstable and destructive of certain moral goods. Finally, I examine briefly Kierkegaard's theological account of living poetically and how it functions in his critique of irony.

4.1   IRONY AS INFINITE ABSOLUTE NEGATIVITY

Kierkegaard's *The Concept of Irony* is a diffuse, subtle, and complex work. The first half of the work, which constitutes the bulk of it, focuses on Socrates and Socratic irony. Socrates is a main topic of Kierkegaard's discussion because Kierkegaard takes Socrates to be the first ironist, that is, the first person who exemplifies irony as an existential stance.[5] Also, Kierkegaard thinks that it is helpful to introduce and clarify the concept of irony through an analysis of the character and personality of its first exemplar. As he explains:

> The concept of irony makes its entry into the world through Socrates. Concepts, just like individuals, have their history and are no more able than they to resist the dominion of time, but in and through it all they nevertheless harbor a kind of homesickness for the place of their birth.[6]
>
> Philosophy is not to look too long at one particular side of its [irony's] phenomenological existence and above all at its appearance but is to see the truth of the concept in and with the phenomenological.[7]

The second half of the thesis offers a more analytical treatment of the concept of irony before moving to a critique of romantic irony. Kierkegaard then concludes his thesis with a terse discussion of the "truth" of irony as a controlled (or mastered) element. For my purposes, it is most instructive to focus on the discussion of irony in the second half of Kierkegaard's thesis.

As noted above, Kierkegaard characterizes irony that is a comprehensive stance as "infinite absolute negativity." For the sake of simplicity, I will refer to this sort of stance as a stance of *pure irony*. According to Kierkegaard, pure irony is a radical and thoroughgoing stance of critical disengagement from human society. As he explains:

> Irony *sensu eminentiori* is directed not against this or that particular existing entity but against the entire given actuality at a certain time and

under certain conditions. . . . It is not this or that phenomenon but the totality of existence that it contemplates *sub specie ironiae* [under the aspect of irony]. To this extent we see the correctness of Hegel's view of irony as infinite absolute negativity.[8]

If we turn back to the foregoing general description of irony as infinite absolute negativity, it is adequately suggested therein that irony is no longer directed against this or that particular phenomenon, against a particular existing thing, but that the whole of existence has become alien to the ironic subject and the ironic subject in turn alien to existence, that as actuality has lost its validity for the ironic subject, he himself has to a certain degree become unactual. The word "actuality," however, must here primarily be understood as historical actuality— that is, the given actuality at a certain time and in a certain situation.[9]

Kierkegaard advances several important claims about pure irony here. First, pure irony (or irony in the eminent sense) is a critical and detached stance against an entire given "actuality." Second, those who take this stance (pure ironists) gain a perspective according to which everything in their given actuality appears vain. Third, as a result, they attain a kind of negative freedom through their recognition of the vanity of everything. So, fourth, since from the standpoint of pure irony "everything becomes nothing," such persons become alienated because actuality "loses its validity" for them.

Several questions emerge at this point. First, what is a given "actuality" and what is involved in being alienated from such a thing? Second, in what sense does everything in this actuality become vain or "nothing" for a person who takes a stance of pure irony, and why does this happen? Third, what sort of freedom does an ironist obtain from such a disengaged standpoint? Fourth, why call this sort of stance "infinite absolute negativity"?

I will take these questions in order. It is likely that by "an entire given actuality," Kierkegaard intends Hegel's notion of *Sittlichkeit* or ethical life. Allen Wood helpfully clarifies Hegelian *Sittlichkeit* as follows:

Hegel uses *Sittlichkeit* to signify two apparently quite distinct things: First, it refers to a certain kind of social order, one that is differentiated and structured in a rational way. Thus "ethical life" is Hegel's name for an entire set of institutions . . . the family, civil society, and the modern political state. Second, however, the term also refers to a certain attitude or "subjective disposition" on the part of individuals toward their social life, an attitude of harmonious identification with its institutions.[10]

Charles Taylor adds:

> "*Sittlichkeit*" refers to the moral obligations I have to an ongoing community of which I am part. These obligations are based on established norms and uses, and that is why the etymological root "Sitten" is important for Hegel's use. The crucial characteristic of *Sittlichkeit* is that it enjoins us to bring about what already is. This is a paradoxical way of putting it, but in fact the common life which is the basis of my *sittlich* obligation is already there in existence. . . .
>
> The doctrine of *Sittlichkeit* is that morality reaches its completion in a community.[11]

Taking these passages together, we have that Hegelian *Sittlichkeit* refers to: (a) a kind of structured social order, which includes institutions such as the family, civil society, other mediating institutions, and the state; (b) a citizen's attitude of harmonious identification with these institutions; and (c) the moral obligations that arise from inhabiting social roles within these various institutions.

Now the stance of pure irony begins to come into focus as a negation of *Sittlichkeit*. Consider first those persons who serve as a foil to pure ironists. These persons identify with the institutions that compose their social order. In a certain respect, they define themselves as persons who inhabit various social roles that contribute to the flourishing of their community; they evaluate themselves in view of the norms and expectations that accompany these roles. Ironists, however, take a standpoint from which the social order appears to lose its meaning and normativity. They no longer find themselves, so to speak, in their various social roles. As a result, they become alienated from social institutions and others who do identify with and take seriously the goals and ideals of these institutions.

But why does this happen? What insight provokes a pure ironist into this sort of radical disengagement? Kierkegaard's answer, at least in his thesis, is subtle and twofold. First, Kierkegaard first notes that to be ironic in a less comprehensive way, to have irony "as a minor element," is to have an "eye for what is crooked, wrong, and vain in existence."[12] Pure ironists, of course, also have this sort of ability to perceive gaps between what is and what ought to be in life. So, in the first place, their recognition of various incongruities in their social environment gives them a kind of critical distance that is not available to others who do not perceive these disparities. By itself, however, this fact does not explain why pure ironists become alienated and disengaged, since other persons who are ironic in this respect do not become alienated and detached from society. To put this point another way, while having an eye for incongruities in life is a necessary condition for being a pure ironist, according to Kierkegaard, it is not a sufficient condition. So, why does the pure ironist radically disengage while others recognize the same incongruities without drawing the conclusion that all the conventions of society and culture are vain?

The difference between a pure ironist and a person who is ironic in this less comprehensive respect is this: pure ironists, according to Kierkegaard, fundamentally want to be free from the obligations, restrictions, and long-term commitments that accompany taking seriously one's given place in a complex social order. They want to have the benefits of living in a social environment in which other persons take these frequently burdensome obligations seriously. However, they themselves do not want to be confined by such things. We can construe this basic desire for negative freedom as an identity-conferring desire that pure ironists have. It motivates them to take the incongruities that they perceive in their social environment as *reason enough* to withdraw from serious commitment to confining social roles. After all, it is not as if, in Kierkegaard's view, ironists must draw the conclusion that everything is vain or that this is the only warranted conclusion. Rather, the evidence underdetermines the leap to radical disengagement. An ironist's basic desire for negative freedom makes up the difference. As Kierkegaard explains:

> Irony is essentially practical . . . if irony gets an inkling that there is something more behind the phenomenon than meets the eye, then precisely what irony has always insisted upon is this, that the subject feel free, so that the phenomenon never acquires any reality for the subject. . . . In irony, the subject continually wants to get outside the object, and he achieves this by realizing at every moment that the object has no reality. . . . In irony, the subject is continually retreating, talking every phenomenon out of its reality in order to save itself—that is, in order to preserve itself in negative independence of everything.
>
> Finally, insofar as irony, when it realizes that existence has no reality [*Realitet*], pronounces the same thesis as the pious mentality, irony might seem to be a kind of religious devotion. . . . Indeed, in the deeper devotional literature, we see that the pious mind regards its own finite personality as the most wretched of all.
>
> In irony, however, since everything is shown to be vanity, the subject becomes free. The more vain everything becomes, all the lighter, emptier, and volatilized the subject becomes.[13]

Thus, according to Kierkegaard, the desire for a radical form of negative freedom is the main motivation for the disengaged stance that ironists take toward their communities and the social roles that they inhabit. The moment an ironist begins to suspect that her detached and unserious attitude may be unwarranted, moreover, she retreats to an even more critical and disengaged standpoint in order to preserve her freedom (by sustaining the "unreality" of the phenomenon, as Kierkegaard puts it). As a result, she becomes more disengaged, more alienated, and even less defined by her social roles—a process that Kierkegaard obscurely, but aptly, refers to as volatilization.[14]

The sketch that Kierkegaard gives us here is a portrait of someone who plays at the various social roles that she inhabits, such as being an employee, friend, daughter, mother, and colleague, for instance.[15] When she begins to feel constrained by one or more of these roles or begins to take them seriously, either she jettisons them or she recurs to a standpoint from which they (once again) appear frivolous or just certain ways of leading a human life, among other ways. For a person to sustain this detached stance, in some cases it also may be necessary for her to mislead some other persons with regard to her attitude toward certain of her social roles, as Kierkegaard recognizes.[16] For instance, an employer who discovers that one of her employees does not take his job very seriously is not likely to retain such a person. A person who discovers that her friend simply plays the role of being a friend, as if there were nothing more to it than playing second base on a softball team, may attempt to persuade her friend to take more seriously the goods and obligations of friendship. The crucial point is that in both cases the person who plays at being an employee or being a friend, and who cannot simply abandon these roles, may find the freedom he desires to be more difficult to obtain and sustain, if his ironic detachment is discovered. So, he may dissemble about his commitments in the presence of certain others in order to enhance his prospects for freedom, as he understands it.

Why would anyone find this sort of freedom attractive? It might seem very unattractive, even repulsive, to us. In the context of noting the various ways in which irony may manifest itself, Kierkegaard suggests the following response:

> But in all these and similar incidents, the salient feature of the irony is the subjective freedom that at all times has in its power the possibility of a beginning and is not handicapped by earlier situations. There is something seductive about all beginnings, because the subject is still free, and this is the enjoyment the ironist craves. In such moments, actuality loses its validity for him; he is free and above it.[17]

In irony, the subject is negatively free, since the actuality that is supposed to give the subject content is not there. He is free from the constraint in which the given actuality holds the subject, but he is negatively free and as such is suspended, because there is nothing that holds him. But this very freedom, this suspension, gives the ironist a certain enthusiasm, because he becomes intoxicated, so to speak, in the infinity of possibilities, and if he needs any consolation for everything that is destroyed, he can have recourse to the enormous reserve fund of possibility.[18]

According to Kierkegaard, then, ironists are attracted to the possibility of shearing off commitments and beginning again, unencumbered, with more interesting and novel relationships and ways of life.[19]

Now that I have clarified what Kierkegaard intends by a given actuality, the negation of actuality in the stance of pure irony, and the sort of freedom that an ironist pursues by adopting such a stance, I will seek to clarify what Kierkegaard intends by referring to irony specifically as "infinite absolute negativity." Although Kierkegaard borrows this description of irony from Hegel, he recognizes that it is apt to be obscure even to his contemporaries. So he clarifies it as follows:

> Here, then, we have irony as the infinite absolute negativity. It is negativity, because it only negates; it is infinite, because it does not negate this or that phenomenon; it is absolute, because that by virtue of which it negates is a higher something that still is not.[20]

Several points emerge in this passage. First, according to Kierkegaard, pure irony is an entirely negative stance. It is not negativity in the service of some higher positive ideal. To adopt a higher positive ideal after seeing through the ideals of one's community is to abandon the stance of pure irony, as Kierkegaard understands it. Second, and closely related, pure ironists are not simply looking for a better set of conventions than the ones that they have inherited. They resist the idea that any given set of conventions ought to be taken seriously, so that they may more efficiently pursue as much freedom as they can get from the confining obligations that arise from social roles and other such conventions. In this respect, the negativity of pure irony is "infinite," or open-ended and without limits.

Kierkegaard's final claim: ironists negate through the invocation of "a higher something that still is not," suggests that although ironists do have absolute commitments of a sort, their absolute commitments are devoid of positive content, since they are commitments to negative freedom and the vanity of all social conventions. Anthony Rudd adds this interpretive suggestion:

> The individual, becoming self-consciously aware of himself as an individual, stands back from all the established conventions of society and

culture, from all that is accepted as wisdom and knowledge by those around him. Without positively asserting that these are invalid or wrong, he undermines those standards by raising questions about them that cannot adequately be answered. What had previously been accepted without question as evidently true and right, is now exposed as simply a groundless prejudice.[21]

So on Rudd's reading, ironists negate without positing something positive in the sense that they simply undermine beliefs and practices by questioning them, without advocating that they are wrong or baseless and without arguing for alternative beliefs and practices. Kierkegaard also recognizes other, subtler ways in which to undermine social conventions without positively asserting that they are invalid or vain. He notes, for instance, that an ironist might undermine what she takes to be an absurd social convention simply by lavishing (ironic) praise on it, which calls the attention of others to it, until it collapses, so to speak, under the weight of closer examination.[22] The central point is that although ironists have a fundamental commitment to negative freedom and the path to it via critique of existing social conventions, no positive ideal emerges from their standpoint.

4.2   THE PROBLEMS OF PURE IRONY

According to Kierkegaard, pure irony is an unstable, self-defeating, and psychologically unhealthy stance. A problem arises first in relation to how ironists are to treat their irony. Are they to take their ironic stance as a serious life choice with its own set of commitments? If they do, then does not this move signal a limit to their irony? If they do not, then is there a sense in which their irony still is not absolute? If so, then why consider them pure ironists rather than persons who use irony as a "minor element," as Kierkegaard puts it? Second, ironists pay a high price for their disengagement. According to Kierkegaard, they lack continuity in their identities, and they eventually become enslaved to the flux of their moods, which leads to boredom.[23] So they fail to attain a basic good that they desire as ironists, the good of "the interesting" or "the novel," precisely because they are pure ironists. In that respect, their ironic pursuits fail even on their own aesthetic terms.[24] Ironists also fail to realize positive freedom, according to Kierkegaard. In other words, they fail to realize the freedom that comes from energetically embracing their social roles, for, according to Kierkegaard, when one commits oneself to responsible community with other persons in this way, one experiences a kind of freedom within the boundaries set by this commitment that cannot be realized outside of these boundaries. This is the freedom that comes from not having to reconsider one's commitments every time one encounters an enticing alternative course of action or way of life. It is also the sort of freedom a morally virtuous person enjoys who does not have to act against the grain of her character in order to fulfill her various responsibilities. In Kierkegaard's view, a pure ironist's pursuit of negative freedom prevents her from experiencing this good of positive freedom.

In this section, I will attempt to clarify more precisely these problems of pure irony and how they arise. In the next chapter, I will discuss in detail Kierkegaard's proposal for resolving these problems in a complex stance that combines irony and moral commitment. For unlike Hegel, Kierkegaard does not dismiss irony on account of the problems that plague unmastered versions of it.

Is pure irony a coherent position? Kierkegaard indicates in *The Concept of Irony* that it is not. He argues that significant problems emerge as ironists attempt to disengage from serious commitment or refrain from taking any self-description seriously. As Kierkegaard explains:

> To be specific, if irony is going to advance a supreme thesis, it does as every negative position does—it declares something positive and is earnest about what it says. For irony, nothing is an established order; it plays helter-skelter *ad libitum* [at will] with everything; but when it wants to declare this, it says something positive, and to that extent its sovereignty is thereby at an end. . . . The difficulty here is that, strictly speaking, irony actually is never able to advance a thesis, because irony is a qualification of the being-for-itself subject, who in incessant agility allows nothing to remain established and on account of this agility cannot focus on the total point of view that it allows nothing to remain established.[25]
>
> Ultimately the ironist always has to posit something, but what he posits in this way is nothing. But then it is impossible to be earnest about nothing without either arriving at something (this happens if one becomes speculatively earnest about it) or despairing (if one takes it personally in earnest). But the ironist does neither, and thus we can also say that he is not in earnest about it. . . . Therefore we can say of irony that it is earnestness about nothing—insofar as it is not earnestness about something. It continually conceives of nothing in contrast to something, and in order to free itself of earnestness about anything, it grasps the nothing. But it does not become earnestness about nothing, either, except insofar as it is not earnestness about anything.[26]

Consider the following line of thought an attempt to recapitulate Kierkegaard's reasoning in these passages. Suppose first that whatever else pure irony is, it essentially is the rejection of earnestness about anything. Immediately a conundrum presents itself: is an ironist earnest about not being earnest about anything? If she is earnest about this, then she no longer is a pure ironist, since pure irony is incompatible with earnestness about anything, including irony itself. If she is not earnest about not being earnest about anything, then she is not seriously committed to being an ironist. In that case, she may be overwhelmed by some relationship and subsequently "handicapped by an earlier situation," as Kierkegaard puts it.[27] In other words, if she is not vigilant about being disengaged from her social roles, she is liable to lose the freedom from serious commitment to them that she desires. As Kierkegaard explains:

> This is the freedom that irony craves. Therefore it watches over itself and fears nothing more than that some impression or other might overwhelm it, because not until one is free in that way does one live poetically, and as is well known, irony's great requirement was to live poetically.[28]

The problem is that an ironist's watchfulness, which is required to maintain her stance of pure irony, is itself a kind of seriousness about maintaining a stance of unseriousness about everything else. That is why Kierkegaard states that the stance of pure irony ultimately involves positing something and therefore is a kind of earnestness, even if it is not earnestness about anything (positive) in particular. If, however, pure irony is incompatible with earnest commitment and earnest commitment to a stance of pure irony is needed to maintain such a stance, then pure irony is an incoherent position. It cannot be realized.

Andrew Cross arrives at a similar reading but from another angle. As he explains:

> As Kierkegaard sometimes puts it, the ironist cannot have any "positive content"; he is nothing but this negating entity, this derogating and disengaging, carried on for its own sake rather than for the sake of some positive alternative. For him to have any such positive content would be for there to be something toward which he is not ironical—and if there is any such thing, then he is not a pure, which is to say total, ironist. . . .
>
> But what of the ironist's attitude toward himself—that is, toward the ironic self, the thing that is held apart from the embodied social being that it playfully manipulates? Does the ironist identify himself with the activity of ironizing, and does he see this activity, the maintaining of this type of orientation, as having some point? Here, it seems,

the ironist has been backed into a corner. If he does take this way of existing seriously, then his irony ceases to be comprehensive; there exists one way of life that he does not "negate" or repudiate, namely, the ironic life. . . .

Thus, if there is to be such a thing as a stance of total or comprehensive ironic disengagement, it must lie in the other possibility, that of dissociation from his own ironizing. This possibility immediately threatens us with an infinite regress of ironic disengagement from ironic disengagement from . . . [But] what is being retreated to is just another position whose suitability as an object of serious concern and identification has been ruled out in advance. The problem is not so much that the retreat is infinite as that it is not a retreat, since there is no material difference between the position retreated to and the position retreated from.[29]

Cross helps to clarify that an ironist's dissociation from her own ironizing is itself a stance that could become a serious commitment. Thus, ironists also need to dissociate from their (initial) dissociation from an ironic stance. This new position, however, will also need to be emptied of its seriousness and so on, *ad infinitum*. Ultimately nothing is achieved in this process. If I determine not to take seriously my stance of not taking anything seriously, what have I accomplished? Do I now take things seriously? Suppose I then determine not to take this stance seriously—the stance of not taking seriously my stance of not taking anything seriously. Do I then not take things seriously, until it occurs to me that I am taking too seriously my attitude of not taking things seriously?

There is a certain intrigue in this way of formulating this particular problem of pure irony. However, if we construe the problem just this way, we might be invited to think that the problem simply is a kind of pseudophilosophical (or metaphysical) problem that can be resolved practically, if not theoretically. That is why it is important to keep in mind the first formulation of the problem as well, which I sketched above. On that reading of Kierkegaard, ironists must be committed to their (original) stance of pure irony in order to maintain it. Its upkeep requires vigilance, which is incompatible with irony, as a comprehensive stance. Consequently, it appears that pure irony carries within it the seeds of its own downfall.

Suppose, however, that ironists ignore or fail to recognize this problem and continue to disengage from their social environments in pursuit of negative freedom. It might not matter much, practically speaking, that they cannot instantiate *pure* irony. They might be able to approximate it enough to satisfy their desire for freedom, as they understand it. So why should they desist from their pursuit of pure irony on account of its unrealizability? Why not instead pursue it as an unachievable but nonetheless worthy ideal?

This question brings us to Kierkegaard's second line of criticism of pure irony. Simply stated, Kierkegaard argues that the pursuit of pure irony: (a) brings about a significant loss of freedom insofar as ironists fail to attain positive freedom and become enslaved to moods; (b) devolves into boredom; and (c) is destructive of the good of individuality.[30] Kierkegaard's critique depends in part on his view that actuality, as clarified above, is both a "gift" and a "task."[31] So, first it is necessary briefly to clarify this idea.

If we recur to the discussion of Hegelian *Sittlichkeit* presented above, the idea that actuality is both a gift and a task begins to come into focus. If I view actuality as a gift, I thereby recognize the place in the given social order that I inhabit *as* the place where my project of selfhood gets underway. I also recognize that the person that I become is inextricably bound up with how I am shaped by and, in turn, how I shape this given place that I inhabit at this given time. That is, I am a self with an inescapable history, with unavoidable relations to other persons and institutions in my social environment. No matter what sort of person I eventually become, this fact about my identity will not change.

A person could view herself, others, and the conventions of her society just this way, however, and still take the project of pure irony as a basic life project. She might simply take her given social environment as a gift in the sense that it provides her with plenty of things about which to be disillusioned and from which to be disengaged. As Rorty notes, "Ironists have to have something to have doubts about, something from which to be alienated."[32] Kierkegaard thinks of actuality as a gift in a different respect, however. It is not a gift in the sense that it is solely for the personal use and enjoyment of the person to whom it is given, in the way that a teddy bear is a gift to a child, for instance. Rather, it is a gift that carries with it a certain moral responsibility for the person who receives it, somewhat in the way that a pet can be a gift to a child. In other words, those who receive this gift are obligated to relate to it properly because of its significant value. It would be immoral of them to dispose of the gift however they please.

This point leads to the related idea that actuality also is a task. Perhaps it is most helpful to clarify this idea through an example. I am a son, grandson, husband, father, employee, colleague, professor, friend, mentor, and nephew, just to note some of the social roles that I inhabit. *My* "actuality" includes these roles and the norms that accompany them, in addition to many other things in my social environment. Consequently, if I am to embrace it as a task, according to Kierkegaard, I must attempt to construct my identity *in* these roles, not in disengagement *from* them. This point does not imply, however, that I simply have to accept these social roles just as my community currently understands them. I might define myself in opposition to my society as someone who is not and will not be what others expect me to be. This stance can be consistent with taking my actuality as a task, if my rebellious attitude is not motivated simply by a desire for negative freedom. After all, a person could have compelling moral reasons for taking such a combative stance. Furthermore, she could continue to take seriously the social roles that she inhabits, even as she attempts to modify her community's understanding of them. Indeed, she might be motivated by an alternative conception of a social role, in the way, for instance, that many persons have opposed a sexist and degrading understanding of being a woman, wife, and mother.

Roughly then, taking actuality as a gift and task, according to Kierkegaard, involves taking seriously one's given place in a complex social order, with the various responsibilities and roles that accompany such a place. A person who relates to her actuality this way accepts that her project of becoming a self occurs within a particular social context, even if she attempts to alter radically the social practices that compose it. She accepts that her socialization carries with it certain responsibilities, which inform her desire to be a novel and autonomous self. As Kierkegaard explains:

> But actuality (historical actuality) stands in a twofold relation to the subject: partly as a gift that refuses to be rejected, partly as a task that wants to be fulfilled. Irony's misrelation to actuality is already sufficiently intimated by the essentially critical stance of irony. . . .
>
> But when I said earlier that actuality offers itself partly as a gift, the individual's relation to a past is thereby implied. This past will now claim validity for the individual and will not be overlooked or ignored. For irony, however, there really never was a past. . . . The actual history, however, in which the authentic individual has his positive freedom because therein he possesses his premises, had to be set aside.[33]
>
> But for the individual actuality is also a task that wants to be fulfilled. . . . In order for the acting individual to be able to accomplish his task by fulfilling actuality, he must feel himself integrated in a larger context, must feel the earnestness of responsibility, must feel and respect every reasonable consequence. Irony is free from this. It knows it has the power to start all over again if it so pleases; anything that happened before is not binding.[34]

These passages are important because they present one of Kierkegaard's main criticisms of pure irony, and they refer to an alternative kind of freedom that ironists fail to realize. So they deserve careful attention.

Notice first that, according to Kierkegaard, ironists misrelate to actuality. This claim implies, of course, that there is a way that they should relate to actuality. They should treat it as a gift and task, but they do not. Ironists fail to treat actuality as a gift in the sense that they attempt to overlook or ignore their relation to "a past." It is likely that Kierkegaard intends by this that ironists view the social order into which they are socialized, with its various practices and traditions, simply as something to be overcome, not as something that has a claim on them. Even if they want to and do see their inherited identities in this way, however, they will not be able to ignore this inheritance, according to Kierkegaard. They will not be able to ignore it in the sense that if they do ignore it they will suffer the consequences. The first consequence that Kierkegaard mentions is the loss of "positive freedom."

Kierkegaard indicates that the "premises" of positive freedom are located in one's "actual history," which ironists set aside. What does this mean? It is very likely that "actual history" is just a synonym for actuality. In that case, one attains positive freedom by "possessing one's premises" in one's given actuality, according to Kierkegaard. In turn, I possess my premises in my given actuality by relating properly to my social roles and the other practices and traditions of my social order.

Interestingly, Kierkegaard uses the term "freedom" to describe the state of a person who properly relates to actuality and in the same context refers to a person's "possessing" his premises. He conveys by these moves that a person's properly relating to her given actuality does not involve her passively becoming just a product of her social environment. Since he wishes to give emphasis to the proper boundedness of freedom in this context, however, he notes that persons need to embrace their "actual history" in order to achieve a certain kind of positive freedom.

This reading is confirmed by Kierkegaard's remarks concerning how persons are to fulfill the *task* of actuality. As noted in the quotation above, according to Kierkegaard, to "fulfill actuality," one must: (a) feel oneself integrated in a larger context, (b) feel the earnestness of responsibility, and (c) feel and respect "every reasonable consequence." Notice how each of these conditions picks out an attitude that contrasts with the stance that a pure ironist takes, so that, as Kierkegaard indicates, irony is "free from this." First, to feel integrated in a larger context is not to be alienated from it and disillusioned by it. Positively, it is to have the sort of harmonious identification with one's social order that is characteristic of (one aspect of) Hegelian *Sittlichkeit*. Second, to feel the earnestness of responsibility is to take seriously the moral obligations that correspond to one's social roles, not to view them as pointless or able to be sheared off at one's convenience. Third, as a result, one accepts the consequences that arise from embracing one's social roles and the norms that govern them. Or, as Kierkegaard puts it, one feels and respects "every reasonable consequence."[35]

Pure ironists, however, fail to meet these conditions, since, for them, "anything that happened before is not binding." The result is that they fail to experience positive freedom—the sort of freedom that one gains by relating properly to actuality, by taking it as a gift and task and fulfilling the task that it presents.

As I intimated above, this line of interpretation suggests that Kierkegaard's sketch in his thesis of ethical life as an alternative to the stance of pure irony anticipates the account of ethical life that he advances as an alternative to aesthetic ways of life in volume two of *Either/Or*, under the pseudonym Judge William. Rudd's analysis of *Either/Or* helps to clarify this point. As he explains:

> The aesthete cannot wholly avoid occupying social roles, but he will refuse to admit that they do anything to define him as a person. . . .
>
> The ethicist is different, in that he chooses to accept social roles, and therefore chooses to accept that the institutionally defined criteria of good and bad performance of these roles are relevant to him. . . . If, by the objective criteria of the society in which he lives, he is bad at being those things, this is not a criticism that he can laugh off . . . such criticism goes to the heart. . . . The reflective ethicist is aware that the social order in which he lives is not immutable; he knows that he can refuse to adopt social positions, or that, even if he does, he can take up an ironically distanced attitude towards them. But he chooses not to. He chooses to commit himself to a certain relationship, to playing a certain part in a social organization. More generally, he chooses broadly to accept the social conventions governing the distinctions between good and evil behaviour.[36]

Rudd accentuates the volitional aspect of "fulfilling actuality" because he has in view Judge William's position, not Kierkegaard's account in *The Concept of Irony*. Still, his reading resonates with the interpretive points sketched above. It indicates that Kierkegaard's first major work after his thesis extends lines of reasoning initially developed in it. Through the construction of "A," Kierkegaard discovers a more provocative and engaging way to display the pursuit of pure irony. Through Judge William, Kierkegaard revisits and elaborates positions first sketched in his thesis, but with a somewhat more personal, informal approach.[37]

Now that we have a grasp of Kierkegaard's view that actuality is both a gift and a task, we can see more clearly why he thinks that those who (at least attempt to) take a stance of pure irony thereby lose the ability to be positively free. We can also begin to see more clearly why Kierkegaard thinks that the pursuit of pure irony is destructive of the good of individuality and leads to boredom and bondage to moods. Here is how Kierkegaard describes the high price that ironists pay, who pursue negative freedom as a basic good pay:

> Irony is indeed free, free from the sorrows of actuality, but also free from its joys, free from its blessing, for inasmuch as it has nothing higher than itself, it can receive no blessing, since it is always the lesser that is blessed by the greater. . . .
>
> But just as commonplace people do not have any *an sich* but can become anything, so also the ironist has none. But this is not simply because he is merely a product of his environment. On the contrary, he stands above his whole environment, but in order really to live poetically, really and thoroughly to be able to create himself poetically, the ironist must have no *an sich*. In this way, irony itself lapses into that which it is fighting the hardest, because an ironist comes to have a certain resemblance to an altogether commonplace person, except that the ironist has the negative freedom with which he stands, poetically creating, above himself. Therefore the ironist frequently becomes nothing. . . . But the ironist continually preserves his poetic freedom, and when he notices that he is becoming nothing, he includes that in his poetizing . . . it is part and parcel of the poetic poses and positions in life that irony promoted—indeed, to become nothing at all is the most superior of them all. . . . For the ironist, everything is possible. Our God is in heaven and does whatever he pleases; the ironist is on earth and does whatever he desires. But we cannot blame the ironist for finding it so difficult to become something, because when one has such a prodigious multitude of possibilities it is not easy to choose. For a change, the ironist finds it proper to let fate and chance decide.[38]

I will take the main claims that Kierkegaard advances in these passages in order. First, consider Kierkegaard's claim that while freedom from serious engagement in social roles and other aspects of one's actuality may have some benefits, it also has much more significant costs. It is not difficult to see what Kierkegaard has in mind. Consider, for instance, a person who takes the social role of being a father to be a burden insofar as it is a serious restriction on his (negative) freedom. Such a person might not be able to avoid some parental duties. He accomplishes them, however, with little earnestness and enthusiasm so that he may hover above serious commitment to parenthood and retain as much freedom from confining relations to his children and their mother as possible. A parent such as this will not experience many of the goods of parenthood. When his children take their first steps and when they learn to read and write, play baseball, graduate from high school and then college, find partners and have their own children perhaps, he will not experience the goods that other persons experience who are engaged parents. Admittedly, when his children suffer, he will not suffer as engaged parents do on account of their children's suffering. However, few if any parents who have experienced even some of these goods of parenthood would trade places with him for this reason.[39]

Kierkegaard's next point is obscure by comparison. He suggests that pure ironists ultimately end up resembling "commonplace people," which is the very thing that they seek to avoid. How, though, do they come to resemble commonplace people? Also, in what sense is this consequence the very thing that they want to avoid?

Kierkegaard states that commonplace people do not have any "*an sich*." The immediate context suggests that this claim means that commonplace persons have not sufficiently developed individuality, since they are unreflective conformists who embrace their social order uncritically.[40] As Kierkegaard states: "By the phrase 'living poetically,' irony not only registered a protest against all contemptibleness that is nothing but a miserable product of its environment, against all the commonplace people who, sorry to say, populate the world in such numbers, but it wanted something more."[41] So to lack "*an sich*" has something to do with lacking the critical insight that distinguishes unreflective social conformists from those who embrace their actuality properly as gift and task. The latter group of persons realizes that their social order is flawed and contingent and, as such, it is resistible. In that respect, these persons resemble ironists. However, they do not disengage as ironists do; rather, they embrace their social roles with earnestness. In this respect, they resemble commonplace people.

In what respect, though, do *ironists* come to resemble commonplace people? It is obvious that, in Kierkegaard's view, pure ironists are not unreflective social conformists. Indeed, Kierkegaard critiques unbridled irony because it fosters *excessive* individuality and criticism of the social order. Presumably, that is why Kierkegaard qualifies as he does his claim that ironists come to resemble commonplace people.

Therefore, the resemblance between an ironist and a commonplace person has to be located somewhere else.

Kierkegaard's claim that ironists frequently "become nothing" provides a helpful clue as to how to understand this supposed resemblance. As I interpret Kierkegaard, ironists "become nothing" because they pursue whatever they happen to desire, and they have no overarching, long-term commitments that provide some sort of focus and critical touchstone for their desires. Consequently, they are awash in possibilities. That is why Kierkegaard states that, in exhaustion and for the sake of novelty, they ultimately "let fate and chance decide" for them what to do. When they let fate and chance profoundly shape their lives in this way, however, they come to resemble commonplace persons, who merely are products of their environment. So, in an ironic twist, an ironist's excessive individuality and hyper-critical attitude eventually put her in the same predicament as that of a mindless conformist.

Here, then, are the relevant similarities between ironists and commonplace persons, according to Kierkegaard. First, in a broad sense, both misrelate to actuality. Commonplace persons fail to take actuality as a gift and task in the sense that they have an excessively passive stance toward it. They simply inherit a social identity and uncritically attempt to conform to it. Ironists, however, attempt to jettison altogether their inherited social identity, or they treat it simply as fodder for their projects of disengagement. Second, ironists and commonplace persons both fail to develop healthy individuality. One main reason is that commonplace persons recognize too little, and ironists too much, possibility.[42] For a commonplace person, the social order as she receives it is necessary. For an ironist, the social order is utterly contingent in the sense that it has no inherent claim on her. So, an ironist's inherited social identity and the social environment in which this identity is embedded give form to her projects of selfhood only in a negative sense—as what she is not to take seriously or as what she is to lampoon and see through. This shared misrelation to possibility causes commonplace persons and ironists alike to fail to become individuals in community with other persons. Commonplace persons fail to become *individuals* in community with others. Ironists fail to become individuals *in community* with others. Kierkegaard takes both outcomes to be distorted or unhealthy forms of individuality or less than desirable ways to be an individual person.

Still the reasoning behind this claim might be a bit unclear. Perhaps it helps to recur to the example of the disengaged father. Suppose that this person treats all his social roles in the way that he treats parenthood.

Suppose as well that the reason that he treats his social roles this way is that he is an ironist seeking negative freedom. It is not difficult to see the sense in which he would "become nothing." If he were consistently to live this way, at the end of his life he could only say that he had been defined by nothing in particular, except his commitment not to be encumbered by commitment. If he were to take seriously being a parent, however, his choices to that extent would gain a kind of focus that they lack otherwise. For starters, some things that might have been possible things to do for him before he began to take parenthood seriously would no longer appeal to him. These options, thus, would be foreclosed by his commitment to parenthood. His life would change in a more radical way, moreover, if he developed the same sort of earnestness about being a husband, employee, friend, colleague, and son, for instance. Each new commitment would bring new focus to his decisions. Of course, there is an extreme to be avoided on the other side of this continuum as well—that of the uncritical conformist who just is the sum total of his social roles. According to Kierkegaard, healthy individuality is to be found somewhere between the stance of an ironist and that of a mindless conformist.[43]

Even if we grant Kierkegaard's twin claims that the pursuit of pure irony brings about a loss of positive freedom and undermines the good of individuality, though, why think that it also yields boredom and bondage to moods? Here is what Kierkegaard has to say in response to this question:

> The ironist stands proudly inclosed within himself, and just as Adam had the animals pass by, he lets people pass before him and finds no fellowship for himself. . . . For him, life is a drama, and what absorbs him is the ingenious complication of this drama. He himself is a spectator, even when he himself is the one acting. . . .
> As the ironist poetically composes himself and his environment with the greatest possible poetic license, as he lives in this totally hypothetical and subjunctive way, his life loses all continuity. He succumbs completely to mood. His life is nothing but moods. . . .
> But since there is no continuity in the ironist, the most contrasting moods succeed one another. . . . His moods are just as occasional as the incarnations of Brahma. And the ironist, who considered himself free, thereby . . . drudges along in the most frightful slavery. . . .
> But since there always must be a bond that ties these contrasts together, a unity in which the enormous dissonances of these moods resolves themselves, upon closer inspection one will reveal this unity in the ironist. Boredom is the only continuity the ironist has.[44]

Kierkegaard's chain of reasoning proceeds as follows. On account of their pursuit of negative freedom, ironists alienate themselves from others in such a way that their relations are superficial, at best. Furthermore, they have no long-term positive commitments or projects. Consequently, their identities lack continuity and depth. This vacuum in their identities is filled by moods—fleeting and momentary attitudes and desires that yield short-lived projects. Since ironists have no other alternative than to opt for this sort of life, if they are to maintain a disengaged stance, ultimately they succumb to boredom and the tyranny of moods. They fail to develop the character traits that are necessary to ward off this outcome. If we look for a common theme in the various and disparate short-lived projects of an ironist, moreover, it is that all these projects are just so many ultimately futile attempts to escape boredom.[45]

Construed this way, Kierkegaard's position has interesting parallels with the position that Bernard Williams advances in his groundbreaking essay, "Persons, Character and Morality." Williams's notions of "ground projects" and "categorical desires" and the roles that these play in relation to personal identity are especially relevant. Williams argues that, as an individual, a person has "a set of desires, concerns or . . . projects, which help to constitute a *character*."[46] Roughly, categorical desires are those desires that "propel one on."[47] That is, these desires are basic desires that endure over time and motivate persons to continue to pursue longstanding projects and/or to initiate new projects. Ground projects are those projects that are (at least relatively) longstanding and, as such, are central to a person's identity. According to Williams, to a significant degree they "give a meaning" to a person's life.[48] Williams's discussion helps to illuminate the fact that some desires and projects are identity-conferring, while others have a more marginal role in the formation of an identity.

With regard to Kierkegaard's critique of pure irony, the significance of Williams's discussion is this: to the extent that ironists have identity-conferring desires and projects, these are mainly *negative* desires and projects—to be free *from* confining social roles and to *avoid* boredom. Consequently, ironists fail to have sufficient continuity in their identities because their categorical desires and ground projects are too thin (or negative) to generate such continuity. To extend Williams's account a bit, we could also say that a person's character ultimately comes to take on the qualities of the basic goods that she pursues, which are reflected in her categorical desires and ground projects. So, if she has narrow and quite trivial ground projects, she likely will *become* a narrow person who is occupied with very trivial concerns. Likewise, if the basic goods that she pursues are fleeting, she will lack depth and continuity in her character. If her most basic ground project is not to have positive ground projects, then she will have no alternative except to find her identity in fleeting novelties. This is the portrait of a person in pursuit of pure irony, according to Kierkegaard. We see from this analysis as well that Kierkegaard's charge that ironists become enslaved by their moods and succumb to boredom is just a variation on the theme that the pursuit of pure irony undercuts the good of individuality (or healthy personal identity).

So, to sum up, pure irony is a stance that is rife with problems, according to Kierkegaard. First, it is an inherently unstable position. To maintain the disengagement that characterizes pure irony, ironists must be watchful and serious about not becoming entangled in and defined by their social roles (or more broadly, their actuality, as Kierkegaard puts it). To the extent that ironists take this task of maintaining ironic disengagement seriously, however, they thereby undermine their goal not to treat anything with earnestness. Second, the pursuit of pure irony has several severe repercussions for ironists. They seek a kind of (negative) freedom, but they become dominated by moods, and they fail to recognize and realize the good of positive freedom. Also, ironists seek to transcend completely their social order and especially the mindset of commonplace persons who are determined by it. According to Kierkegaard, however, they come to resemble commonplace persons, for in exhaustion and for the sake of novelty, ironists eventually yield to social influences. In this way, along with commonplace persons, they fail to become individuals. Ironists struggle, moreover, to have continuity and depth as persons. The reason is that their ground projects and categorical desires center around the pursuit of fleeting and thin (or negative) goods.

4.3   Something Theological about Kierkegaard's Critique of Pure Irony

If Kierkegaard's analysis of irony concluded with these criticisms, his overall conclusion would be the same as MacIntyre's—there is no place in a good life for irony. However, that certainly is not Kierkegaard's considered position. In the next chapter, I will explain how Kierkegaard stakes out a position between acceptance of pure irony and outright rejection of irony. Before I turn to Kierkegaard's mediating position, however, I discuss briefly here a distinctly theological aspect of Kierkegaard's critique of pure irony, which heretofore I have set to the side.

To clarify this feature of Kierkegaard's account, I begin by distinguishing two perspectives from which he critiques pure irony. The first perspective is the broadly ethical perspective that I attempted to convey in the previous section. The second is an ethical–religious perspective that turns decisively on certain tenets of Christian theism. The set of criticisms that Kierkegaard presents from the first perspective do not crucially rest on theological presuppositions. Even if Kierkegaard himself advances these criticisms because he is a Christian,[49] and even if these criticisms resonate with most forms of orthodox Christianity, these facts (if they are facts) do not imply that one must be a Christian in order to concur with Kierkegaard's criticisms. As far as I can tell, even the view that actuality is a gift and task does not *require* a theological reading. Kierkegaard takes actuality to be a gift and task likely on account of his Christianity. However, a person without any religious faith could hold at least a very similar view.

This is important because, unlike Kierkegaard perhaps, we have to contend with what Rawls refers to as "the fact of reasonable pluralism."[50] This fact has many implications. One implication that is relevant here is this: it is especially important for us to practice the virtues of civility and tolerance, and even, perhaps especially, in our philosophizing. One way to practice these virtues in this context is to distinguish those features of Kierkegaard's account that could be endorsed by a person who does not share his theological convictions from those features that require these convictions as a point of departure. One advantage of this approach is that it helps to reveal the substantial common ground that persons may share with Kierkegaard, even if they do not embrace his Christian theism.[51] Another advantage of this approach is that it reminds us that there are certain features of Kierkegaard's position that others could not reasonably be expected to accept, unless they converted to his Christian theism.

Of course, Kierkegaard himself is *acutely* aware of the decisive role that religious faith often plays in his account. Moreover, in his writings, he distinguishes between a broadly ethical and a distinctly ethical–religious perspective. Indeed, he attempts to write from both perspectives in order to illustrate the similarities and differences that exist between them.[52] So, there is a precedent in Kierkegaard's own writings for distinguishing a broadly ethical viewpoint from a distinctly religious one.[53]

With these caveats in mind, I now turn to an important, but decidedly theological, element in Kierkegaard's critique of pure irony. Kierkegaard distinguishes between two competing conceptions of living poetically, an ironist conception and a Christian conception.

Ironists think that to live poetically is to "compose oneself poetically."[54] The problem with this view, according to Kierkegaard, is that it largely ignores the fact that the self that is to be poetically composed has an inherited social and religious identity, which cannot simply be jettisoned. In Kierkegaard's Christian conception, to live poetically is, by contrast, "to be composed poetically."[55] Obviously there is an accentuated passivity in this way of living poetically. This passivity derives from the belief that God is the creator of human beings. As a result, human nature has a given *telos* of union with God. This *telos* cannot be realized through just any way of life. More specifically, one cannot realize it through pursuit of pure irony. As Sylvia Walsh explains:

> As Kierkegaard sees it, human existence is not merely a process of becoming or simply a matter of becoming whatever we happen by chance or will to become, as in the case of the romantic ironists; rather, it is a process of becoming something in particular—namely, ourselves, that which we are originally defined as being and are intended to become. . . . From a Christian standpoint we are not totally free, as the romanticists think, to make ourselves into anything we wish. Instead we must become, as it were, "accomplices" of God, lending assistance in a synergistic fashion to perfecting the "seeds," or potentialities, implanted in us by the Creator. These God-given traits constitute the limit in which poetic freedom and artistic productivity are to be exercised in relation to the personal life. For Kierkegaard, then, living poetically is a matter not of self-creation but of self-development in accordance with one's given nature.[56]

So Kierkegaard's view of poetic living is a decidedly Christian view that contrasts sharply with the view of (romantic) ironists.[57] Walsh's remarks suggest as well that Kierkegaard's account of poetic living goes well beyond a broadly ethical perspective.

On Kierkegaard's view, human nature generates norms for distinguishing self-realizing from self-destructive ways of life.[58] Self-destructive ways of life do not count as examples of truly poetic living. Furthermore, according to Kierkegaard, a life of pure irony is a self-destructive kind of human life. So, strictly speaking, pure ironists do not live poetically. Rather, they take extreme poetic license with their lives as they attempt to disengage from human community and, more importantly in this context, relation to God. As Kierkegaard explains:

> Irony's great requirement was to live poetically.
> But by "living poetically" irony understood something more than any sensible person who has any respect for a human being's worth, any

sense for the originality in a human being, understands by this phrase. . . . It did not understand it to be what the pious Christian thinks of when he becomes aware that life is an upbringing, an education, which, please note, is not supposed to make him into someone completely different . . . but is specifically supposed to develop the seeds God himself has placed in man, since the Christian knows himself as that which has reality for God. Here, in fact, the Christian comes to the aid of God, becomes, so to speak, his co-worker in completing the good work God himself has begun.[59]

I find it instructive that Kierkegaard invokes the perspective of a "sensible person" who respects "a human being's worth and originality" in order to lend support to his critique of pure irony here. Does Kierkegaard intend to equate the perspective of a "sensible person" with that of "the pious Christian"? If so, then he inscribes distinctly Christian commitments into the common sense of his day. This move would be understandable, given Kierkegaard's historical context. I doubt, however, that Kierkegaard intends to equate these perspectives, since he also refers in the same context to a view of living poetically that is located between his Christian conception and the ironist conception. Kierkegaard states:

The Christian lets himself be poetically composed, and in this respect a simple Christian lives far more poetically than many a brilliant intellectual. But also the person who in the Greek sense poetically composes himself recognizes that he has been given a task. Therefore it is very urgent for him to become conscious of what is original in him, and this originality is the boundary within which he poetically composes, within which he is poetically free.[60]

For my purposes, what is crucial about living poetically "in the Greek sense," for Kierkegaard, is that, unlike the ironist conception, it recognizes that the social identity that a person inherits represents a *task* for her in an important respect. She is not to compose herself poetically through ironic disengagement from her social roles but through responsible choice within them.[61] However, this task does not have an additional distinctly theological component. Still it counts as a way of living poetically, for Kierkegaard, even if it is not the best way to live poetically. So we can construe this conception of poetic living as a broadly ethical conception that has much in common with a decidedly Christian conception, even if it does not recur to a Christian view of human nature and destiny. If this reading is accurate, then even when Kierkegaard relies on explicitly Christian premises in his critique of pure irony, he recognizes that it could be criticized merely from a broadly ethical perspective as well. In other words, one need not become a Christian in order to concur with Kierkegaard that pure irony is ethically problematic. So, Kierkegaard recognizes much common ground between a person who takes a broadly ethical perspective and one who adopts an explicitly Christian view of pure irony.[62]

There is one remaining point in Kierkegaard's account of poetic living that I would be remiss to pass over. According to Kierkegaard, "anyone can live poetically who truly wants to do so."[63] Kierkegaard thinks that this feature of his position is another advantage that it has over an ironist understanding of poetic living. For, if poetic living requires the kind of highly reflective disengagement that is characteristic of pure irony, uneducated and common persons will find it very difficult, if not impossible, to live poetically. As Kierkegaard states in another context, "Irony presupposes a very specific intellectual culture, which is very rare in any generation."[64] If to live a good life is to live a poetic life or if a poetic life is the best kind of good life, then educated, intelligent, and relatively wealthy persons will have an overwhelming advantage over others in their pursuit of a good life. Kierkegaard will have none of this. As a Christian, he takes offense at the idea that this sort of moral luck plays such a decisive role in the pursuit of a good life.[65]

Whatever we make of Kierkegaard's position here, his own account of poetic living faces a problem that is similar to the one he claims to find in the ironist's position. For it is dubious to think that anyone can live *Christianly* who truly wants to do so.[66] In that case, contra Kierkegaard, not everyone will be able to live poetically who truly wants to live this way, except perhaps in a broadly ethical sense. Perhaps Kierkegaard has something like this in mind. It is possible that he believes that persons can live *Christianly* without consciously *being Christians* by exemplifying many virtues that Christianity endorses. In that case, many more persons will be able to live poetically, as Kierkegaard understands living poetically (as opposed to how ironists understand it).

Kierkegaard's remarks in the concluding section of his thesis give some credence to this reading. In the context of praising Shakespeare and Goethe for the "controlled irony" that their works display, he states, "the poet does not live poetically by creating a poetic work . . . but he lives poetically only when he himself is oriented and thus integrated in the age in which he lives, is positively free in the actuality to which he belongs. But anyone can live poetically in this way."[67] Note that Kierkegaard here equates living poetically with becoming positively free. In the previous section, we saw that, for Kierkegaard, a person becomes positively free when she relates properly to her actuality, when she recognizes it as a gift and task and lives responsibly within it. Kierkegaard does not suggest that one has to become a Christian in order to realize positive freedom this way. It follows then that, for Kierkegaard, one can live poetically even if one is not a religious person or, more specifically, a Christian. Now we can see more clearly why Kierkegaard believes that anyone can lead a truly poetic life. Perhaps the most that we can say in Kierkegaard's behalf, then, is that most persons can live poetically *up to a point*, in his view. Those who can embrace an explicitly Christian way of life can move beyond this point to a higher kind of poetic existence, according to Kierkegaard.[68]

4.4 CONCLUSION

I have argued that, for Kierkegaard, pure irony or irony as a comprehensive stance is an entirely negative position. As such, it also is a highly problematic position. First, according to Kierkegaard, the stance of pure irony is inherently unstable. Ironists attempt to disengage from commitment to anything in order to pursue negative freedom. In order to maintain this disengaged stance, though, they must commit themselves to its upkeep. Otherwise they are liable to be "handicapped by earlier situations," or confined in some way by their relations to others. The upshot is that pure irony is not realizable.

Second, the pursuit of pure irony brings in its train not a few negative consequences that ironists seek to avoid. For starters, ironists seek in the first place a kind of freedom. However, according to Kierkegaard, they become less free through their pursuit of pure irony. They fail to recognize and realize the positive freedom that comes from (a) being integrated in some way into one's society, not wholly or mainly alienated by it and (b) being committed to others through responsible choice in one's social roles. Moreover, eventually ironists become prisoners of their moods. This occurs because they fail to develop and sustain long-term projects and relationships, which are necessary to develop continuity in identity. Furthermore, ironists seek to be superior to commonplace persons, as they attempt to transcend the trivialities that define such persons. However, according to Kierkegaard, they come to resemble commonplace persons in certain important respects. Their lack of commitment to anything (other than irony) breeds so much possibility that, out of exhaustion and for a change, eventually ironists simply acquiesce to the social influences in their environment. In this way, their highly reflective disengagement collapses into crude social conformity. Furthermore, like commonplace persons, who uncritically embrace their inherited roles and the social practices of their society, ironists misrelate to their social environment. Both kinds of persons fail to become individuals in community with other persons but for different reasons, according to Kierkegaard. The upshot of all this is that ironists develop a very unhealthy kind of individuality, which also is destructive of certain communal goods.

As far as I can tell, these criticisms do not crucially depend on Kierkegaard's Christian understanding of human nature. Even if Kierkegaard himself arrives at these criticisms because he is a Christian and even if Kierkegaard bases these criticisms on his view that actuality is both a gift and a task, it does not follow that these criticisms are plausible only from a religious or distinctly Christian viewpoint. So, as I have explicated Kierkegaard's position, I have tried to keep separate these broadly ethical lines of criticism of pure irony and the line of criticism that depends crucially on Kierkegaard's Christian understanding of poetic living. These lines of criticism admittedly are found together in *The Concept of Irony*. However, that fact may simply confirm my reading. As I have argued, it may help to show that, for Kicrkegaard, there is much common ground between those who take a broadly ethical and those who take an ethical–religious critical approach to pure irony.

Finally, the reading of *The Concept of Irony* that I have sketched here indicates that it provides a foreshadowing and first in-depth look at some central themes that Kierkegaard develops in his later writings, especially his pseudonymous works. *Either/Or*, in particular, stands out as a work that closely parallels and extends themes from Kierkegaard's thesis. Consequently, it especially should not be interpreted in isolation from *The Concept of Irony*. MacIntyre makes this very mistake when he argues that Kierkegaard presents us with a criterionless choice between aesthetic and ethical modes of existence in *Either/Or*.[69] In view of the close affinities between Kierkegaard's sketch and analysis of pure irony in his thesis and the presentation and evaluation of the way of life of "A" in *Either/Or*, it is very likely that, for Kierkegaard and not simply Judge William, the ironic detachment of "A" comes up short as a way of life because it fails to realize the same ethical, aesthetic, and psychological goods that Kierkegaard invokes in his thesis in his critique of pure irony.[70] As a result, the case for an underlying unity in Kierkegaard's various writings, which Kierkegaard claims retrospectively in *Point of View*, is made stronger.[71] *The Concept of Irony* turns out to be a pivotal work that sets the stage for Kierkegaard's pseudonymous authorship.

CHAPTER 5

Kierkegaard on Mastered Irony

As I argued in the previous chapter, much of Kierkegaard's thesis is devoted to a critique of pure irony. This extended and incisive critique leaves us with this question: if pure irony has the significant problems that Kierkegaard says it has, why then does he not simply dispense with irony altogether, as Hegel does and as MacIntyre does in his most recent work, *Dependent Rational Animals?* The answer is that Kierkegaard believes that irony can be mastered. When it is mastered, moreover, it becomes an indispensable component in an ethical way of life. This idea is the "truth of irony" that Kierkegaard attempts to preserve in the concluding section of his thesis.[1]

In this chapter, I attempt to clarify Kierkegaard's account of mastered irony. I proceed as follows. First, I untangle the suggestive analogy that Kierkegaard posits between poets who gainfully employ mastered irony in their work and persons who profit from utilizing mastered irony in their "individual existence," as Kierkegaard puts it.[2] Second, I examine four illuminating metaphors that Kierkegaard uses to convey the benefits of mastered irony in the life of a person who is committed to moral ideals. In the process of explicating Kierkegaard's position, I also address how irony is properly mastered. I suggest that, for Kierkegaard, it is mastered through moral commitment. Furthermore, I propose that we construe this commitment broadly as an ultimate commitment to the good of persons in general and to goodness and moral obligation.[3] The overall conclusion that I reach in this chapter is that Kierkegaard offers an interesting and suggestive account of the role of irony in ethical life.

5.1 Mastered Irony in *The Concept of Irony*: Artists and Ironists

To clarify the positive role that irony has in ethical life, Kierkegaard draws an analogy between a poet's employment of irony in relation to her work and, more generally, a person's utilization of irony in her life. With regard to the former, Kierkegaard suggests that poets are free in relation to their work and that their work, in turn, is free in some respect, if they employ irony in the proper way in it and toward it. As he explains, "The more irony is present, the more freely and poetically the poet floats above his artistic work. . . . Therefore irony simultaneously makes the poem and the poet free. But in order for this to happen, the poet himself must be master over the irony."[4] This passage can be taken in many ways. I will focus on just a few of its implications.

First, poets (or more broadly artists[5]) are "free" in relation to their work when they strike the proper balance between being infatuated with it and overly disengaged from it. When an artist maintains some ironic distance from her work, she does not treat it as if her identity and worth are entirely bound up with it. Persons who cannot countenance criticism of their work do not have this sort of detachment. As a result, they are bound to the provisional and limited perspective that it embodies. In this respect, such persons are significantly unfree in relation to their work. There is another extreme to be avoided here as well, though. Artists who take a completely insouciant, breezy attitude toward their work seldom produce great work. The mean between these extremes, according to Kierkegaard, is the position of the artist who takes a stance of controlled irony in relation to her work.

Second, an artist liberates herself and her work in certain respects when she recognizes that its meaning, value, and implications are not bound by her understanding of it. Artists are not completely clear about their own intentions, after all. Furthermore, a piece of art can have many implications. It is quite dubious to think that the artist who produced it must have these implications in mind in order for others legitimately to find them in her work. An artist who recognizes and embraces this fact frees herself from the pettiness and drudgery that accompany not acknowledging it. She also frees *her work* in a certain respect insofar as she encourages others to explore its meaning from multiple perspectives.

However, just as with the previous point, there is another extreme to be avoided here as well, according to Kierkegaard. Even if an artist's conscious intentions in regard to her work do not capture all that it represents, still they are important in discerning the meaning and significance of it. If she fails to control the irony that she employs in her work, moreover, she may not be able to convey whatever she intends through it.[6] In that case, others will not be able to decipher the meaning and significance of her work as *she* understands it. The uncontrolled irony in her work will act as a barrier that prevents others from grasping the ideas that she seeks to express through it. If a work exhibits total irony, for instance, but the author intends for it to convey lesser ironies, the total irony in the work likely will undermine these lesser ironies. As C. Stephen Evans notes, "A 'global' sense that 'everything in the text is ironical' can, ironically enough, make it impossible for us to recognize whatever ironical elements are present."[7] In this regard, consider Kierkegaard's remarks about Shakespeare:

> Shakespeare has frequently been eulogized as the grand master of irony, and there can be no doubt that there is a justification for that. But by no means does Shakespeare allow the substantive worth to evaporate into an ever more fugitive sublimate, and as for the occasional culmination of his lyrics in madness, there is an extraordinary degree of objectivity in this madness. When Shakespeare is related ironically to what he writes, it is precisely in order to let the objective dominate.[8]

For Kierkegaard, Shakespeare is a master of irony in an artistic sense because he controls the irony that he employs. Consequently, he is able to convey something "objective" in his work. In other words, Shakespeare controls his irony in such a way that it helps his work achieve a higher goal of conveying meanings that can be shared. His work does not collapse into an ironic chaos, even when he employs madness within it to disclose a larger point.

When an artist controls the irony within her work in order to "let the objective dominate," she moves herself out of the way and invites others (and herself) to consider her work for its own sake, on its own terms.[9] Her work can be considered on its own terms because it does not reduce to her uncontrolled ironic playfulness. It is widely believed by Kierkegaard scholars that Kierkegaard uses pseudonyms in some of his own works in part to let the reader alone with them. For instance, *Either/Or* is a pseudonymous work that presents its audience with a choice between (at least) two alternative ways of life, an aesthetic and an ethical existence.[10] One reason that Kierkegaard employs pseudonyms in this work is to encourage his readers to consider this choice for themselves. In this way, Kierkegaard takes a feature of mastered irony that he observes in his thesis and employs it in his later writings.

Now, what do these points about an artist's employing mastered irony in her *work* have to do with a person's use of irony in her *individual existence*? In order to get the analogy off the ground, the key move is to think of an individual human existence *as* a work of art. Furthermore, it is helpful to think of the given features of an individual person's identity as the raw materials out of which she constructs a character and personality (a "self") through choice. This self that she constructs is her work of art, even if it is not constructed *ex nihilo*. Just as an artist may fail in her attempts to create significant works of art, moreover, so also a person may fail in the task of selfhood through the irresponsible use of choice, according to Kierkegaard. Kierkegaard gets at these points through his concept of "living poetically." As he explains:

> The poet does not *live* poetically by creating a poetic work . . . but he lives poetically only when he himself is oriented and thus integrated in the age in which he lives, is positively free in the actuality to which he belongs. But anyone can live poetically in this way.[11]

Now the analogy between mastered irony in poetry and in an individual human life begins to come into focus.[12] First, just as an artist who takes a stance of controlled irony in regard to her work gains a kind of freedom in relation to it, so also an individual who masters irony in her existence thereby becomes positively free or enhances her possession of this freedom. As Kierkegaard explains:

> As soon as irony is controlled, it makes a movement opposite to that in which uncontrolled irony declares its life. Irony limits, finitizes, and circumscribes and thereby yields truth, actuality, content; it disciplines and punishes and thereby yields balance and consistency. . . . Anyone who does not understand irony at all . . . he lacks the bath of regeneration and rejuvenation, irony's baptism of purification that rescues the soul from having its life in finitude even though it is living energetically and robustly in it.[13]

Consider first the claim that mastered irony's "disciplining" brings a kind of "balance and consistency" to an individual's life, which is an important component of positive freedom, according to Kierkegaard. One clear sense of "balance" in this quotation is the balance that a person achieves who "makes a movement opposite to that in which uncontrolled irony declares its life," while also avoiding "having her life in finitude." This "balance" is the mean between the radical disengagement of a pure ironist and the unreflective social conformity of a commonplace person. The person who strikes this balance in her life or hits this mean is said to be positively free in her actuality. Through her controlled use of irony, she embraces in a morally responsible way her social roles. She recognizes that she can resist these roles to a certain extent and that they are not above critique. But by critically engaging them, by closing off certain possibilities through reflective commitment to them, she actually enhances her freedom, according to Kierkegaard.

Ronald Hall offers a related but somewhat different reading of Kierkegaard on this point. He argues that mastered irony causes a person to be positively free by giving her the power to repudiate her given actuality.[14] For this "power of repudiation" gives her the *ability to do otherwise* than embrace her actuality. She must have this ability to embrace or not embrace her actuality, moreover, in order for her choice to embrace it to be a free choice. As Hall explains:

> Mastered irony does not repudiate (negate) the given actuality, but tells me that I could. This momentary realization that I could repudiate the given actuality has the ironic effect of deepening my positive embrace of it. For to know that I could say "no" to actuality, deepens my capacity to say "yes" to it. . . .
>
> I am taking it as obvious that I can accept a gift (or give one) only if I can refuse it (or to give it).[15]

While Hall's reading of Kierkegaard certainly is interesting and suggestive, a few difficulties attend it. First, it hitches Kierkegaard's position to the principle of alternative possibilities. This move is not necessary.[16] Since it is not, it should not be made, on account of the fact that it weakens Kierkegaard's position by making it more objectionable than it has to be. Second, Hall simply assumes what he takes to be the obvious truth of the principle of alternative possibilities. But this principle is hardly obvious anymore, especially in view of numerous Frankfurt-style counterexamples to it.[17] Suppose we ignore these problems, though. Still a third problem presents itself. That is, irony need not be mastered to play the role that Hall envisions for it here—that of equipping a person with the "power of repudiation." It is not *mastered* irony that tells me that I have the power to repudiate my given actuality. Rather, it is irony, whether mastered or not.

Nevertheless, Hall is right to point out that a person who employs mastered irony has a different orientation to actuality than a mere conformist who has not awakened to the possibilities of critically evaluating and disengaging from her social roles. A person who employs mastered irony, moreover, is neither an unreflective conformist *nor* a pure ironist. Her irony delivers her from uncritical social conformity,[18] while her mastery of her irony delivers her from the vicious extremes of pure irony. As Vincent McCarthy explains, "Mastered irony finds and actualizes the elusive 'golden mean' which was so much the ideal of another age."[19] This is one "truth" of irony that heretofore has not surfaced in Kierkegaard's critique of it.

In order to see a second main way in which an artist's beneficial employment of mastered irony in her work parallels an individual's gainful use of mastered irony in her life, consider the claim that an artist who takes a completely ironic attitude toward her work usually fails to produce significant work. The other side of this claim, so to speak, is that artists who employ mastered irony are able to create significant works of art. (Kierkegaard mentions in this context Shakespeare and Goethe, in particular.) To clarify the analogy, I will begin with the negative point about artists who do not control the irony with which they view their work. The implied analogy between these *artists* and pure *ironists* is this. Pure ironists, as I argued in the previous chapter, fail to fulfill the task of actuality because they fail to embrace their social roles responsibly, and they fail to develop positive ground projects that define them over time as individuals in community with others. In this respect, just as artists who fail to control their irony do not tend to produce great works of art, pure ironists often *become* nothing, according to Kierkegaard.[20] But this is only half the story, as Kierkegaard sees it. Another "truth" of irony now emerges. Just as artists who employ mastered irony are able to create significant works of art, so also persons who master irony in their individual lives are able to fulfill the task of actuality. As Kierkegaard puts this point:

> Irony as a controlled element manifests itself in its truth precisely by teaching how to actualize actuality, by placing the appropriate emphasis on actuality. In no way can this be interpreted as wanting to deify actuality in good St. Simon style or as denying that there is, or at least there ought to be, a longing in every human being for something higher and more perfect. But this longing must not hollow out actuality; on the contrary, life's content must become a genuine and meaningful element in the higher actuality whose fullness the soul craves.[21]

We need not get distracted by Kierkegaard's somewhat obscure phrase "actualizing actuality." He simply has in mind fulfilling the task of actuality, which I clarified in the previous chapter. With this in mind, note that this passage adds the idea that one who employs mastered irony thereby is able to "place the appropriate emphasis on actuality." But what does this amount to, for Kierkegaard?

For starters, actuality should not be deified, as unreflective persons deify it in certain respects. For, if one deifies actuality, then it will seem beyond critique. Persons who view their social order this way usually come to have servile personalities. They also tend to develop hostile and condescending attitudes toward others who live in very different social contexts, with foreign practices and different basic values. However, actuality should not be "hollowed out" either, according to Kierkegaard. Presumably, pure ironists hollow out (their) actuality through their *overly* critical attitudes toward it, which underwrite their disengagement from it. They find their social roles empty and meaningless instead of viewing them as the arena for responsible selfhood.

The positive analogy here between artists and individuals who employ mastered irony is this. The artist is enabled to create significant works of art partly because she has the right sort of attitude toward her work—she takes it seriously, but she is not infatuated with it. Somewhat analogously, an individual who employs mastered irony in her existence becomes a well-adjusted and morally responsible person because she takes an appropriate attitude toward her actuality. She neither divinizes her social order nor carelessly deconstructs it in order to disengage from it. As Richard Summers puts this point: "Irony in this sense thus plays an essential role in the accomplishment of the human task, as Kierkegaard conceives it. It is the condition for correctly appraising the dimension of givenness in our situations, and for discerning the shape of the personal task that each of us has to accept."[22]

A third analogy that Kierkegaard suggests between artists and ironists in this context is just a very slight variation on this theme. We have seen that, for Kierkegaard, when an artist properly employs irony in and toward her work, not only is she then free in relation to it, but also she frees *her work* in such a way that "the objective" comes to "dominate" in it. Now, as we unpack the analogy, it is likely that "the objective" has this role in an individual's existence when she embraces actuality both as a gift and task. Kierkegaard may have in mind that just as an artistic work has ramifications that exceed the grasp of the artist who created it, so also an individual person's life has a significance that goes beyond whatever value *she* might happen to attribute to it. This idea resonates with the view that we are socially embedded selves and that our social context is a basic source of value and normativity for us, whether we recognize it as such or not.[23] Furthermore, our inherited social roles and other features of our social environment set an ineliminable context for our projects of selfhood. These features, we might say, are objective criteria in a certain sense, criteria that persons should not ignore as they construct an individual character through their choices.[24]

Consider, for instance, a person who is a parent. He has value as a person who is a parent; and his value as a parent does not depend on his recognizing or appreciating it. Moreover, for Kierkegaard, it is also true that he should not avoid or ignore this objective criterion, being a parent, which partly defines him. Even if he somehow modifies how this criterion is understood in the communities to which he belongs, still he should not avoid taking it seriously as a defining feature of his identity. (Indeed, this is one way in which to take seriously a criterion of this sort.)

How does mastered irony help such a person? Roughly, the irony in mastered irony helps him to maintain an ability to evaluate critically the objective criteria that others (in the communities to which he belongs) use to evaluate him. In other words, the irony in mastered irony helps him not to take an obsequious and uncritical attitude toward what are, after all, *human* criteria—the norms that accompany the role of parent and other social roles that persons may have. The mastery of irony in mastered irony helps him take seriously such criteria, nonetheless.

The question still lingers: *How* can mastered irony play the sort of role that Kierkegaard envisions for it? *How* can it help one become a responsible person in community with others? I have sketched a general and partial response to these questions. Mastered irony wards off both the uncritical social conformity that characterizes commonplace persons and the radical and cynical disengagement of pure ironists. As a result, it enables one to hit the mean between these extremes—a mean of critical or reflective engagement. Yet this response calls for more explanation. So, in order to clarify more how mastered irony enables persons to fulfill the task of selfhood, I now turn to several suggestive metaphors that Kierkegaard uses to describe the positive role of mastered irony.

I must first offer a disclaimer, however. Kierkegaard merely begins to work out the "truth" of irony in the concluding section of his thesis. In *Postscript*, under the pseudonym Johannes Climacus, he offers a fuller account of the positive role that irony plays in human life. So when I have examined Climacus's discussion of irony, then we will have a more complete answer from Kierkegaard's corpus to the questions raised above. Nevertheless, here is the rest of Kierkegaard's account of mastered irony in *The Concept of Irony*.

5.2   Four Instructive Metaphors

Kierkegaard employs a number of interesting metaphors to convey the positive role that irony plays when it is mastered. I will focus on four of them. First, he refers to mastered irony as a "disciplinarian."

Second, he likens mastered irony to "an excellent surgeon." Third, he compares momentarily retreating to an ironic stance with having a "bath of rejuvenation and regeneration [in] the sea of irony."[25] Fourth, he refers to mastered irony as a "guide."[26]

The first two metaphors mainly concern mastered irony as a stance one takes toward oneself. In other words, Kierkegaard intends for us to think of mastered irony as "a disciplinarian" and "an excellent surgeon" primarily when it is turned inward. On the other hand, when mastered irony is turned outward, when it is directed toward other persons, social practices, and the social order in general, the person who employs it takes a refreshing "irony bath," so to speak. I will take these metaphors in order.

How is mastered irony a helpful disciplinarian and an excellent surgeon? Here is what Kierkegaard has to say in response to this question:

> As soon as irony is controlled, it makes a movement opposite to that in which uncontrolled irony declares its life. Irony . . . disciplines and punishes and thereby yields balance and consistency. Irony is a disciplinarian feared only by those who do not know it but loved by those who do.[27]
>
> In every personal life there is so much that must be thrown out, so many wild shoots to be pruned. Here again irony is an excellent surgeon, because, as stated, when irony has been put under control, its function is extremely important in enabling personal life to gain health and truth.[28]

So, according to Kierkegaard, controlled irony, brings about a kind of personal disciplining that produces "balance and consistency." But what exactly does he have in mind? In order to clarify what Kierkegaard intends by referring to mastered irony as a disciplinarian, it helps to consider first how irony itself is properly disciplined. Then the discipline that *comes from* irony, when it is disciplined or controlled, becomes clear.

So what is controlled or mastered irony, anyhow? The partial answer that is suggested by my analysis thus far is this. Since irony is infinite, absolute negativity, it stands to reason that mastered irony is negativity that is circumscribed or controlled. It is not negativity for its own sake (or for the sake of obtaining negative freedom), but negativity with a positive purpose. Pure irony, moreover, produces radical disengagement, according to Kierkegaard. Mastered irony, however, observes limits within which some disengagement or critical detachment occurs but in order to promote a higher good. Which higher good? In other words, mastered irony is negativity that is circumscribed within the parameters of *what*? For Kierkegaard, it is clear that individual persons are the agents who *do* the circumscribing. The question is this: what is it within the confines of which they circumscribe irony?

Kierkegaard's answer is that irony is to serve is the higher good of fulfilling the task of actuality.[29] But this is just Kierkegaard's way of talking about leading an ethical life—a morally responsible life in community with other persons. Consequently, we also can state Kierkegaard's position this way. Mastered irony is irony that is circumscribed by moral commitment. Moral commitment should not be conflated with commitment to a particular view of morality, even though a person's moral views obviously shape her moral commitments. For one's understanding of morality and one's community's understanding of morality are things that are not *always* to be treated nonironically, according to Kierkegaard. Moral commitment itself, however, or commitment to the good of persons and to goodness and moral obligation, has an ultimacy that trumps these things. As Robert Adams argues, an ultimate commitment of this sort "ought to be a stance in relation to something larger [than] a verbal formulation."[30] According to Adams, it is "a stance in relation to goodness and duty, and in relation to possibilities of human action, thought, and feeling and their larger context in human life and in the universe."[31] Of course, when we define such a stance, we recur to propositions about what goodness and duty are and the central role that they have in human life. However, these propositions have a different, nonultimate status. As Adams observes, "We can hardly talk about such a stance without articulating its content verbally; but the adequacy of any verbal formulation, as an articulation of the stance, can always be questioned."[32] Here Adams articulates a view that resonates with Kierkegaard's position, as I understand it. Moral commitment has this ultimate status even though it is often helpful to scrutinize the *particular* moral commitments in one's life and commonly held views *of* moral commitment (including one's own view, of course).[33]

So, the disciplining that irony undergoes that makes it fit for the promotion of "personal life" is the disciplining provided by moral commitment. This idea in turn sheds light on the disciplining that disciplined irony provides. A morally committed person will use irony to promote her ethical way of life. How might irony be used in this way? Certainly if it is turned inward, in a controlled way, it can help to reveal inconsistencies in one's behavior—gaps between one's ideals and one's actions and desires. A person who takes morality seriously will be bothered by these gaps. If she then attempts to bring her desires and behavior into greater conformity with her ideals, then her character and personality (her self) likely will have more consistency.

Another sense in which mastered irony produces "balance" emerges from this reading as well. Consider the differences among (a) a person who takes toward herself an entirely negative attitude, (b) a person who carefully limits the negativity to which she subjects herself, and (c) a person who refuses to reflect critically on her desires and actions. The first person likely will suffer from low self-esteem. We could refer to her low self-esteem as an *imbalance* in her view of herself. She has value that she does not recognize. She also fails to see that no human being can withstand an entirely negative self-assessment, nor should she. The third person, on the other hand, likely will be insufferable because her personality is imbalanced in the other direction. However, the second person will not be as likely to suffer either sort of imbalance in her personality. The fact that she critically assesses herself and controls the negativity (or irony) that she employs when she evaluates herself accounts for the difference. In this way, mastered irony can bring "balance" to an individual's personal life when it is employed as a disciplinarian. This reading also explains why Kierkegaard notes that only those who do not know these beneficial effects of mastered irony fear irony. They fear the negativity that they perceive in irony. And they are right to fear it, if it is unbridled. But they fail to see that when it is controlled, this sort of negativity has very beneficial results.

The idea that irony is an excellent surgeon is closely related. As Kierkegaard notes, there is much in every personal life that needs to be "thrown out," many "wild shoots" that need to be pruned. Mastered irony turned inward helps to reveal these "wild shoots," which can then be excised. For instance, a morally committed person likely will desire to have desires that conform to and reflect her ideals. If she critically examines her desires, she almost certainly will find desires that are at odds with her ideals. She cannot prune these desires from her set of desires and herself, so to speak, until she recognizes them *as* alien. Insofar as mastered irony helps her to locate and excise these desires, it functions as an excellent surgeon on her behalf. It promotes her moral identity or the health of her "personal life," as Kierkegaard puts it. Consider, for instance, a person who, having been socialized into a racist community, defines herself now as adamantly opposed to racism. Such a person likely will desire not to have desires that are racist, even if this basic desire is inchoate, as it often is with persons in this situation. If she critically examines her desires, she might discover that she harbors desires that are inconsistent with the nonracist ideals to which she aspires. She may discover, for instance, that she desires that her daughter not marry an African-American man. If she is sufficiently critical of herself, she might discover as well that she harbors this desire simply as a vestige of racism that she has failed to "prune" from her character. In that case, the revelation that she has this desire, although painful to her, will motivate her to root it out along with other remnants of inherited racism that remain in her character. In this way, mastered irony functions as a surgeon for such a person. The result, as Kierkegaard puts it, is that her personal life gains "health and truth."

Mastered irony also has beneficial effects when it is turned outward, according to Kierkegaard. As I briefly indicated above, Kierkegaard uses the metaphor of taking a bath in the "sea of irony" to convey this idea. As he explains:

> Anyone who does not understand irony at all, who has no ear for its whispering, lacks *eo ipso* [precisely thereby] what could be called the absolute beginning of personal life; he lacks what momentarily is indispensable for personal life; he lacks the bath of regeneration and rejuvenation, irony's baptism of purification that rescues the soul from having its life in finitude even though it is living energetically and robustly in it. He does not know the refreshment and strengthening that come with undressing when the air gets too hot and heavy and diving into the sea of irony, not in order to stay there, of course, but in order to come out healthy, happy, and buoyant and to dress again.[34]

The imagery here suggests that there are occasions when it is very helpful for a person to step back from energetic and robust engagement in the affairs of life—those things that are involved in taking seriously the task of actuality (or selfhood). As every reflective person who is committed to his or her social roles knows, they can become stifling. It is not difficult for persons who take their responsibilities seriously to lose sight of a larger perspective from which these duties can be transcended momentarily in order for one to gain a better perspective on them. Kierkegaard uses the imagery of undressing to capture the kind of controlled disengagement that is needed in such cases. This is an apt metaphor. For taking seriously the task of actuality involves, as we have seen, embracing one's social roles in such a way that one comes to be defined by them, at least to a very significant extent. They are, so to speak, the covering that gives substance and content to human agency. When a person undresses and dives into the "sea of irony," as Kierkegaard puts it, she momentarily and partially takes off this covering in order to be refreshed by some distance from it.[35]

This distance can and sometimes should be a *critical* distance as well, according to Kierkegaard. This idea is suggested by several of the metaphors that Kierkegaard employs, including metaphors of baptism, purification, regeneration, and salvation from "finitude" with its stifling environmental conditions (the hot and heavy air of finitude).[36] So, persons need "irony baths" not simply to have a refreshing break from the sometimes tedious and exhausting work that accompanies serious commitment to social roles, but also so that they can maintain a *critically* engaged perspective on them.

However, even when it is mastered, irony does not provide a positive perspective from which to assess critically one's social roles. Rather, it merely is a "guide."[37] As Kierkegaard somewhat cryptically puts it, "Irony as the negative is the way; it is not the truth but the way."[38] How then does a person manage to attain a critical perspective on her actuality without succumbing to the *absolute* negativity of pure irony? Kierkegaard does not address this question in much detail in his thesis. His partial answer is that moral commitment halts the slide into pure irony. But this answer does not tell us where we are to find a criterion that enables us to evaluate critically our social roles. Nevertheless, several possibilities quickly emerge. A person can take an "irony bath" simply by comparing her community's ideals to the ideals of other communities with which she is familiar. Or she may evaluate her community's current practices in view of its stated ideals. Moreover, a person can critically assess current ideals and practices in view of the ideals and practices of the past. She might also explore philosophically the negations of the ideals of her community in order to determine what things might be like if these ideals were overturned. Or she might seek a transcendent source of value as a touchstone for evaluating her social order's ideals and practices (or those of all human social orders). Kierkegaard recognizes all these ways of achieving a critical perspective on the ideals and practices of one's community, even if he says little about them in his thesis. For my purposes here, the crucial point is that irony itself functions merely as a "guide" in the sense that it does not provide any positive ideal that serves as a criterion for evaluating social roles or the norms that accompany them, even when it is mastered. In this respect, it points beyond itself to the need for a positive set of ideals.[39] Where we are to locate these ideals is an issue that Kierkegaard addresses in much more detail in other writings.

The four metaphors that I have discussed here help to clarify the important role that mastered irony plays in ethical life, according to Kierkegaard. Simply stated, the irony in mastered irony helps persons to realize their own shortcomings and the fallibility and mutability of their social order. It also helps persons who are very much engaged in the tasks of actuality to be able to disengage from them occasionally in order to be rejuvenated for better engagement in these tasks in the future. The mastery of irony in mastered irony helps persons not to become overly critical of themselves and their social order.[40] It helps persons not to become disengaged in an unhealthy and unethical way from their social roles and the communities in which these roles are embedded. For these reasons, Kierkegaard believes that mastered irony is crucial for "health and truth in personal life."

There is a remaining point about Kierkegaard's treatment of irony in the concluding section of *The Concept of Irony* that merits our attention. Summers makes an interesting case for the claim that mastered irony, as Kierkegaard conceives it, cannot have the critical role that Kierkegaard attributes to it, if those who employ it are not in community with other persons.[41] In other words, there is a kind of sociality implicit in the *irony* of mastered irony, which is easy to overlook. As Summers explains:

> Like conscience, "controlled" irony has to remain a force that we cannot dominate if it is to fulfill its role of challenging and chastening. It cannot therefore lose its edge as irony; it is just that its barbs are now seen to be necessary. And the way these barbs will come, most of the time, will be through other people. Thus controlled irony actively acknowledges our need for others. It presupposes a community.[42]

The beneficial effects of mastered irony cannot be obtained by persons who employ it in isolation, according to Summers. He concludes, "All these actions, however, require the involvement of other people for their accomplishment: individuals cannot realistically do them for themselves on the basis of simple self-reflection. Controlled irony is thus necessarily intersubjective."[43] We can add that the refreshment and critical distance that occasional "irony baths" provide also cannot be procured in isolation. It is important not to overlook this implicit sociality of mastered irony not least because it helps to offset the tendency to understand the employment of mastered irony as a highly individualistic activity.

5.3 Conclusion

Although Kierkegaard, in his thesis, merely sketches the positive role that irony has in ethical life, he offers an intriguing account of mastered irony, nonetheless. When we unpack the analogy that Kierkegaard evokes between artists who employ mastered irony in their work and persons who utilize mastered irony in their individual lives, we see that, for Kierkegaard, mastered irony helps persons hit the mean between unreflective social conformity and radical disengagement. In other words, mastered irony enables persons to fulfill the task of ethical selfhood, as Kierkegaard understands this task. Unlike pure irony, which fails to deliver on its promise to promote individual freedom, mastered irony helps persons to realize positive freedom, the sort of freedom that accompanies responsible community with other persons.

When mastered irony is employed in the task of self-examination, according to Kierkegaard, it functions as a disciplinarian and excellent surgeon. In this employment, it brings balance and consistency to personal life, as it helps persons accurately assess themselves according to norms and ideals related to their social roles. This enhanced self-knowledge enables persons to prune from their characters attitudes, desires, and beliefs that they reject as foreign and immoral in their more reflective moments. Yet persons who are energetically involved in fulfilling the tasks that accompany their social roles and other features of ethical life frequently need refreshment and critical distance from these things. Kierkegaard alludes to this need through the metaphor of undressing and taking rejuvenating baths in the "sea of irony." An "irony bath" is not to be confused with a stint as a pure ironist, however. For the goal of such refreshment is renewed and more vigorous engagement in ethical life, not negative freedom. Furthermore, the critical reflection that one undertakes while bathing in the "sea of irony" is not the wilting reflection of searing, absolute negativity. Rather, it is critical reflection within the boundaries of commitment to the good of other persons, one's own good, and goodness and moral obligation. Moreover, as Summers points out, in order to engage in this sort of critical reflection we need to draw from the perspectives of other persons. So there is an implicit sociality in mastered irony.

Yet, as beneficial as mastered irony is, according to Kierkegaard, it does not itself provide a positive moral ideal. Mastered irony still is negativity, even if it is controlled negativity. That is why Kierkegaard refers to it as a "guide." In his thesis, Kierkegaard does not discuss at length where we are to locate positive moral ideals to utilize as criteria when we employ mastered irony. But a person who employs mastered irony will look to her community and other communities for such criteria. Especially from the vantage point of Kierkegaard's later writings, there is the additional possibility that she will seek a transcendent ideal from which to critique her entire social order. For Kierkegaard, mastered irony may be used in conjunction with a number of different moral ideals, stemming from various sources of normativity. Consequently, mastered irony may be successfully employed by persons from multiple and competing ethical and ethical–religious traditions.

In *Postscript*, under the guise of Johannes Climacus, Kierkegaard refines his view of irony. In addition to expanding his view of the role that irony has within ethical life, he offers an account of irony as a developmental stage between aesthetic and ethical ways of life. These discussions help to clarify and explain more adequately the final thesis that Kierkegaard defends in *The Concept of Irony*, namely, that "no genuinely human life is possible without irony."[44] Clearly the sketch of mastered irony that I have provided in this chapter helps to explain this thesis, so long as we take "irony" to refer to "mastered irony" and "genuinely human life" to refer to "ethical life" in this claim. However, this claim raises complexities that can be sorted out much more clearly when it is analyzed also against the backdrop of *Postscript*. So I now turn to the account of irony advanced in *Postscript*.

CHAPTER 6

Climacus on Irony and
Moral Commitment

In *Postscript*, under the pseudonym Johannes Climacus, Kierkegaard modifies and extends the account of irony that he offers in his thesis. Some of Climacus's positions illuminate certain features of Kierkegaard's original position. Climacus also clarifies and elaborates the developmental role that irony has in helping persons recognize their unique moral agency, which prepares them for ethical life, in his view. Furthermore, Climacus expands the function that irony has in ethical life, when it is mastered, by developing an interesting account of irony as an incognito for ethical passion. He also attempts to show that there is no problem of moral luck generated by his claim that irony is a crucial element in a good life, but seems exclusive to reflective and intelligent persons.

Some of Climacus's views, however, represent a step backwards in comparison to Kierkegaard's account in his thesis. For example, Climacus's pure ironists oddly seem less ironic than Kierkegaard's, who are distinguished by their thoroughgoing negativity. Kierkegaard's ironists bootstrap their way to freedom from social roles and inherited vocabularies via their withering critical stance, which seizes on incongruity. Climacus's ironists, however, come to their stance by holding steady an "ethical infinite requirement" that trumps and relativizes all merely social sources of normativity. Their route to irony is curiously top-down. Climacus's view of ethical life, moreover, is extremely rigorous. He consigns certain kinds of persons who clearly seem to be ethical to a pre-ethical mode of existence. Kierkegaard's more Hegelian account of ethical life in his thesis is both more organic and more generous.

After providing a preliminary analysis of several key passages on irony in *Postscript*, my discussion proceeds as follows. I first address how Climacus's view of irony as a *confinium* or transition zone between aesthetic and ethical ways of life both complicates how we are to interpret Kierkegaard's final thesis in *The Concept of Irony* and also shows us how to resolve a conundrum created by this thesis. Then I offer a critical analysis of Andrew Cross's reading of Climacus on irony as a transition zone. Specifically, I assess the merits of Cross's view that, for Climacus, the radical disengagement of pure irony is a necessary precursor to ethical life. I also discuss Climacus's way around his and Kierkegaard's apparent problem with moral luck through his distinction between simple and intellectual routes to ethical existence and self-realization. Then I examine Climacus's view of the role of irony within ethical life as a disguise for ethical commitment. I conclude by highlighting some significant problems in Climacus's position and with a brief summary of my findings.

6.1   IRONY AS A TRANSITION ZONE: A PRELIMINARY SKETCH

In *Postscript*, in the context of distinguishing ironists from ethical persons and also pre-ethical persons who have not reached the developmental stage of irony, Climacus advances an important developmental claim about irony. He states:

> There are three existence-spheres: the esthetic, the ethical, the religious. To these there is a respectively corresponding *confinium* [border territory]: irony is the *confinium* between the esthetic and the ethical; humor is the *confinium* between the ethical and the religious.
>
> Let us take irony. As soon as an observer discovers an ironist, he will be attentive, because it is possible that the ironist is an ethicist. The immediate person is distinguishable at once, and as soon as he is recognized it is a certainty that he is not an ethicist, because he has not made the movement of infinity. The ironical rejoinder, if it is correct (and the observer is assumed to be a tried and tested man who knows all about tricking and unsettling the speaker in order to see if what he says is something learned by rote or has a bountifully ironic value such as an existing ironist will always have), betrays that the speaker has made the movement of infinity, but no more. The irony emerges by continually joining the particulars of the finite with the ethical infinite requirement and allowing the contradiction to come into existence. The one who can do it with proficiency and not let himself be caught in any relativity, in which his proficiency becomes diffident, must have made a movement of infinity, and to that extent it is possible that he is an ethicist. . . . He is an ethicist only by relating himself within himself to the absolute requirement. Such an ethicist uses irony as his incognito.[1]

This is a challenging passage to interpret. I begin simply by noting the key claims that are made in it.

Climacus first claims that irony is a developmental stage between aesthetic and ethical ways of life, whereas humor is a developmental stage between ethical and religious (or ethical–religious) ways of life. I am not concerned here with Climacus's views on humor. So, I will set to the side this part of his account. Climacus suggests that, as a developmental stage, irony represents an advance beyond aesthetic ways of life but is a pre-ethical mode of existence, nonetheless. Therefore, the sort of irony that Climacus has in view as a "border territory" is not mastered irony. Climacus also implies that in order to become an ethical person, it is necessary to progress from aesthetic ways of life through irony into ethical life. Consequently, for Climacus, it appears that irony is a necessary precursor to ethical existence.

Climacus also indicates that it is possible to confuse an ironist with an "ethicist," or a person who has progressed through irony and into ethical life. Both, however, are easily distinguished from an "immediate person." The reason that an immediate person is not easily confused with an ironist or ethicist, according to Climacus, is that she has not made "the movement of infinity." Whatever exactly this movement is, when one makes it one is no longer "caught in any relativity." Thus, immediate persons are caught in relativities of one sort or another. Ironists and ethicists, however, are not, according to Climacus. That is one reason why it is not difficult to confuse ironists and ethicists with each other. Another reason is that an ethicist may employ irony as an incognito or as a disguise for her ethical passion. So, she may outwardly appear to be an ironist while she inwardly "relates herself within herself to the absolute requirement."

To make progress in sorting out Climacus's position, we must get a handle on these claims. I begin with the claim that irony is a transition zone between aesthetic and ethical ways of life. For Climacus and Kierkegaard, an aesthetic way of life roughly is equivalent to a life of immediacy. That is why "immediate" persons are contrasted with ironists and ethicists in this passage. Kierkegaard uses the concept of immediacy in several different ways in his writings. As Andrew Cross helpfully explains:

> Immediacy and its cognates have several distinct usages in Kierkegaard's writings, usages that are linked by the notion of something's being unmediated, directly given. In the first usage, one's immediate nature (or one's immediacy) is simply those features of oneself that are merely given over to one's self: one's physical body and

its characteristics, one's temporal position, one's socially determined identity, and so on. In the second usage, for one to stand in an immediate relation to something is for one's relation to it to be unmediated by critical reflection. . . . In this usage, a person is always in an immediate relation to some *x* if that person lacks the detachment from *x* that comes from reflecting critically on it and his relation to it.

In the third usage, to live a life of immediacy is to take life as it comes, to take one's life as a kind of happening in which one finds oneself, whose nature is determined by various conditions that are also, unreflectively, accepted as just "the way things are." One finds oneself in a given society, with certain dispositions and preferences, obligated to comply with various social norms; good things sometimes happen to one, and that's good luck, bad things happen to one, and that's bad luck. . . . The immediate person pursues what he takes to be the good without reflecting or calling into question its goodness; he lives a life whose content is determined by his given desires and ideals, by the norms of his society, without considering, in abstract reflection, whether his conception of the good has any genuine merit, whether his desires and ideals should be transformed or modified, whether his society's norms have any genuine authority over him. He stands in an immediate relation both to his environing world and to himself: for his not calling "externalities" such as his societal norms into question— indeed, his failure to recognize these as externalities—is a manifestation of his failure to consider, in a detached and critical way, himself, whether the manner of life in which he "finds himself" is the only one available to him, whether he is living a type of life that is genuinely worthy of being lived.[2]

According to Cross, then, Kierkegaard employs the concept of immediacy in three distinct but closely related ways. First, Kierkegaard uses it to refer to the givens of a person's identity—her physical constitution, determinants in her social environment, and so on. Second, he also invokes immediacy to refer to lack of critical reflection in a person's relation to something. For instance, if I stand in a relation of immediacy to my religious beliefs, then I have not critically reflected on them. Third, Kierkegaard uses "immediacy" to refer to a person's lacking the critical distance from something that emerges when she reflects critically on it and her relation to it.

The third sense of immediacy that Cross distinguishes is the sense that Climacus has in mind when he claims that immediate persons are readily distinguishable both from ironists and ethicists. It also represents what Climacus intends by an aesthetic existence-sphere. A person who lives in an immediate or aesthetic way has not critically reflected enough on (a) the social practices and norms of her society, (b) herself and her place in her social order, or (c) both a and b.[3] The goods that she purses are goods that are immediately available to her apart from sustained, critical reflection on these features of her social environment and/or herself. Furthermore, she organizes her life around these goods, which is reflected in the character that she comes to have.

Climacus classifies such a person as an aesthete for two reasons. First, the goods that are immediately accessible to persons apart from this sort of critical reflection tend to be aesthetic goods, most notably, pleasure. Second, moral goods cannot be intentionally pursued and realized apart from the kind of critical reflection that an immediate person lacks. For example, Climacus suggests that an ethicist is distinguished by her sustained reflection on and internal appropriation of a fundamental moral ideal—she "relates herself within herself to the absolute requirement." A kind of Kantian rigor in Climacus's position is revealed here. Climacus thinks that a person who just happens to pursue and realize a moral good on account of her social conditioning is not morally praiseworthy for pursuing and realizing this good. In a certain respect, she is not an ethical person until she *intentionally* seeks moral goods because they are moral goods. As Evans explains:

> There is certainly a Kantian strain here in Climacus' thought. . . . The truly ethical person not only does his duty, he does it because it is his duty. And just as was the case with Kant, the absolute duty cannot be identified with any particular set of moral rules; the absolute duty is to duty itself. And, somewhat like Kant, Climacus thinks that this formal principle itself gives the key to the content of the ethical life.[4]

Climacus also believes that, in order to strive to realize moral goods because they are moral goods, a person must critically reflect on the basic goods that she pursues. No one intentionally seeks moral goods as moral goods apart from the sort of critical reflection that immediate persons fail to do. So, in Climacus's view, it is possible that a person who outwardly appears to be ethical is, in fact, at a stage of personal development that is pre-ethical because of the way in which she pursues and realizes moral goods. Consequently, a person counts as existing in a state of immediacy, according to Climacus, if she meets one or both of the following conditions: (a) the basic goods that she pursues are aesthetic goods; (b) she pursues moral goods, but not because they are moral goods. That is why Climacus emphasizes recognition of the "ethical infinite requirement" as a necessary condition of entry into ethical existence. This idea is Climacus's way of conveying that persons who do not recognize the unique and categorical nature of moral goods are not yet ethical persons, no matter how ethical they may appear to be. Climacus and Kierkegaard associate the absence of a certain kind of critical reflection with immediate modes of existence because this reflection brings persons to the point where they can recognize and choose moral goods as unconditional goods and nonmoral goods as conditional goods.

One apparent difficulty with this reading of Climacus is that it implies that it may not be easy to distinguish immediate persons and ethicists. Yet he suggests that it is not difficult to differentiate such persons. Either Climacus exaggerates when he states, "the immediate person is distinguishable at once," or he thinks that immediate persons *obviously* fail to lead ethical lives.

There is no reason to think that Climacus holds the latter view. In fact, there is reason to believe that he does not.[5] Furthermore, we should not attribute this view to Climacus unless it is clear that he holds it, since it is an extremely dubious position. Persons can be socialized into a way of life that outwardly resembles an ethical way of life even if they do not inwardly appropriate the "ethical infinite requirement," as Climacus thinks they must in order to be ethical persons. As I argue below, some of Climacus's remarks in the same passage, moreover, are to be taken in a nonliteral way—for instance, his remarks about ironists being distinguished by their speech. I propose here that we make the same move in regard to Climacus's comments about the ease with which immediate persons are distinguished from ironists and ethicists. It is likely that Climacus simply exaggerates when he advances this idea. Perhaps he speaks with hyperbole in order to make the point that immediate persons are on the other side of a very important divide, developmentally speaking, that separates them from both ironists and ethicists.

At any rate, it is more plausible to think that Climacus simply overstates his point than to think that he holds that immediate persons are obviously pre-ethical in their mode of existence, especially since he accentuates *inward* appropriation of the "ethical infinite requirement" as the defining characteristic of an ethical person. As he explains in another passage:

> True ethical enthusiasm consists in willing to the utmost of one's capability, but also, uplifted in divine jest, in never thinking whether or not one thereby achieves something. As soon as the will begins to cast a covetous eye on the outcome, the individual begins to become immoral—the energy of the will becomes torpid, or it develops abnormally into an unhealthy, unethical, mercenary hankering that, even if it

achieves something great, does not achieve it ethically—the individual demands something other than the ethical itself. A truly great ethical individuality would consummate his life as follows: he would develop himself to the utmost of his capability; in the process he perhaps would produce a great effect in the external world, but this would not occupy him at all, because he would know that the external is not in his power and therefore means nothing either *pro* or *contra*.[6]

So Climacus believes it is wrongheaded to hold that, as a matter of course, an ethical person clearly will be recognizable on the basis of the outward effects of her inward, ethical passion. I conclude, then, that the apparent problem that attends my reading of Climacus on immediacy is no real problem at all.

Another potential difficulty is that readers familiar with *Either/Or* may wonder how "A," who is a highly reflective aesthete, could count as an *immediate* person, given the view of immediacy that I have sketched and endorsed as Climacus's and Kierkegaard's position. The reason is that, for Climacus and Kierkegaard, there are more and less reflective ways of life within the existence-sphere of immediacy or aestheticism. Both take "A" to be an aesthete because he is not sufficiently reflective about himself. As Cross explains:

First, A's absorption in reflective experience is still an absorption in experience; the fact that the experiences he absorbs himself in are the products of his own imagination does not differentiate his activity in any significant way from the person who absorbs himself in direct sensory experience. Whether his experiences are generated by reflection or by perception is of no importance; experience, as such, is always something that is directly given. Second, and more importantly, as a reflective aesthete his reflection does not "penetrate into the personality itself"; while A reflects on his life, on the variety of experiences he has had, on the variety of experiences he can have, he does not reflect critically upon his own devotion to experience. . . . The pursuit of enjoyment is a project that he simply inherits, one might say, from the earlier stage of immediate pleasure-pursuit. He concocts increasingly elaborate and reflective means of carrying out that project, but that this project itself is to be carried out is, for him, simply a given.[7]

Cross suggests that it is oversimplified to construe Climacus's immediate person simply as an unreflective person. Such a person has need of a certain *kind* of critical reflection. She needs to reflect critically on her culture's social practices and her social roles and on herself and the basic goods that she pursues. If she is sufficiently reflective about the former, but insufficiently reflective about the latter, then she still will fail to "penetrate into the personality itself" in her critical reflection. In that case, she is not an ethical person, according to Climacus's schema, because she aims at whatever goods she pursues just because she has been socialized to seek them and just because these goods happen to be available to her as goods to be sought. As a result, even if she is highly reflective in certain respects, according to Climacus, she still is a mere product of her social environment and not a responsible moral agent, because her capacity for moral agency remains unrealized.

Now that we have a rough idea of what Climacus intends by an immediate person or aesthete and, to a lesser extent, what he intends by an ethicist, we can begin to unpack some of his other key ideas. Consider first Climacus's sketch of ironists. He focuses on the speech of persons as a guide to discerning whether they are ironists. I think it is helpful not to opt for a very literal reading of what he intends by this, however. For in the same context, Climacus states, "Irony is an existence-qualification, and thus nothing is more ludicrous than regarding it as a style of speaking or an author's counting himself lucky to express himself ironically once in a while. The person who has essential irony has it all day long and is not bound to any style, because it is the infinite within him."[8] For Climacus, then, irony primarily is a way of existing, not a mode of speech. Furthermore, in some sense irony is "the infinite" within a person.

This claim harks back to Climacus's remark that ironists and ethicists have made the "movement of infinity." What is this movement? According to Climacus, ironists and ethicists have made a discovery that immediate persons have not made. They have discovered an absolute moral ideal, which Climacus vaguely refers to as "the ethical infinite requirement." Apparently this ideal trumps, relativizes, and contrasts with all merely cultural ideals, practices, and norms—the "particulars of the finite." Because an ironist recognizes this overarching, absolute requirement and reevaluates social practices, norms, and her own self-understanding in view of it, she is not "caught in any relativity." In other words, she does not make the mistake of treating something that has merely relative value as if it is unconditionally good or right. Perhaps Climacus refers to someone who has made this discovery and who has adjusted her valuations accordingly in light of it as having "the infinite" within her because she has discovered the unconditional nature of morality; and she has discovered her status as a moral agent who is bound by morality but only provisionally or conditionally bound by the "particulars of the finite"—all merely cultural norms, practices, and ideals.

Climacus clarifies the "movement of infinity" in a footnote that corresponds to the passage in which he refers to this concept. He states:

> If the observer is able to catch him[9] in a relativity that he does not have the strength to comprehend ironically, then he is not really an ironist. In other words, if irony is not taken in the decisive sense, every human being is basically ironical. As soon as a person who has his life in a certain relativity (and this definitely shows that he is not ironical) is placed outside it in a relativity that he considers to be lower (a nobleman, for example, in a group of peasants, a professor in the company of parish clerks, a city millionaire together with beggars, a royal coachman in a room with peat cutters, a cook at a manor house together with women who do weeding, etc.), then he is ironical—that is, he is not ironical since his irony is only the illusory superiority of relativity, but the symptoms and the rejoinders will have a certain similarity.[10]

This passage suggests that "getting caught in a relativity" roughly is equivalent to treating something that has relative value as if it has unconditional worth. For instance, a nobleman gets caught in a relativity when he takes this status too seriously, that is, when he thinks that it makes him superior in a moral respect to peasants. From a higher perspective, he is not morally superior to peasants by virtue of being a nobleman. If he thinks that he is, then he is snared in a silly relative valuation, a fact that becomes clear when one takes into account the "ethical infinite requirement." Apparently Climacus thinks that this requirement illuminates not only the "relativity" of cultural practices and norms but also the equality, in a moral respect, of all persons. That is another reason for associating this ideal with the principle that human persons should recognize and realize their unique moral agency through moral commitment.

Climacus's remarks also help to clarify the sort of irony that is a transition zone between aesthetic and ethical modes of existence. He notes that every person is an ironist in a relative sense. He has in mind that every person who is even mildly reflective notices that she differs from others in certain ways and usually concludes that at least some of these other persons are inferior to her in certain respects. This sort of irony, however, is not the sort that indicates a progression out of a life of immediacy. It is merely the "illusory superiority of relativity." It is not comprehensive enough to reveal the relativity of all valuations and distinctions that are not based on the "ethical infinite requirement." This suggests that the irony that is associated with the perception of the relativity of every practice, norm, and ideal, save the "ethical infinite requirement," is pure or comprehensive irony. In other words, the kind of irony that is a *confinium* between aesthetic and ethical modes of existence is pure irony, not relative irony and not mastered irony, either. Furthermore, interestingly Climacus associates pure irony with the recognition of the "ethical infinite requirement" and not with "infinite absolute negativity," as Kierkegaard does.

As Evans helpfully explains:

> The same type of negativity that is present in irony and humor as existential life-possibilities is present in ordinary irony and humor. This ordinary irony and humor is irony and humor as an element or component in existence rather than as a sphere or zone of existence. Its distinguishing mark is relativity. A man who from a superior position looks ironically on others, such as a city sophisticate who ironically undermines the values held dear by a group of uneducated rurals, is engaged in negating what he regards as lower on the basis of his resumed higher position. All such irony Climacus designates as relative irony, which everyone has a little of, since everyone finds someone to feel superior to. This relative irony, since it is possessed by everyone, is not the distinguishing mark of Climacus's ironist, who does not merely dissolve one relativity on the basis of higher relativity, but dissolves "every relativity" through his discovery of the absolute.[11]

How do persons discover this absolute? Although Climacus does not give us many details about the process of discovery, he suggests that it is not a terribly complicated undertaking. In the context of discussing ethical passion, he states:

> What I am writing here must be regarded as ABC reading, not in the speculative but in the simple sense. Every child knows it, even though not with quite the same experience; everyone understands it, even though not with quite the same definiteness; everyone can understand it, because the ethical is quite consistently always very easy to understand, probably in order that no time will be wasted on understanding but one will be able to begin immediately. But, in return, it is very difficult to accomplish—just the same for the sagacious as for the simple, since the difficulty does not lie in understanding, for in that case the sagacious would have a great advantage.[12]

This passage suggests that, like Kant, Climacus thinks that the central difficulty in becoming an ethical person is realizing moral ideals, not discovering them. Climacus is led to this conclusion by his conviction that intellectual persons have no advantage over simple persons with regard to the task of leading an ethical life. Of course, Climacus states in this passage that "the ethical," not the "ethical infinite requirement," is easy to grasp. So, unless Climacus also believes that in order to understand "the ethical" it is necessary to understand the "ethical infinite requirement," this passage will not give us a clear reason to believe that Climacus also thinks the "ethical infinite requirement" is easy to understand.

I think that Climacus is committed to the view that one cannot understand "the ethical" unless one also grasps the "ethical infinite requirement." Consider what follows if one does not grasp this requirement. According to Climacus's remarks in the first passage cited in this section, one cannot possibly avoid getting caught in a relativity of one sort or another unless one recognizes this requirement, which *discloses* the relative validity of merely social practices, norms, and ideals. Furthermore, if one is caught in a relativity, if one treats a merely relative norm, practice, or ideal as an unconditional good or as an absolutely binding obligation, then it is not even possible that one is an ethical person, according to Climacus. One also can be caught in a relativity by treating the "ethical infinite requirement" as if it merely is conditionally binding. It follows from these claims that, for Climacus, a person cannot understand what is involved in leading an ethical life if she does not grasp the "ethical infinite requirement" and grasp it *as* an unconditional requirement. For if a person fails properly to grasp this requirement, she likely will come to the mistaken view that ethical life simply involves fulfilling the obligations that accompany her social roles, however these obligations are construed in her society. Furthermore, if recognizing the "ethical infinite requirement" and recognizing it as an unconditional requirement are crucial in coming developmentally to a point where entry into ethical life is possible, this requirement must be easy to grasp, if "the ethical" is as easy to understand as Climacus takes it to be. Otherwise intellectually gifted persons will have an advantage over simple persons in recognizing and embracing the "ethical infinite requirement" and in recognizing and embracing it *as* an unconditional requirement. Both of these conditions are necessary conditions for entry into ethical existence, according to Climacus. So, unless the "ethical infinite requirement" is easy to understand, intellectual persons will have an advantage over simple persons in gaining entry into ethical life. But Climacus will have none of that. Consequently, the "ethical infinite requirement" must not be difficult to comprehend, in his view.

The idea that the "ethical infinite requirement" is easy to grasp might seem to create problems for the view that immediate persons do not grasp it because of their paucity of critical reflection. If this requirement is not difficult to understand, then it appears that moral goods can be intentionally pursued and realized apart from the sort of critical reflection that immediate persons fail to do. For if this requirement is easy to grasp, why is critical reflection needed in order to comprehend it? If Climacus's account is consistent, the answer has to be that the sort of critical reflection that is required to pursue and realize moral goods is not difficult to undertake. Immediate persons are capable of this kind of reflection. But they fail to do it. After all, that is why they are morally culpable for not becoming ethical persons, according to Climacus (and Kierkegaard). As I suggested in regard to Cross's remarks about "A"'s highly reflective kind of immediacy, moreover, it is not necessarily elaborate or complicated critical reflection that is missing in the lives of immediate persons. Rather, it is critical reflection on one's social order and oneself, especially the basic goods that one pursues. Apparently Climacus thinks that this sort of reflection does not have to be very involved in order for one to discover the "ethical infinite requirement" through it.

In Climacus's view, then, ironists and ethicists recognize the "ethical infinite requirement," which reveals the relative validity of merely cultural norms, practices, and ideals. As a result, they are not "caught in a relativity." Immediate persons, however, do not properly recognize this requirement, even though they could. They do not engage in the requisite sort of critical reflection. Consequently, their moral agency lies fallow—unrecognized and unrealized. Or, as Climacus puts it, they fail to make "the movement of infinity."

Then what is the difference between (pure) ironists and ethicists, in Climacus's account? The difference is that ethicists not only recognize the "ethical infinite requirement"; they also embrace it and attempt to realize it in their lives. As a result, they are motivated to be critically engaged in their social roles and the other duties that they have as moral agents who are in community with other moral agents. Ironists, on the other hand, merely perceive this requirement and employ it in their pursuit of negative freedom. In other words, ironists disengage radically from society on the basis of their realization that all merely cultural norms, practices, and ideals are relatively valid—an insight they gain from recognizing the "ethical infinite requirement."

There is an implicit assumption here in Climacus's position that needs to be made explicit. That is, if a person recognizes the "ethical infinite requirement," she is not necessarily going to embrace it and strive to realize it in her life. That is why there can be persons who exist as pure ironists and not as ethicists, on Climacus's account. To put this point another way: the perception of the "ethical infinite requirement" is a necessary condition of ethical existence, but it is not a sufficient condition of it. As Evans puts these points:

> Irony and humor are boundary zones in which the individual has acquired an intellectual understanding of a truth that he has not yet existentially realized. This understanding is sufficient to undermine the relativities of the individual's past and present existence, but it does not in itself make an existential advance to the next sphere a reality. Being essentially reflective, humor and irony are only achievable by reflective individuals. The intellectual understanding that is their content makes possible the existential jump to a higher sphere. But since there is always a gap between thought and action, it follows that the possession of such an understanding by no means guarantees that the individual's intellectual understanding will become concretized in her life. Hence irony and humor are not only transition points, but existential zones in their own right, the sphere of a cultured individual whose understanding is more advanced than her existence.[13]

Evans's reading of Climacus, with which I concur, clarifies that it is quite possible on Climacus's account to progress into the transition zone of irony and then to hover there without progressing farther into an ethical existence. In such cases, irony becomes an existential zone, not merely a momentary transition point.

Climacus's construal of pure irony is markedly different from Kierkegaard's description of pure irony as "infinite absolute negativity" in *The Concept of Irony*. The possibility of radical disengagement remains, however, according to Climacus. For persons who perceive the absolute ethical requirement may simply remain in a stage of canceling, negating, and attempting to transcend all merely cultural norms and ideals without embracing this absolute requirement as a defining commitment.

In this preliminary sketch of Climacus's position, I have attempted to clarify several of his central concepts. A few of these ideas generate perplexities that require more clarification. I will attempt to unravel as many of these difficulties as possible in subsequent sections as I fill out Climacus's position. It will become apparent, I hope, that his position illuminates and extends certain features of Kierkegaard's initial discussion of irony. I now turn to an important claim in Kierkegaard's thesis that is complicated and illuminated by Climacus's account.

6.2   A Conundrum That Links
The Concept of Irony and *Postscript*

As I noted in the conclusion of the previous chapter, in the final section of his thesis, Kierkegaard states that "no genuinely human life is
possible without irony."[14] This claim explicitly introduces into the
body of *The Concept of Irony* the final thesis that Kierkegaard defends
in it. This thesis is advanced in the same passage in which Kierkegaard
describes the process of being rejuvenated through baths in the "sea
of irony." Thus, it is closely related to his claim in the same context
that to lack an appreciation for irony is to lack "the absolute beginning of personal life," or "what momentarily is indispensable for personal life."[15] It is not clear, though, how we are to understand
Kierkegaard's final thesis and the other claims noted here, which are
very similar to it.

My discussion of Kierkegaard's thesis in the previous chapter suggests that by "genuinely human" Kierkegaard intends "ethical." In
other words, Kierkegaard employs the concept "human person" in a
normative sense. One advantage of this reading is that Kierkegaard
does employ this concept in this way in his later writings and he uses
it this way in other sections of his thesis. So, I will assume for the
moment that by "genuinely human" Kierkegaard intends "ethical."

Kierkegaard advances his final thesis about irony in a section
devoted to an explication of the benefits of mastered irony. This fact
suggests that it is mastered irony, not pure irony or some other form
of irony that which marks "the absolute beginning of personal life" or
makes possible a "genuinely human life." In that case, Kierkegaard's
final thesis more specifically is that no genuinely *ethical* life is possible
without *mastered* irony.

John Lippitt interprets Kierkegaard's position this way. He argues:

> Kierkegaard's central claim in this section, then, can be seen as being
> that the *use of irony from a position of rootedness* is fundamentally different
> from when that irony is symptomatic of "infinite absolute negativity." It
> is on the basis of this assumption—that the irony under discussion is
> *mastered* irony—that he claims irony is necessary for a "genuinely
> human life." . . .
>   The key point to note is how irony here is "mastered." Rather than it
> being one's master . . . , one masters *it*, in the sense that one's use of irony
> is always in the service of one's wider ethical or religious existence.[16]

The larger context for Lippitt's remarks indicates that by "a position
of rootedness" he intends the position of a person who has embraced

actuality as gift and task. A person who occupies this sort of position has a "wider ethical or religious existence" that informs and regulates her employment of irony. It is this form of irony, moreover, that is necessary for a "genuinely human" life, on Lippitt's reading of Kierkegaard. So, Lippitt takes "genuinely human life" to be equivalent roughly to "ethical life." He also argues that mastered irony is the form of irony that is essential to this sort of life.

Lippitt's reading of Kierkegaard is insightful and very plausible. There is some reason to think, however, that it is incomplete. For starters, there seems to be something incoherent about Kierkegaard's position, if we take it just this way. On the one hand, mastered irony makes possible ethical life. On the other hand, in order to master irony in the first place, a person already must be leading an ethical life, since irony is mastered through moral commitment.

It is possible that Lippitt feels this tension. For he immediately adds, "Given what follows it in the text, this claim[17] seems to be related to the claim that a life of immediacy is less than fully human."[18] This suggestion is helpful. For when we examine the idea that Kierkegaard's claim that "no genuinely human life is possible without irony," is related to the claim that a life of immediacy is less than fully human, an *alternative* reading of Kierkegaard's final thesis quickly emerges.

Kierkegaard and Climacus both view a life of immediacy as a pre-ethical form of existence. Moreover, Climacus construes irony as a mode of existence that represents a developmental advance over immediacy and brings one to the threshold of ethical existence. Climacus puts it this way: "Irony is the cultivation of the spirit and therefore follows next after immediacy; then comes the ethicist, then the humorist, then the religious person."[19]

The alternative reading now is easier to clarify. A person who has broken free from a life of immediacy is not necessarily an ethical person. If moving beyond a life of immediacy makes one more fully human, however, then perhaps the phrase "genuinely human" in Kierkegaard's final thesis is not equivalent to "ethical." Rather, it may be roughly equivalent to "truly individual." The "cultivation of the spirit" that occurs when one enters into the transition zone of irony can be construed as the emergence of individuality. This development occurs as persons come to recognize that they are moral agents. But if by "a genuinely human life," Kierkegaard intends "a truly individual life" or "a critically reflective life," an alternative reading of Kierkegaard's final thesis now presents itself: irony makes possible truly individual life. This claim is very different from the claim that mastered irony makes possible ethical life. Furthermore, as my analysis of Climacus's account of irony as a transition zone suggests, there is some reason to believe that Kierkegaard holds this alternative view, at least in *Postscript*, if he concurs with Climacus. If (a) irony is the transition zone between aesthetic and ethical modes of existence; (b) an aesthetic life is a life of immediacy; and (c) a life of immediacy is less than fully human; then it follows that irony delivers one into a more fully human way of life. However, this way of life is not necessarily an ethical way of life. For irony is a pre-ethical stage, according to Climacus. Moreover, as intimated above, Climacus (and Kierkegaard) famously denies that transitions through stages of existence are logically or psychologically necessary. So a person could move beyond immediacy into the transition zone of irony via her recognition of the "ethical infinite requirement" without choosing to commit herself to this requirement. In that case, Climacus's account implies that she would be an individual, since she has transcended immediacy. However, she would not yet be an ethical individual. From the vantage point of *Postscript*, then, irony makes possible "genuinely human" life in the sense that it gives rise to truly individual life. If Climacus's account of irony may be employed in this way to clarify the account that Kierkegaard presents in *The Concept of Irony*, then Kierkegaard's final thesis in this work amounts to the claim that irony makes possible truly individual life.

A slightly different reading of Kierkegaard's final thesis also is possible here, namely, that irony makes possible ethical life, since it makes possible the sort of individuality that is required for ethical life. This way of construing Kierkegaard's claim that "no genuinely human life is possible without irony," clearly jibes with Climacus's view that irony is a transition zone between aesthetic and ethical ways of life. Notice, however, that it still differs from Lippitt's reading. For the irony that makes possible ethical life, according to Lippitt, is mastered irony. Whereas, the irony that makes possible ethical life, according to this third possible reading, is pure irony, as Climacus construes this. Moreover, Climacus concurs with Kierkegaard that pure irony is a pre-ethical form of irony. So, Climacus's pure irony is not at all Kierkegaard's mastered irony.

Andrew Cross recently has articulated a slight variant of the alternative readings that I have briefly sketched here.[20] He begins his discussion by focusing on the relation between irony and immediacy in Kierkegaard's thesis. Then he offers an interpretation of Climacus's claim that irony is a transition zone between aesthetic and ethical ways of life. He states:

> For Kierkegaard, ceasing to live such a life of immediacy . . . requires that one dissociate oneself from, and regard as external to oneself, the whole of one's immediate or merely given nature. And this radical disengagement from what one has hitherto regarded as one's self is the movement or adoption of irony. The ironist separates himself from the self and the life that have hitherto been his; he ceases to identify himself with the identity and goals delivered to him by virtue of his particular location in a particular society, that is, his own history and upbringing, and so on.[21]

From what has been said so far, it should be clear why Climacus sees irony as a border zone between immediacy (which includes the aesthetic) and the ethical. Between the position of the person who takes his given immediate nature as brute data for the pursuit of a meaningful life (and as determining what would constitute a meaningful life) and the person who takes his immediate nature as an object of choice,[22] there is the position of the person who has dissociated himself from his immediate nature but not yet achieved the partial reintegration with that nature that ethical self-choice involves. This intermediary position in which one is entirely dissociated from one's immediacy, without identifying oneself with anything other than this dissociating, is the position of irony.[23]

According to Cross, progressing beyond immediacy requires detaching oneself in a wholesale way from the givens of one's identity. When a person achieves this sort of radical dissociation, she inhabits the position of irony, as Climacus sketches it.

Cross's interpretation of Kierkegaard and Climacus suggests that there is a very close link between *The Concept of Irony* and *Postscript*. On this reading, it is natural to take the concluding thesis of *The Concept of Irony* to be a seed that gives rise in Kierkegaard's thinking to the idea that Climacus advances later in *Postscript* that irony is a transition zone between aesthetic and ethical ways of life. Cross's reading also suggests that, for Kierkegaard, persons need to move through a stage of radical disengagement before they can embrace and fulfill the task of ethical selfhood. Indeed, Cross explicitly affirms this position. As he explains, "Climacus, like Kierkegaard, sees in the ironic life a kind of radical detachment of oneself from all others and from one's surrounding world; as he somewhat obscurely puts it, "In irony there is no sympathy; it is self-assertion" (*CUP* 553), the asserting of oneself as a radically independent entity."[24] And immediately following this passage Cross adds that Climacus takes this radical detachment to be "an important stage in the maturation of the individual."[25] It corresponds roughly to the emergence of individuality, as sketched above. So, Cross takes the irony that is, for Climacus, a transition zone between aesthetic and ethical forms of existence to be pure irony. Moreover, he thus takes Climacus to hold that a stance of pure irony is an important developmental stage between aesthetic and ethical forms of existence. For persons who take such a stance assert themselves as "radically independent entities." They progress from immediacy into a state of individuality, which is a prerequisite for becoming an ethical individual. In support of this reading Cross cites Climacus's assertion that irony is self-assertion that lacks sympathy. This characterization captures the mode of existence of a person who has seen through the "relativity" of social practices and norms, who has awakened to individuality, so to speak, but who has not yet become an ethical person.

It should be clearer now why Lippitt suggests that Kierkegaard's claim that irony is necessary for a genuinely human life seems to be related to the idea that a life of immediacy is less than fully human. We can also see why this suggestion needs careful elaboration. There is a crucial difference between taking Kierkegaard's final thesis to be a thesis about the vital role of *mastered* irony in *ethical* life and taking it to be a thesis about the essential role of *pure* irony in *pre-ethical* life, which makes possible ethical existence. The merit of Cross's reading is that it provides a clear and illuminating interpretive bridge from *The Concept of Irony* to *Postscript*. Moreover, it avoids the problems that are generated by the pair of claims that (a) mastered irony makes possible ethical life and (b) we master irony in the first place though moral commitment. The merit of Lippitt's position is that it provides an accurate and insightful reading of *The Concept of Irony* on its own terms. For the paragraph in which Kierkegaard advances his final thesis about irony is a paragraph about the benefits of mastered irony in a concluding section that focuses almost entirely on this form of irony. Moreover, in the context of *The Concept of Irony*, it makes sense to take "genuinely human" as a synonym for "ethical." So, who is right?

In certain respects, both Lippitt and Cross offer plausible readings of Kierkegaard on this point. I think there is an explanation for the disparity in their readings, which traces back to an ambiguity in Kierkegaard's original account of irony in his thesis. We can begin to get to the bottom of this ambiguity by noting that in his thesis Kierkegaard suggests, albeit implicitly, that there are two positive roles for irony, not one. In the previous chapter, I discussed the positive role that irony plays when it is mastered. That is the role that Lippitt has in view. There is another positive role that irony has, however, that needs to be disentangled from the role that irony plays when it is mastered. From a developmental perspective, before a person can employ mastered irony in her life, she needs to realize her capacity for moral agency. According to Kierkegaard, irony plays a crucial role at this stage of personal development.[26] When a person develops an ironic sensibility, she begins to discover disparities or incongruities—gaps between what is and what ought to be—in her social environment that enliven her critical faculties. As a result, with respect to her identity as a person socialized into particular communities with other persons, the process of individuation gets underway. She begins to think independently and to become an individual in this sense. This is the developmental role of irony to which Cross alludes. It is somewhat implicit in *The Concept of Irony*, especially in the concluding section of this work. Since Kierkegaard suggests to his readers that the "truth" or "validity" of irony is disclosed in this section, it is not difficult to overlook the fact that irony has this positive function even apart from the role that it plays when it is mastered.

Perhaps Kierkegaard himself is a bit vague about this distinction in *The Concept of Irony*, especially in the final section. In the context of discussing mastered irony, he refers to the role that irony has in bringing about the "absolute beginning of personal life." But "personal life" is ambiguous between a "truly individual life" and an "ethical life." The absolute beginning of personal life could plausibly be construed as the beginning of individuality. When Kierkegaard uses the phrase "personal life," sometimes he has "individual life" specifically in view and at other times "ethical life." Cross rightly points out that an ironist can be an individual, a person who has transcended an insufficiently reflective life of immediacy, without becoming an ethical person, as Kierkegaard understands this. So, it is important to keep separate these senses of "personal life." The same point holds for "genuinely human life" as well.

If this more complicated reading is on the right track, it follows that Kierkegaard's claim that "no genuinely human life is possible without irony," can plausibly be taken in two ways. First, it refers to the idea that persons need to become ironic in order to develop as individuals, which is a crucial step on the path toward ethical individuality. Second, it refers to the idea that mastered irony is crucial for ethical life in the various ways discussed in the previous chapter. It is not clear which of these two readings best captures the meaning of Kierkegaard's final thesis, all things considered. Perhaps Kierkegaard intends both ways of understanding this claim. We do not have to choose between them. So, why not take Kierkegaard's final thesis about irony in *The Concept of Irony* to be a complex claim that can be broken down into two simpler claims, which reveal a close connection between *The Concept of Irony* and *Postscript?*

Whether or not one concurs with this reading, it does offer a viable solution to the original puzzle generated by Lippitt's reading. Becoming ironic is a precursor to becoming ethical, for Kierkegaard. Once a person decisively opts for an ethical way of life, moreover, if she continues to utilize irony within the confines of her more ultimate ethical commitments, she will find that it promotes her ethical way of life. In this way, irony precedes ethical existence and makes it possible, for Kierkegaard and Climacus, but mastered irony arises in conjunction with ethical existence and promotes it.

6.3 PURE IRONY AS A TRANSITION ZONE: AN ANALYSIS OF CROSS'S READING OF CLIMACUS

What sort of irony constitutes a transition zone between aesthetic and ethical modes of existence? The sketch of Climacus's account that I have provided thus far suggests that the answer is pure irony. What exactly does this answer imply? On Cross's reading, a person cannot pass through irony as a transition zone without having to become, at least momentarily, a pure ironist. Or to state this position another way: radical disengagement is a necessary precursor to ethical life, according to Cross's reading of Climacus (and Kierkegaard).[27]

Cross partly bases this reading on Climacus's claim that irony is unsympathetic self-assertion. However, most of the support that Cross offers for this reading, in fact, turns on a controversial reading of *Either/Or*. Cross argues that Judge William advances a Kantian view of ethical self-choice, which also is embraced by Kierkegaard and Climacus. On Cross's reading, Judge William holds that ethical self-choice involves something very much like one's noumenal self's accepting the given characteristics of its embodied or phenomenal self "as a task—as, so to speak, raw material to be shaped in accordance with an ideal posited in freedom."[28] He states:

> The core idea is that of an unrestricted taking of responsibility for oneself, a taking of responsibility extending toward one's immediacy, one's past, and one's future. This taking of responsibility involves a double movement toward one's empirical self in both its physical and social aspects. The first movement is a ceasing to identify with this self; one

regards oneself as essentially not such-and-such an embodied person but an autonomous will, a thing with an unbounded capacity for choice. The second movement, which is the actual "choosing" in ethical self-choice, is a partial reunification of this willing self with the embodied person; being this embodied person is taken on as an act of one's own will.[29]

Cross identifies a person who has made the first movement mentioned here but not the second as a pure ironist.[30] One advantage of this identification is that it helps to explain why irony is post-aesthetic but pre-ethical on Climacus's account. For a person who has taken the first step mentioned above is beyond immediacy. Until she takes the second step, she remains in a pre-ethical way of life, according to Climacus (and Kierkegaard). So, Cross's reading of Judge William clarifies Climacus's position to a certain extent. Yet there is reason to think that it is flawed, nonetheless.

Although Kierkegaard clearly endorses in *Either/Or* and in other writings the idea that the given features of one's character and social location set a task for one, to read into his position a kind of Kantian split between noumenal and phenomenal selves, as Cross does, is an important mistake. As an ethicist and moral psychologist, Judge William appears to be more of an Aristotelian and Hegelian than a Kantian. As Westphal explains:

The aesthetic sphere embodies a philosophy of self-choice. Judge William does not deny that this is a philosophy of freedom. But he complains that the aesthetic self chooses itself only in terms of its immediate interests and inclinations, where immediate means the whim of the moment. The result, he suggests, is an unstable self. He understands the ethical to enact a philosophy of self-choice, but it is a choice of the self in relation to the difference between good and evil, or, as he sometimes puts it, an *absolute* choice of the self in its *eternal* validity (EO 2:166–69, 178, 188–90, 214–19, 223–24).

These references to *absolute* choice and *eternal* validity should not lead us to think that Judge William understands the ethical in Platonic or Kantian terms as involving the apprehension of an abstract, formal principle by an intellect that has somehow become pure reason. Judge William is an Aristotelian, for whom right reason is to be defined in terms of the man of practical wisdom rather than the reverse, and a Hegelian, for whom ethics is always a matter of *Sittlichkeit*, the laws, customs, practices, and institutions of a people. The right and the good are to be found, not abstractly in a rational principle but concretely within one's social order, which is, for each individual, the essential mediator of the absolute and eternal.

Accordingly, Judge William immediately embeds his theory of self-choice in a theory of marriage, the first moment of Hegel's theory of *Sittlichkeit*.[31]

If Westphal's reading is accurate, as I take it to be, then according to Judge William, the self that embraces actuality as a gift and task is not a noumenal self, but is always a socially embedded self with a capacity for critical reflection and responsible choice.

Nevertheless, Cross's reading of Judge William's notion of ethical self-choice illuminates Climacus's notion of irony as a transition zone between aesthetic and ethical modes of existence. Climacus does identify pure irony with the position of someone who has dissociated from her social roles, who has made, according to Judge William, the first move in taking complete responsibility for herself, as Cross suggests. However, we need not take this stance of dissociation in such a dualistic way or as a stance of a being who regards its essential self as disembodied—a notion that is foreign to Kierkegaard even if it is familiar to Kant.

What about Cross's related claim that radical disengagement is an element in the pure irony that constitutes, for Climacus, a transition zone between aesthetic and ethical modes of existence? I have a somewhat complicated view of Cross's reading on this point. First, I find it somewhat odd that Cross takes what seems to be an exegetically circuitous route to this view and fails to utilize more direct and more compelling textual evidence in *Postscript* in support of it. Second, the textual evidence in *Postscript* to which I refer does support the view, which Cross espouses, that pure irony is the sort of irony that constitutes a transition zone between aesthetic and ethical forms of existence. However, it does not sustain the view that, for Climacus, persons must become *radically* disengaged as a precursor to leading an ethical way of life.

It seems that by taking such a position I am arguing very oddly that Climacus takes pure irony to be and not to be a transition zone between aesthetic and ethical modes of existence. For is not radical disengagement a feature of pure irony? If it is, and if pure irony is the sort of irony that is a transition zone between immediacy and ethical life, then radical disengagement is an important developmental stage beyond immediacy and prior to ethical life, on Climacus's account. I concur with Cross that radical disengagement is a feature of pure irony and that pure irony is the sort of irony that is a transition zone, on Climacus's account. I do not believe, however, that Climacus takes radical disengagement to be a crucial stage in personal development. Obviously this requires some explanation.

Climacus suggests that it is not even possible that a person could be an ethicist if she dabbles in irony only in a relative sense. The reason is that relative ironists do not recognize the "ethical infinite requirement," which reveals the conditional goodness or rightness of cultural norms, practices, and ideals. Pure ironists do perceive this requirement. Indeed, Climacus suggests that this perception helps them progress out of the existence-sphere of immediacy. So what pure ironists and ethicists have in common, according to Climacus, is the recognition of the "ethical infinite requirement" and the adjustment in valuations that this recognition brings. Notice that Climacus's account of pure irony differs in an important way from Kierkegaard's account of pure irony in *The Concept of Irony*. As Climacus states, "the irony emerges by continually joining the particulars of the finite with the ethical infinite requirement and allowing the contradiction to come into existence."[32] For Climacus, a pure ironist's seeing through the relativity of social conventions comes on the heels of her discovery of the "ethical infinite requirement." It is only in view of this overarching, unconditional requirement that the conditional value of everything else becomes evident. So, in a certain respect, Climacus has a *top-down* approach to pure irony. However, Kierkegaard suggests a different route to pure irony in his thesis. His pure ironists do not hold steady a positive, absolute moral ideal as they critique and dissociate from everything else. Rather, they simply employ searing and withering negativity toward everything, except their own ironic stance, in order to realize negative freedom through radical disengagement. Their path to pure irony is a kind of *bootstrapping*, thoroughgoing negativity.

Consequently, for Climacus, to say that a person must pass through a stage of pure irony in order to become an ethical person is not precisely to say that she must become radically disengaged from society and her social roles as she embraces a stance of "infinite absolute negativity." Rather, it is to say that she must recognize the "ethical infinite requirement" and recognize it *as* an absolute ideal that trumps and renders relative all merely social norms, practices, and commitments. One might think that someone who recognizes the *relative* validity of a practice, norm, or ideal, thereby begins to dissociate or disengage from it. If this dissociation or disengagement is unchecked by commitment to an ideal that promotes critical *reengagement* in one's social roles and other features of the communities to which one belongs, it may become radical. This is the position of someone who recognizes the "ethical infinite requirement" but does not embrace and attempt to realize it. In other words, this is the position of a pure ironist, as *Climacus* construes pure irony. However, it is possible to pass through (pure) irony as a transition zone without becoming a pure ironist in this respect.

Pure ironists and ethicists both recognize the "ethical infinite requirement." In regard to pure ironists, this recognition leads to radical disengagement because these persons reject this requirement as an ultimate, identity-conferring commitment. They come to recognize it simply as a device for deconstructing societal norms, practices, and ideals. In this way, in an odd twist, a pure ironist's recognition of the "ethical infinite requirement" promotes and, in some cases, may even initiate her pursuit of negative freedom, according to Climacus. So, her stance still is a stance of negativity, even though she utilizes a positive, absolute ideal to critique societal conventions. However, a person might embrace and commit herself to the "ethical infinite requirement" when she recognizes it, or at least once she decides how to respond to the reorientation to her actuality and herself that accompanies her discovery of this requirement. In that case, she would not go through a stage of radical disengagement before she becomes an ethicist.

A person who embraces the "ethical infinite requirement" takes seriously the norms, practices, and ideals that she perceives to have merely relative validity, but from a standpoint of critical commitment. She takes these "relativities" seriously because the "ethical infinite requirement" to which she is committed is a requirement of ethical self-realization. As Evans explains:

> It might be thought that Climacus has two different ethical views which are not completely congruent. On the one hand he talks about self-actualization; the ethical task is the task of existing, of becoming oneself. On the other hand he talks of the absolute character of duty in a way reminiscent of Kant. The key to understanding his view is to recognize that he is saying both of these things: Actualize yourself and do your duty for the sake of duty. They are unified in this way: The essential self that you are to become is your ethical self; the person only realizes himself through ethical commitment. Ethical commitment is the decisive criterion of "selfhood."[33]
>
> Climacus assumes that the aesthetic, immediate elements in life provide a multiplicity of content; it is up to the individual to discover and select that content given to him *through which* he can express his commitment to the eternal.[34]

For Climacus, then, a person realizes herself as a moral agent by fulfilling the "ethical infinite requirement." She fulfills this requirement by responsibly engaging her social roles and the norms, practices, and ideals that accompany these roles. She cannot be committed to the "ethical infinite requirement" as an unconditional commitment, if she radically disengages from the norms, practices, and ideals of her culture. She does not absolutize these social conventions, however, as commonplace persons do who do not recognize their relative validity. In this respect, just like a pure ironist, she is not "caught in any relativity." Unlike a pure ironist, however, she manages not to "get caught in any relativity" through *commitment* to the "ethical infinite requirement," not through radical disengagement from societal conventions or "relativities," which is underwritten by *mere recognition* of this absolute ideal.

The alternative reading that I have offered here, in summation, goes as follows. Pure irony is the irony that constitutes a transition zone between aesthetic and ethical modes of existence. Furthermore, although Climacus modifies and extends Kierkegaard's account of irony, it remains the case for Climacus that pure irony is characterized by radical disengagement. Cross incorrectly deduces from these facts that, on Climacus's view, radical disengagement is a crucial stage in personal development. I contend, on the contrary, that what is crucial for personal development, for Climacus, is that persons come to recognize the "ethical infinite requirement," which trumps and relativizes all merely social norms and practices. Furthermore, it is possible and, for Climacus, vastly preferable, to embrace and appropriate this ideal when one perceives it, or at least before one becomes radically dissociated from society by virtue of the significant readjustment in one's valuations that comes with its discovery.

Admittedly, in a certain respect, it is true that persons who bypass the radical disengagement of pure irony in this way still go *through* pure irony as a transition zone. But they do this only in the sense that they come to see the merely relative validity of social norms and practices. They do not even momentarily disengage *radically* from society, however. So they never are pure ironists or persons who hover in the transition zone of pure irony on account of not embracing the absolute moral ideal that they use to deconstruct social norms and practices. Consequently, for Climacus, the radically disengaged stance of pure irony may be a developmental phase that some persons go through into ethical existence. It does not have to be, however. In fact, it clearly is not a good thing, in Climacus's view, to fall into the radical disengagement of pure irony when one comes to recognize the merely relative validity of social norms and practices. This lapse into radical disengagement marks a failure to progress into ethical existence.

Therefore, for Climacus, once a person enters into the transition zone of irony, her recognition of the "ethical infinite requirement" leaves her with the choice of moving forward into ethical existence or radically dissociating from social conventions, which she now sees through. If she opts for the latter alternative, she will become a full-fledged pure ironist, at least for as long as she exists in this way. Of course, such a person also could simply attempt to ignore and forget about her discovery. In that case, she would devolve back into immediacy, according to Climacus. The best scenario, however, for Climacus, is the one in which a person progresses straightforwardly into ethical existence.[35]

This implication ought to be welcomed by those who sympathize with Kierkegaard and Climacus, since it is doubtful that persons must go through a stage of radical disengagement in order to become ethical. Many ethical persons have not gone through a period of radical disengagement in their lives, even if they have experienced *some* dissociation from social norms and practices as a result of discovering what they believe is an absolute moral ideal. All such persons would stand as counterexamples to Climacus's position, if he posited that radical disengagement is a necessary prerequisite to ethical life.

How does the reading that I have sketched here in response to Cross's position modify how we are to understand Kierkegaard's claim that irony makes possible genuinely human life? I have argued that this claim is perhaps intentionally ambiguous between the claim that mastered irony is necessary for ethical life and the claim that irony is necessary for truly individual life, which precedes ethical individuality. Now in view of my clarification of Climacus's position in *Postscript*, we can modify this latter claim as follows. Irony makes possible individuality and ethical individuality in the sense that one needs to see the relative validity of social norms and practices in order truly to become an individual, that is, in order to progress beyond immediacy. In order to see the relative validity of social norms and practices, moreover, Climacus suggests that one must recognize the "ethical infinite requirement," which trumps and relativizes these things. However, this particular claim goes well beyond the account of irony that Kierkegaard advances in his thesis. As far as I can tell, it is, at most, barely implicit in Kierkegaard's thesis, where irony is said to be merely a "guide."[36] Therefore, when Kierkegaard states in his thesis that irony makes possible genuinely human life, it is unlikely that he has in mind that irony brings with it the discovery of an absolute moral ideal. Rather, what he implicitly suggests by this claim in *The Concept of Irony* and then explicitly argues (through Climacus) in *Postscript* is that recognizing the relative validity of social norms and practices is a crucial step in becoming a moral agent. In *Postscript*, Climacus adds that this discovery turns on perceiving an "ethical infinite requirement."

6.4 CLIMACUS ON IRONY AND MORAL LUCK

Although Climacus does not hold that it is necessary to adopt a stance of radical disengagement in order to pass from aestheticism through irony into ethical existence, he does believe that to make the complete transition into ethical existence it is necessary to recognize that all merely social practices, norms, and ideals are conditionally good or right in comparison to the "ethical infinite requirement." Furthermore, he associates this discovery with a person's progressing beyond immediacy into the transition zone of irony. However, if irony is exclusive to well-educated or intelligent persons, then Climacus's position appears to imply that only persons with a certain kind of good fortune can become ethical persons.

Kierkegaard clearly is very uncomfortable with the idea that a person needs a bit of good fortune, especially of this sort, to be able to lead an ethical life. As I explained in chapter 4, in his thesis Kierkegaard faults views of poetic living that posit requirements for this sort of life that are not attainable for uneducated, simple persons. As we have seen in regard to his view that "the ethical" is easy to understand, Climacus clearly shares this sentiment as well. It would be surprising, then, if his account of irony collided with this sentiment. In fact, it does not. Climacus offers, albeit very briefly, a way around this problem.

Evans helpfully points us to an extended passage in *Postscript* in which Climacus argues that both simple and intellectual persons are able to live ethically and ethical–religiously; but they understand and realize these ways of life in different ways.[37] In the context of discussing "becoming subjective" or ethical and ethical–religiously passionate, Climacus states:

> First then, the ethical, the task of becoming subjective, and afterwards the world-historical. I do not doubt that even the most objective person is at bottom in tacit agreement with what has here been set forth, that it is right and proper for the wise man first to understand the same thing that the plain man understands, and to feel himself obligated by the same considerations that obligate the simple . . . .Now if I could only contrive an opportunity to speak with the wise man for still another moment, I should gladly be content to be the plain man who

asks him to pause a moment over the following simple remark: *Is it not the case that what is most difficult of all for the wise man to understand, is precisely the simple?* The plain man understands the simple directly, but when the wise man sets himself to understand it, it becomes infinitely difficult. . . . The more the wise man thinks about the simple (and the fact that a prolonged occupation with it is conceivable, shows already that it is not so easy), the more difficult it becomes for him. And yet he feels himself gripped by a profound humanity, which reconciles him with the whole of life: that the difference between the wise man and the simplest human being is merely this vanishing little distinction, that *the simple man knows the essential,* while the wise man little by little learns *to know that he knows it,* or learns *to know that he does not know it.* But what they both know is the same. . . .

But the ethical is not merely a knowing; it is also a doing that is related to a knowing.[38]

Climacus employs a bit of sarcasm in this passage in regard to the "world-historical" intellectual aspirations of Hegel and Danish Hegelians. For my purposes, it does not matter whether his characterization of these persons is accurate. So I will set aside this issue.

How does this passage suggest that Climacus has a solution to the problem of moral luck that his account of irony generates? Note first that Climacus posits a distinction between knowing "the essential" and knowing that one knows it. In the first place, "the essential" refers to the ethical, that which needs to be known in order for one to fulfill the task of "becoming subjective." Climacus refers to this kind of knowledge this way because it is "truth that is related essentially to existence."[39] In other words, ethical and ethical–religious knowledge are forms of knowledge of how one should live. Thus, they have certain preeminence. It is good to know theoretical physics, for instance, but knowledge of theoretical physics is not essential knowledge, according to Climacus, because one can lead a good life without such knowledge. However, one cannot lead a good life without knowledge of how to lead a good life, knowledge of what is crucially important in life and what is less important. So, this sort of knowledge, ethical and ethical–religious knowledge, is essential.

Climacus also claims that intellectual persons and simple persons know the same thing, even though intellectual persons little by little come to know that they know it or gradually come to know that they do not know it, in cases where they do not know it. Simple persons, however, do not possess this second-order knowledge of what they know directly (or fail to know directly). It follows that it cannot be knowledge of what they know that intellectual and simple persons share, since simple persons lack this knowledge. So what is it that both types of persons know? The answer is that both types of persons know "the essential." In other words, what Climacus intends is that both intellectual persons and even simple persons *can* know "the essential," even though intellectual persons also might gradually come to know *that* they know it or that they do not know it if, in fact, they do not.

One might get the impression from these claims that Climacus is concerned only with cognitive differences between simple and intellectual persons. That is why I have included in the quotation Climacus's qualification, "the ethical is not merely a knowing" but also is "a doing that is related to a knowing." This qualification introduces another important distinction that Climacus makes between simple and intellectual persons. Just as simple persons know "the essential" in a more direct way than intellectual persons, so also they *do* "the essential" more directly than intellectual persons. But what does this mean?

Climacus's remarks at a later point in the same section of *Postscript* provide a helpful clue. He notes: "What the simple religious man does directly, the simple man of knowledge does only through humor."[40] As we have seen, for Climacus, humor is the *confinium* between ethical and religious (or better, between ethical and ethical–religious) modes of existence and irony is the *confinium* between aesthetic and ethical modes of existence. Furthermore, according to Climacus, just as irony as a minor element is an important feature of an ethical way of life, so also humor as a minor element is an important feature of an ethical–religious way of life. That is why, in this passage, Climacus juxtaposes the actions of a simple religious person and the actions of an intellectual person who employs humor while performing these same actions. But he just as easily might have said: what the simple ethical person does directly, the intellectual ethical person does only through irony.[41] Still it is not entirely clear how to understand this claim or the corresponding claim about religious action and humor.

Climacus suggests that there is a difference between the way that simple persons realize ethical or ethical–religious ideals in their lives and the way that intellectual persons realize these ideals. Just as intellectual religious persons employ humor in the process of living ethical–religiously, so also intellectual ethical persons employ irony in the process of living ethically. Simple persons, however, do not employ irony or humor, whether they are ethical or ethical–religious persons, as Climacus construes these ways of life. Yet simple persons do not fail to realize the same ideals that their more reflective counterparts realize.

There is more to say about this distinction between simple and intellectual paths to realization of moral ideals. However, it is clear enough to clarify Climacus's solution to his particular problem of moral luck. Without employing irony, simple persons are able to know and appropriate the same moral ideals as intellectual persons, who do employ irony in these tasks. Consequently, if a person is socialized into a nonintellectual culture, a culture where irony is not to be found, according to Kierkegaard, she is not any less able to become an ethical person than a person who is socialized into a highly ironic culture, such as our own. Such a person is able to recognize the "ethical infinite requirement" just as an intellectual person recognizes it. Her recognition of this requirement, however, is more direct and much less complicated than that of a pure ironist or an ethical person in an intellectual culture. Her appropriation of this requirement, moreover, is more direct and less complicated than that of an ethical person in an intellectual culture. What accounts for this difference is that an ethical person in an intellectual culture employs irony as a minor element (or mastered irony) in realizing this ideal.

Climacus's taking such a position commits him to the view that one can recognize and embrace, albeit in a direct and uncomplicated way, the "ethical infinite requirement" without being either a pure ironist or an intellectual ethical person. Is Climacus suggesting that one can lead an ethical life without being a reflective person? It seems that he is. If so, why does he also argue that any life of immediacy is a *pre-ethical* way of life? How can Climacus argue, on the one hand, that persons ought to progress from immediacy through irony into an (intellectual) ethical way of life, in which they recognize and embrace the "ethical infinite requirement," and also argue, on the other hand, that persons who directly and unreflectively recognize and embrace this requirement are, all other things being equal, morally indistinguishable from their critically reflective counterparts? Is not critical reflection itself a moral good? Does not the "ethical infinite requirement" of ethical self-choice imply that one should realize one's capacity for critical reflection, if one has such a capacity? If so, simple ethical persons and intellectual ethical persons who realize the "ethical infinite requirement" are not morally indistinguishable, even if simple ethical persons are not morally blameworthy for not being critically reflective.

Suppose, for instance, that Joe is a simple person who happened to be socialized into a pietistic culture. Joe simply and directly recognizes and appropriates the same absolute moral ideal as Nick, who lives in an intellectual culture. However, Nick is much more reflective about his views and way of life than Joe. Whether or not Joe is morally blameworthy for being unreflective, it is not true that he is morally indistinguishable from Nick, all other things being equal. Nick possesses his moral beliefs in an importantly different way than Joe possesses his. The way that one possesses one's beliefs, moreover, especially one's moral beliefs, is not morally irrelevant. For all we know, Joe could just as easily be an extreme racist, since he never has considered any other view. Nick, however, has considered and rejected racist views as morally repugnant.

Evans defends Climacus against this line of criticism. He argues that Climacus does not hold that simple persons are unreflective. Rather, according to Evans's reading, reflection is not *prominent* in the way of life of simple persons, but it is present, nonetheless. As Evans argues:

> If the spheres of existence are thus universally achievable, why are irony and humor, which are not, regarded as boundary zones of the spheres? The answer is that there are two ways of realizing oneself. The ethical and religious passion that makes a human being a self is achievable by the simple person in a direct or straightforward way. There are also people, however, who because of talent and education become intellec-tually reflective about life to a special degree. Climacus believes that these people have essentially the same task as the simple and that they have no real advantage over the simple in carrying out that task. But the way they accomplish the task is different. It is this latter group for whom irony and humor form transition zones in their existential development. . . .
>
> The distinction between these two classes of people is not a sharp one, and probably in our day of practically universal education it has to a certain extent been erased. But one can still recognize a difference between the factory worker or farm laborer who lives his life on the basis of values and beliefs that are firmly rooted in his personality but who can perhaps not give a clear intellectual account of them, and the sophisticated intellectual who . . . wonders whether all moral values are the product of cultural conditioning. Climacus is not implying that the simple person is totally unreflective or unconscious about his beliefs. The difference is not between a person who thinks and one who does not. What distinguishes the intellectual is the primacy given to thought in his life, which leads to the danger that critical thought will paralyze his practical life or even that thought will become a substitute for living.[42]

Evans's remarks are instructive. If his reading is on the right track, then Climacus does not disregard the good of critical reflection.

Furthermore, Evans surely is right to think that Climacus is concerned about an intellectual person's allowing reflection on moral ideals to become a substitute for living ethically. He also is right to suggest that Climacus posits two ways to realize moral ideals: a simple, direct way and a complicated, intellectual way. He adds that these distinct paths to realization of moral ideals also are distinct paths to self-realization, for Climacus. If the simple route to self-realization and realization of moral ideals still counts as a reflective way of life, as Evans argues, it follows that, for Climacus, a person cannot realize herself and lead an ethical life unless she becomes at least a mildly reflective person.

This reading suggests that the simple route to self-realization and ethical existence is an alternative route that represents a departure from Climacus's standard paradigm, since irony and humor are not transition zones for simple persons. How then do simple persons progress out of mindless conformity to mildly reflective ethical existence? Kierkegaard and Climacus consistently seem to associate this kind of progression with irony, even if not pure irony. There is reason to think, moreover, that even in the case of simple persons this relation holds. Recall that, for Climacus, "if irony is not taken in the decisive sense, every human being is basically ironical."[43] It follows that Climacus holds that even simple persons are relative ironists. This reading confirms Evans's view that, for Climacus, simple persons who realize themselves and become ethical are reflective persons to some extent. Notice, moreover, that this qualifier "to some extent" corresponds to such persons being *ironic* to some extent or *relative* ironists. So even if Climacus holds that irony is not a transition zone for simple persons, as Evans argues, elementary forms of irony may play a role in helping simple persons to become at least mildly reflective. Otherwise Climacus is faced with another problem with moral luck, namely, that simple persons are just lucky that they happen to perceive and understand the "ethical infinite requirement," and not some perversion of this requirement, since (in this case) they do not reflect at all on their beliefs.[44]

So, Climacus has a response to the problem that is raised by his and Kierkegaard's view that irony has important developmental and ethical roles to play in human life, but not everyone is capable of being ironic to the same degree. This response turns on distinguishing simple and intellectual routes to self-realization and ethical existence. Furthermore, Climacus takes every person to be "basically ironical" or ironical in a relative sense, which is sufficient to insure the level of critical reflection needed for ethical formation.[45]

6.5 IRONY AS THE INCOGNITO OF THE ETHICAL

Thus far I have focused on Climacus's account of the *pre-ethical* role that irony has in human life. Climacus thinks that irony also has an important role to play in ethical life. Indeed, his discussion of irony as an incognito of the ethical helpfully supplements Kierkegaard's account of mastered irony.[46] In this section, I briefly sketch this feature of Climacus's position—his version of mastered irony.

As noted above, Climacus takes an ethicist to be someone who "relates himself within himself to the absolute requirement." He then observes that such a person "uses irony as his incognito." In section one, I suggested that Climacus's first claim here refers to a person's discovering and inwardly appropriating the "ethical infinite require-ment" as an unconditional requirement, which relativizes all merely social norms, practices, and ideals. Climacus also has in mind that when a person undergoes such an experience she awakens to and begins to realize her moral agency. For Climacus, this move is a decisive step forward on the path to self-realization. But why should this experience lead a person then to *hide* her ethical passion under an ironic stance? Furthermore, what exactly is involved in employing irony in this way? Also, is Climacus suggesting merely that ethical persons do, in fact, use irony as a disguise or that they *should* use irony this way?

Climacus is fond of contrasting inward ethical passion and outward, overt displays of ethical commitment—a contrast, as he draws it, between inwardly and outwardly accentuating one's own *I* in relation to the "ethical infinite requirement."[47] To accentuate *outwardly* one's own *I* in relation to this requirement is to focus one's energies on *appearing* ethically earnest, presumably in order to reap the benefits that come with seeming to others to be an ethical person. To accentuate *inwardly* one's own *I* in relation to this requirement is to focus on *being* ethically earnest, which involves examining oneself in view of this requirement. For Climacus, irony has a role to play in helping persons, who desire to be ethical, ward off the temptation of settling merely for the appearance of ethical commitment.

There is something odd about a person who brags to others about her moral strivings, according to Climacus. If such a person truly is self-reflective, then she should realize that her public self-righteousness tends to encourage a kind of arrogance that is at odds with ethical passion, as Climacus understands it. She should also realize that such a stance repels others and may discourage them from pursuing the goods to which she is committed. So there is not much to be gained from wearing one's ethical passion on one's sleeve, so to speak, and not a little to be lost by this posture.[48]

But how is a person to employ *irony* as a disguise in order to counteract the deleterious effects that sometimes attend overt ethical passion? Does one act immorally in public once in a while so that other persons will not take one to be ethically earnest? One might get this impression from another passage in *Postscript*, which is somewhat removed from Climacus's main treatment of irony. Climacus states:

> With regard to the observational question about ethical interiority, irony and hypocrisy as antitheses (but both expressing the contradiction that the outer is not the inner—hypocrisy by appearing good, irony by appearing bad) emphasize that actuality and deception are equally possible, that deception can reach just as far as actuality. Only the individual himself can know which is which.[49]

Despite what appears to be the case, there are several clues in this passage that suggest that we should not take Climacus to hold that utilizing irony as an incognito of the ethical involves occasionally acting immorally in the presence of others in order to disguise one's ethical passion. Climacus contrasts irony and hypocrisy. So, a person who has "ethical interiority" and who employs irony as an incognito is not being a being a hypocrite, according to Climacus. Yet, for Climacus, it appears that the only difference between a hypocrite and a person who employs irony in this way is that the hypocrite appears good when she is not and the ethical person appears bad when, in fact, she is good. But why think that a person who acts as if she is immoral when in fact she is ethically passionate is *not* a hypocrite?

The key to understanding Climacus's position lies in a second clue that he provides in this passage. He observes that a person who employs irony in this way merely *appears* bad. Being a hypocrite *is* bad. Since the ethical person only appears bad, she is not a hypocrite. But why is she not a hypocrite? For Climacus, taking into account a person's motivations is crucial in accurately assessing whether she is acting ethically. In this case, a person's motivations make all the difference. One can appear bad but not really be bad, if one's appearing bad is motivated by moral reasons that justify one's appearing bad. The person who merely appears to be good is a hypocrite because she does not have motivations that morally justify her appearing to be good. The ethical person who merely appears to be bad, however, does have reasons that justify her behavior, according to Climacus.

But what exactly does Climacus intend by "appearing bad"? It still seems as if he intends to suggest that ethical persons publicly act immorally at times just to disguise how seriously they take their moral obligations. What sort of reasons could morally justify this sort of behavior?

We cannot get to the bottom of what is involved, for Climacus, in employing irony as an incognito of the ethical without understanding *why* a person would use irony in this way. Climacus himself discusses these points in tandem. But I have something more in mind. I mean that we have to examine the reasons that ethical persons have for employing irony as an incognito in order to understand why Climacus thinks that such persons only appear bad and to discern what they do that makes them appear this way.

So why does an ethical person use irony as an incognito? Climacus answers:

> Because he comprehends the contradiction between the mode in which he exists in his inner being and his not expressing it in his outer appearance. The ethicist certainly becomes open insofar as he exhausts himself in the tasks of factual actuality, but the immediate person also does this, and what makes the ethicist an ethicist is the movement by which he inwardly joins his outward life together with the infinite requirement of the ethical, and this is not directly apparent. In order not to be disturbed by the finite, by all the relativities in the world, the ethicist places the comic[50] between himself and the world and thereby makes sure that he himself does not become comic through a naïve misunderstanding of his ethical passion. An immediate enthusiast bawls out in the world early and late; always in his swagger-boots, he pesters people with his enthusiasm and does not perceive at all that it does not make them enthusiastic, except when they beat him. . . . If such an enthusiast is contemporary with an ironist, the latter naturally makes comic capital of him. The ethicist, however, is sufficiently ironical to be well aware that what engages him absolutely does not engage the others absolutely. He himself grasps this misrelation and places the comic in between in order to be able more inwardly to hold fast the ethical within himself. Now the comedy starts, because people's opinion of a person like that will always be: for him nothing is important. And why not? Because for him the ethical is absolutely important; in this he is different from the generality of people, for whom so many things are important, indeed, almost everything is important—but nothing is absolutely important.[51]

Climacus posits several reasons that ethical persons have for employing irony as an incognito. In the first place, ethical persons recognize that there is a great disparity between their outward behavior and the moral ideals that they seek to realize in their lives. They take these ideals very seriously because they take them to be categorically different from other goods that they pursue and obligations that they recognize. We could say that, for Climacus, an ethical person's commitment to these ideals is an identity-conferring commitment. Her project of realizing these ideals is, in Bernard Williams's terminology, a ground project around which her life is organized. So, ethical persons are very bothered by the fact that their outward behavior does not measure up to their ideals. Consequently, they fundamentally desire to bring their lives into greater conformity with their ideals. That is why they do not want to be "disturbed by the finite."

Climacus has in view at least two kinds of obstacles. First, an ethical person's inability to realize her ideals in the practical affairs of her life might overly discourage her. She then might cease trying to realize her ideals. Second, in the process of energetically embracing her social roles and other "tasks of factual actuality," she might get entangled in and distracted by projects in which she pursues lesser goods and fulfills lesser obligations. So, Climacus has it that ethical persons employ irony in such a way that they are able to retain a complex stance of *critical* engagement and detachment while fulfilling these tasks. Such persons are not reluctant to critique and even lampoon their roles and tasks and their own performances in attempting to accomplish them.

As a result, ethical persons, as Climacus construes them, may appear not to take seriously the obligations and responsibilities that attend their social roles and other moral obligations, especially when they are juxtaposed with ethical enthusiasts, whose entire identities are bound up with these things. Ethical persons realize, however, that enthusiasts are apt to discourage others from embracing the goods about which they are so decidedly nonironic. Thus, they do not take the same publicly enthusiastic approach, especially since they are so far from realizing their ideals anyhow. Consequently, they may not appear to be very enthusiastic about their ideals. This behavior leads persons who judge by appearances to think that they do not *have* ideals—that "nothing is important" to them. But apparently Climacus thinks that it is better, all things considered, for an ethical person to allow others who judge by appearances to draw this false conclusion than it is for her to attempt to correct this misperception by publicly attesting to her ethical passion.

Evans provides a helpful gloss on this passage that draws out a few additional points. He notes:

> The reason the ethicist must use irony as his incognito is that it preserves his inwardness and isolation, ensuring that he seriously is

attempting to become a self and not merely to appear to be a self in other people's eyes. He also thereby frees other people from dependent relationships that would hinder their own spiritual development. And finally the ethicist understands that he can never adequately express his ethical commitment in the relativities of the external life. He does attempt to do this; it is a misunderstanding to see the ethical life as a withdrawal from the world. The ethicist who has found his eternal self attempts to express his commitment in his actual life. But he sees that he may outwardly resemble someone from whom he may be radically different. There is a discrepancy between his inner life and his outer life. His life always contains more than can be seen, and he therefore views his outward efforts ironically. . . . Because of this the ethicist never allows his life to be fully identified with the outward tasks. . . . Therefore, in the midst of the most strenuous activity he maintains a detached attitude toward the significance of these achievements.[52]

Evans's allusion to an ethicist's finding his "eternal self" refers to a person's discovering her capacity for moral agency, which he then seeks to realize in the concrete affairs of his life. Moreover, as Evans points out, Climacus suggests that persons are not able to express or realize fully their inner moral commitments in their external behavior. So there is always a gap between what they aspire to be as moral agents and what they are in reality. Their irony about themselves helps them not only to perceive this incongruity but also not to be defeated by it.

Now it is clear why Climacus thinks that ethical persons who employ irony as an incognito merely *appear* bad. First, they have moral reasons for not wanting to reveal to others just how seriously they take their commitments. Second, they do not engage in immoral behavior in the presence of other persons. Rather, they simply do not disclose to others the full measure of their ethical passion. Third, they are not moral busybodies. They do not invest their entire identities in their outward performances and in attempting to convert others to their point of view. In fact, because they are ironical about the practices to which they are committed and their own inability to measure up to their ideals, they are liable to be confused with ironists, who do not inwardly appropriate the "ethical infinite requirement." As Westphal explains:

> *What* the mere ironist and mere humorist do is the same as what the truly ethical and religious persons do when comedy becomes their incognito—they point out the discrepancy between the ideal and the real in human life. But *how* they do it is radically different. And this difference is radically inward, not publicly visible.[53]

Westphal points out that, for Climacus, ironists and ethical persons who use irony as an incognito may be indistinguishable outwardly since both seize on the incongruities that exist in human society. Ironists cite these incongruities in order to justify their radical dissociation from human community, a point that Kierkegaard elaborates at length in his thesis. Ethical persons, by contrast, keep them in view in order to maintain some critical distance from their social roles and their own moral strivings.

Do ethical persons employ irony this way as a matter of course, though? It is doubtful that Climacus intends this. He is pessimistic about our ability to realize moral ideals, which is unsurprising since he is, after all, a pseudonym of Kierkegaard, a Danish Lutheran.[54] Of course, one does not have to be a Lutheran to be pessimistic about the moral prowess of human beings. But it is important to recognize Climacus's pessimism here, for it suggests that in *Postscript*, he intends to offer an idealization of ethical personhood, even when he describes how ethical persons employ irony as an incognito. Actual human beings may do and may have done many of the things that Climacus says ethical persons do when they employ irony as an incognito. Nevertheless, we should construe the ethical use of irony, as Climacus understands it, as a *goal* of ethical life. Climacus's sketch of irony as an incognito of the ethical is supposed to be taken as a broad prescription for how to appropriate inwardly the "ethical infinite requirement."

It might seem odd, of course, to advise persons to employ irony as an outward disguise for inward ethical passion. However, if we keep in view, as alternatives to Climacus's ethicist, a person such as Climacus's superficial and annoying ethical enthusiast and the narrowly moral sort of person that Susan Wolf describes in her provocative essay, "Moral Saints,"[55] we can understand better and perhaps even appreciate why Climacus thinks that ethical persons ought to employ irony as an incognito.

6.6   Some Problems in
Climacus's Account

I have focused mainly on explicating and clarifying Climacus's account of irony and its relation to moral commitment. I also have attempted to illuminate Kierkegaard's final thesis about irony in *The Concept of Irony*. At this juncture, however, I want to take note of some problems in Climacus's view of ethical life and in his construal of pure irony. These problems congeal around his "ethical infinite requirement."

There is some ambiguity about what Climacus intends by this requirement. As Evans explains:

> Climacus actually does not say very much about the content of the ethical task, and one looks in vain in his writings for something resembling contemporary normative ethical theory. . . . The content of the ethical life was not something he had to invent, since on his view he could presume that every one of his readers would already have knowledge about it.[56]

I do not fault Climacus for this ambiguity and presumption. It is noteworthy, however, that not a little interpretation is involved in clarifying the nature of his "ethical infinite requirement." Following Evans and Cross, among others, I have construed this requirement as a fundamental obligation that persons have to realize their moral agency through critical engagement in their social roles and other features of their actuality. In order to fulfill this task of self-realization, Climacus suggests that persons need (a) to recognize a firm distinction between moral goods and imperatives and merely cultural norms, practices, and ideals; (b) to treat the former as unconditionally good or right and the latter as having conditional worth; (c) to pursue moral goods and observe moral obligations because they are unconditionally good or right. This position amounts to a very rigorous conception of ethical life. As Evans notes:

> Climacus makes a sharp distinction between what one might call "civic morality" and the ethical in the true sense. It is quite possible for a person to grow up in a culture, learn the prevailing social rules and taboos, and live by them, thus acquiring a reputation as a fine, upstanding citizen, without ever discovering the ethical in the deepest sense. The problem with such a person is not necessarily so much what she does, but why she does it. If she follows the principles she does only because "everybody else does," then she fails to discover the ethical in its "infinity." Even if the cultural principles she follows are ethical, the individual is not truly ethical if she does not follow them *because* they are ethical.[57]

Persons who follow ethical principles simply on the basis of sentiments that they have acquired through good moral education and nurturing as children and adolescents also do not count as ethical, on Climacus's account.

This excessive rigor in Climacus's position is objectionable. It would be less objectionable if Climacus simply were to reserve a *higher* form of ethical existence for persons who meet the stringent requirements for ethical life that he posits in *Postscript*. As it stands,

Climacus's account consigns persons who are actively engaged in responsible civic life because they have been well-socialized and are fundamentally motivated by affection and sympathy for other persons to a *pre-ethical* form of existence. This move is rather extreme and harsh.[58] It may represent in its own way an overreaction to the problem of moral luck, since not everyone is the recipient of a psychologically healthy and affirming form of socialization. At any rate, on this particular point Aristotle holds a more defensible position than Climacus.

There also is something objectionable about Climacus's account of pure irony. His pure ironists are markedly less ironic than Kierkegaard's pure ironists, whose irony is characterized as "infinite absolute negativity." It is not surprising or strange that Climacus takes the form of irony that is a transition zone between aesthetic and ethical forms of existence not to be characterized by radical disengagement and thoroughgoing negativity. After all, the developmental transition that Climacus has in mind is supposed to be positive, as it brings one closer to ethical existence and self-realization. However, consider those persons who get to this developmental point but fail to move forward into an ethical way of life, whose irony becomes an existence-sphere and not simply a momentary transition zone. From the vantage point of Kierkegaard's sketch of irony in his thesis, these persons are on their way to becoming the purest ironists conceived in *Postscript*. They recognize the "ethical infinite requirement" and perceive that it trumps and relativizes all merely cultural norms, practices, and ideals. That is how they come to be ironists, in more than a relative sense, in the first place. But they do not embrace and attempt to realize this requirement. That is why their personal development comes to a halt in the transition zone of irony. Notice how much less ironic they are than Kierkegaard's pure ironists, however. They still recognize the "ethical infinite requirement." It is what they hold steady in order to deconstruct social norms and practices. They also recognize the distinction it yields between moral and nonmoral goods and obligations or between absolute and relative validity. These positions could all be correct. But there is no doubting that they also are controversial. So, it is odd that Climacus's pure ironists are not very sceptical of the "ethical infinite requirement" and the distinction between relative and absolute validity that it supposedly yields. Why does their critical negativity end when they come up against these ideas?

Perhaps it does not end. Evans argues that, for Climacus, a person who devolves into pure negativity and radical disengagement as a result of not moving forward into ethical existence eventually becomes a nihilist.[59] What Evans has in mind is that eventually Climacus's pure ironists begin to deconstruct the "ethical infinite requirement" itself. Notice that, at this point, it is not the case that their irony "emerges by continually joining the particulars of the finite with the ethical infinite requirement and allowing the contradiction to come into existence." So, how do pure ironists who reach this stage of devolution manage to get out from under the "ethical infinite requirement"? The answer, I think, is that they become *Kierkegaard's* pure ironists—their irony becomes "infinite absolute negativity."

This line of reasoning helps to reveal an interesting fact. Kierkegaard and Climacus posit significantly different routes to pure irony. Kierkegaard's pure ironists are thoroughly negative from the outset. They fundamentally desire negative freedom and will apply withering negativity toward any commitment, ideal, or practice that stands in their way as an obstacle to their obtaining this (apparent) good. Climacus's pure ironists only reach this point only after (a) failing to embrace and appropriate the "ethical infinite requirement" and then (b) eventually coming to question the very idea of such a requirement. They resemble persons who become disillusioned after coming to see through absolute ideals that they once recognized as valid. Such persons never are quite able to recover and commit themselves again to what they take to be the trivial tasks of actuality.

I do not question that these two paths to the purest form of irony both represent possible routes to this sort of radically disengaged stance. However, as I suggested above, Climacus's route begins as a top-down approach, insofar as it gets underway with the recognition of an overarching "ethical infinite requirement," which discloses the relative validity of merely social norms and practices. Kierkegaard's route, however, is a kind of bootstrapping approach. His ironists apply searing negativity to whatever stands between them and negative freedom at the time. If they need to hold some ideal steady in order to critique something else that could be a threat to their pursuit of negative freedom, then they employ that ideal for this purpose. When its utility has run its course, however, they discard it. As Kierkegaard construes them, they do not hold steady a single, overarching positive ideal over time, which functions as an absolute ideal, except insofar as negative freedom functions as a fundamental good for them.

On this point, Climacus's position is less comprehensive and incisive than Kierkegaard's. This claim is borne out by the fact that in order to realize the purest form of irony, Climacus's ironists have to abandon their original stance and adopt the stance of Kierkegaard's pure ironists. That is how they finally rid themselves of the "ethical infinite requirement" and all that comes with recognizing it as an absolute, overarching ideal. I conclude, then, that Kierkegaard's account of irony as "infinite absolute negativity" more adequately captures what irony proper is. It is not merely avoiding relativities of one sort or another, which entangle relative ironists but not pure ironists, according to Climacus. It is a stance of sheer negativity motivated by an identity-conferring desire for negative freedom. That is why Kierkegaard argues that once a person becomes ironic in more than a relative sense she must master her irony through moral commitment. Otherwise she will neither become morally virtuous nor self-realized. Climacus concurs with this idea. But the somewhat parochial way in which he construes irony can lead us to lose sight of Kierkegaard's insight into its radical and volatile nature.[60]

6.7   Conclusion

Although Climacus's account has some significant flaws, it clearly is an imaginative, subtle, and provocative treatment of irony and moral commitment. I hope that my analysis of it has managed to draw out these qualities. There is a kind of Kantian rigor in Climacus's account of ethical life that helps to distinguish it from Kierkegaard's more Hegelian (and Aristotelian) thesis. Whether this feature of Climacus's account represents an improvement over Kierkegaard's is a controversial matter, of course. I have argued that in certain respects it does not represent an advance but rather a regression.

Climacus reveals a less severe side when he allows that simple persons can lead ethical lives and thus, realize themselves, apart from the complicated machinations that accompany an intellectual person's route to ethical existence and self-realization. Furthermore, his account of irony as a transition zone between aesthetic and ethical modes of existence complicates but also clarifies Kierkegaard's cryptic claim in his thesis, "no genuinely human life is possible without irony." Climacus, more explicitly than Kierkegaard, brings out the developmental role that irony has in helping persons discover and realize their moral agency. He does not hold, however, that in order to become ethical it is necessary to go through a stage of radical disengagement, as Cross suggests. And it is a relief that Climacus is not committed to this view, since it is dubious. Given the severe criticisms that Kierkegaard offers in his thesis of the pursuit of negative freedom through radical disengagement, it would be very surprising if Climacus then endorsed radical disengagement as a crucial developmental stage.

With regard to the role that irony has within ethical life, Climacus's discussion of irony as an incognito helpfully supplements and extends Kierkegaard's account of mastered irony in his thesis. Climacus mentions several goods that are promoted by an ethical person's employing irony as an incognito for her ethical passion. Here is another one. In pluralistic, liberal democracies, utilizing irony as an incognito in this way may be a way of fostering greater civility and tolerance. For instance, suppose that a Parent Teacher Association (PTA) meeting is held in a pluralistic community and the topic of the meeting is homosexuality. Suppose also that the parents at the meeting are randomly split into two large discussion groups. In the first group, persons behave like Climacus's ethical enthusiasts. In the second group, persons behave like Climacus's ethicists who employ irony as an incognito. It stands to reason that persons in the second group are much more likely to have a civil discussion of issues that are liable to be very divisive and explosive. Now I admit that the fix is in, so to speak, with this example and that it is oversimplified. Nevertheless, it illustrates my point that employing irony as an incognito of the ethical may have certain benefits in a pluralistic democracy, which Climacus could not have foreseen.

This analysis brings to a conclusion my sketch of Kierkegaard's overall account of irony and moral commitment. I hope that it is now clear that it merits careful consideration alongside Rorty's liberal irony. Just as with Rorty's position, it is not necessary to embrace all of it in order to appreciate and appropriate much of it. The specific problematic elements in Climacus's account, for instance, do not prevent us from appropriating his insights into the developmental and ethical benefits of irony. We can combine these insights with the position that Kierkegaard advances in his thesis in order to arrive at a fairly compelling Kierkegaardian account of irony and moral commitment.

I now turn to some concluding remarks on my explication and analysis of the accounts of Rorty and Kierkegaard. I will consider how Kierkegaard's position compares with Rorty's. Then I will draw some overall conclusions based on my findings.

CHAPTER 7

Irony and Moral Commitment: Concluding Reflections

Kierkegaard and Rorty not infrequently have suffered the fate of being categorically dismissed—Kierkegaard on account of his association with fideistic Christianity, Rorty on account of his strident antirealism. If I have accomplished nothing else, I hope that at least I have avoided this facile way of handling these figures and have demonstrated how unnecessary and uncharitable such an approach is. Both of these philosophers offer interesting, provocative, and insightful accounts of irony and moral commitment. We should not, then, dismiss irony out of hand, as MacIntyre does, because of the alleged incompatibility between Rortian irony and moral commitment. Rorty's position deserves a more careful response. Other positions, such as Kierkegaard's, do as well.[1]

In this chapter, I offer some orienting and evaluative remarks concerning where my explication and analysis of Rorty's and Kierkegaard's accounts leave us. I do not prefer to choose sides between Rorty and Kierkegaard any more than is necessary to promote a critical appreciation for and engagement of both. My overall view is that Kierkegaard offers a broader, more probing, and less objectionable account of irony and moral commitment than does Rorty. However, Rorty captures a number of important points about irony and moral commitment that are lacking or underemphasized in Kierkegaard's position. For instance, even though I find fault with some of the implications that Rorty's draws from the recognition of contingency, there is something profound about this discovery, which is either absent or too implicit in Kierkegaard's position. Kierkegaard may have the resources to account for or accommodate this insight about contingency. Whether he does is a very controversial issue among Kierkegaard scholars that, in my view, turns on how much place is given to Kierkegaard's Christian theism and how best to interpret the influence of Kierkegaard's faith on his thought. Still there is no doubt that Kierkegaard does not accentuate contingency as Rorty does, even though he is a keen observer of human finitude.

I proceed in two main steps. First, I compare the accounts of irony proper that Rorty and Kierkegaard advance. With this backdrop in place, I then argue that Kierkegaard's construal of irony ultimately is more encompassing and incisive than Rorty's, which is overly preoccupied with the realist/antirealist debate in contemporary philosophy and other features of Rorty's antimetaphysics program. Second, I consider how Rorty, Kierkegaard, and MacIntyre all recognize the need to master irony, though each responds to this recognition in different ways. I argue that Rorty and Kierkegaard offer the right sort of response, in a general sense, insofar as they propose that we master irony through moral commitment. When we consider the details of their proposals, Kierkegaard's approach emerges as having a few more advantages than Rorty's. I conclude by suggesting that we consider Kierkegaard's account of irony and moral commitment a viable and promising counterpart to Rorty's position.

7.1 CONTINGENCY, NEGATIVITY, AND INCONGRUITY

Now that I have sketched Rorty's and Kierkegaard's positions independently of each other, I think it is worthwhile to consider how they compare. This task is complicated by the fact that Kierkegaard sketches in his writings *two* kinds of pure ironists and two other kinds of ironists. There are the pure ironists of Kierkegaard's thesis, who clearly are the most radical, volatile, and negative ironists that Kierkegaard conceives. There also are the pure ironists of *Postscript*, whose irony turns on their recognition of the "ethical infinite requirement." These persons may devolve into the absolute negativity of their counterparts, but as sketched in *Postscript*, they do not exhibit this characteristic. Kierkegaard also offers sketches of relative ironists and ethical persons who employ mastered irony. So the phrase "a Kierkegaardian ironist" is quite ambiguous.

There is a way to simplify Kierkegaard's account on this point. All his ironists exemplify negativity to a greater or lesser extent. On one end of the spectrum is the pure ironist of Kierkegaard's thesis, who personifies "infinite absolute negativity." She takes a severely critical stance toward everything except her thoroughly negative stance itself. She also comes to identify herself with her activity of annulling, negating, and dissociating. As a result, she is radically disengaged from her social roles and other features of her social environment. On the other end of the spectrum is an unreflective, immediate person, who manages to find something or other from which to be alienated but otherwise hardly recognizes that she is not simply the sum total of her social roles, as she has inherited them through socialization. Such a person has very little, if any, critical distance from her inherited social identity. She just is the person that she has been socialized to be and is largely unaware that this identity is revisable and not above criticism.

On this continuum of negativity, where are we to locate Kierkegaard's ethical person who employs irony within the boundaries of moral commitment (or mastered irony)? The answer depends crucially on which account of ethical life we have in view, the account of actuality as gift and task that Kierkegaard advances in his thesis or the more rigorous view of ethical existence that Climacus offers in *Postscript*. According to Climacus, in order to become an ethical person, it is necessary to see through social practices and norms on the basis of one's recognition of the "ethical infinite requirement." In his thesis, however, Kierkegaard suggests that an ethical person simply is someone who responsibly engages her social roles, who critically embraces her actuality as a gift and task and sets herself to fulfilling this task. Such a person needs to be critically reflective about the norms and ideals that accompany her social roles and others that she encounters. But she does not need to be suspicious in any systematic way of the affections, loyalties, and sympathies that have been socialized into her, since she does not observe a sharp distinction between motives that issue from recognition of the "ethical infinite requirement" and morally impure motives, as Climacus's ethicist does. Consequently, she does not need to be as systematically critical of her social order and inherited identity as Climacus's ethicist.

Where then does Rorty's liberal ironist stand in relation to Climacus's ethicist, Kierkegaard's ethical person, who also masters her irony, and also Kierkegaard's *pure* ironist? On the one hand, if we focus on a Rortian ironist's basic commitment to liberalism, then she appears to have more in common with Kierkegaard's ethical person. She accepts her liberal sympathies, likely socialized into her, as appropriate sources of motivation. Her commitment to liberalism, moreover, is a fairly specific, local kind of commitment. It is much more particular than a commitment to the "ethical infinite requirement." To borrow Kierkegaard's language, we might say that it is part of her actuality. In these respects, a liberal ironist more closely resembles Kierkegaard's ethical person, who employs mastered irony, than Climacus's ethicist. Still her Kierkegaardian counterpart might think that she comes too close to absolutizing her social order by being "frankly ethnocentric" in regard to her liberalism.

On the other hand, if we focus on a Rortian ironist's irony, then she has more in common with Kierkegaard's pure ironist, who pursues negative freedom as a basic good. After all, a Rortian ironist *qua* ironist fundamentally desires to get out from under inherited vocabularies and construct her own terms for understanding and evaluating her life, the lives of others, and the meaning of human existence in general. When we abstract from a Rortian ironist's liberalism and the modifications that Rorty makes in his Nietzschean account of ironic self-creation on account of his commitment to liberalism, then a Rortian ironist appears not very different from a Kierkegaardian pure ironist.[2]

But what is so surprising about that? A Kierkegaardian pure ironist lacks moral commitment. So her irony is unmastered. But when we add moral commitment to her life, as Kierkegaard construes it, she then turns out to be a very different person. The same holds true in many respects for a Rortian ironist. If we inspect the sort of person she is without her commitment to liberalism, she is not remarkably different from Kierkegaard's pure ironist. But when we take account of her commitment to liberalism, the impression we have of her changes significantly.

However, a liberal ironist is a more peculiar kind of person than an ethical person who employs mastered irony, as Kierkegaard depicts such a person.[3] This fact is not insignificant. It helps to show that Kierkegaard's account of irony and moral commitment has a wider scope and broader appeal than Rorty's. This claim, though, needs a bit more explanation and support.

Consider the sort of person a liberal ironist is and what it is about her that makes her an ironist, according to Rorty. Although others who are not ironists may recognize contingency, she is distinguished by and identifies with her acknowledgment and acceptance of contingency. Furthermore, she is defined as much by her doubts as she is by her positive views. She wonders whether her final vocabulary ultimately is a hindrance in her quest for novel self-creation. Such a person also tends to find the vocabularies of other persons and cultures interesting, enticing, and nonthreatening. We should not illicitly deduce from this point, however, that a liberal ironist has this sort of response to all other vocabularies, including extremely illiberal ones. As we have seen, this mistake leads to extremely uncharitable and unwarranted readings of Rorty.

The humility, sense of finitude, tolerance, and openness of a liberal ironist are very attractive. Gutting rightly accentuates this *epistemic* irony in Rorty's account. Kierkegaardian ethical ironists affirm this kind of irony too. There also is something attractive about a liberal ironist's understanding of and desire for novel self-creation. Rorty's reflections on the self-creative aspirations and projects of Proust, for instance, are illuminating and suggestive. I see no reason why we should not join Rorty in endorsing self-creation as a basic good, especially if we observe the qualifications that he places on his endorsement of it.

Still there is something parochial about the way Rorty casts his ironist's recognition of contingency. This turns out to be much more than recognition of human finitude, fallibility, and fragility. It serves as a springboard for the inculcation of a narrow sentiment in liberal ironists: disgust with metaphysics and other classical philosophical disciplines, such as epistemology. For Rorty, the recognition of contingency somehow implies the end of metaphysics and epistemology, not to mention many kinds of moral philosophy. This is an extreme reaction to the demise of classical foundationalism and the recognition that we are socially embedded beings. As Thomas McCarthy explains:

> That we now understand our capacities for reasoning to be rooted in culturally variable and historically changing forms of social practice can mean the end of the Enlightenment only for thinkers who remain so captivated by absolutist conceptions of reason, truth, and right that their passing means there is nothing left that really makes a difference— the "God is dead, everything is permitted" fallacy of disappointed expectations.[4]

In a similar vein, contrasting Kierkegaard and Rorty, Evans notes:

> He [Kierkegaard] rejects an often unnoticed premise that is common both to the classical foundationalist and the antirealist postmodernist. Both agree that *if* there is to be knowledge of objective reality, there must be some method of obtaining certain knowledge about that reality. The classical foundationalist, from Descartes through Husserl, concludes that since there is objective knowledge there must be such a method. The antirealist concludes that since there is no such method there is no knowledge of objective reality. We can see lurking behind Rorty's antirealism the dashed hopes and disappointments of the classical foundationalist.[5]

McCarthy's and Evans's plausible genealogies of Rorty's position suggest that contingency, as he construes it, turns out to be a very loaded concept.

I tend to concur with critics of Rorty, such as McCarthy and Evans, who believe that coping with contingency does not at all *require* or fully justify Rorty's extreme hostility to metaphysics and epistemology, although I appreciate and have considerable sympathy for Rorty's main concerns here. Coping with contingency does require abandoning classical foundationalism, as Rorty argues. But even Alvin Plantinga, hardly an opponent of metaphysics, concurs with Rorty on this point. Also, why not leave alone philosophers who have been chastened by the failures of the Enlightenment, but who want to pursue the traditional questions of metaphysics and epistemology in a humbler way? Rorty's own position suggests that such persons are trying to create themselves, trying to come to terms with their inherited identities through projects that he happens to find futile. Unless Rorty thinks that such persons are violating their obligations to others by failing to take up more fruitful questions, however, perhaps he should ratchet down his invective.[6] After all, the possibility of self-creation does not stand or fall with the success or failure of Rorty's or anyone else's antirealist and antimetaphysics program.

A deeper problem here is that this sort of dismissive and deflationary attitude may make us more vulnerable to the contingencies that we want to overcome by making us less thoughtful and articulate about them. Charles Taylor expresses this concern with Rorty's position in a recent essay. He states:

> Now Rorty and I have an old debate going. This is the *n*th round; I have lost count. But what seems constant throughout is an agreed-upon basis—that we both see ourselves as getting out from under the Cartesian, representational epistemology—and within this a difference. This latter might be put in the following way: that for Rorty we escape . . . mainly by getting rid of certain traditional distinctions and questions: for example, the scheme-content way of talking or the issue of correspondence with reality; while I think that these distinctions and questions have to be recast. Rorty is a minimalist: he thinks we had best just forget about the whole range of issues that concern how our thought relates to reality, the relation of Mind to World, if I can lapse again into those great uppercase terms about which Rorty loves to wax ironic. I am a maximalist: I think that we badly need to recast our distorted understanding of these matters inherited from the epistemological tradition.
>
> My reason is that you don't just walk away from these deep, pervasive, half-articulated, taken-for-granted pictures that are embedded in our culture and enframe our thought and action. . . . You can't free

yourself from them until you identify them and see where they're wrong; and even then it's not always easy. Just saying you've abandoned them, and then not giving them any further thought, à la Davidson, is a sure recipe for remaining in their thrall.[7]

The objection that Taylor advances here is most forceful, in my view, when it is taken as an *internal* criticism of Rorty's position. Rorty clearly wants desperately to get out from under inherited contingencies that have long since lost their utility. He writes as if to liberate his readers in this way as well. And there is reason to believe that not a little of what he says *is* liberating in this regard. Taylor alleges that Rorty's way of simply dismissing in total certain deeply ingrained but half-articulated distinctions, questions, and understandings is not really a way of overcoming them. Rather, it is a more insidious way of failing to relate to them autonomously. The challenge for Rorty, then, is to show that dismissing out of hand these inherited contingencies is a better path to autonomy than the one that Taylor commends. Certainly Taylor's route is more difficult. But Rorty's can seem hollow and superficial in certain respects. How can one overcome inherited contingencies, some of which are inchoate, others barely articulated, simply by walking away from them and without carefully working through and revising them? This seems analogous to thinking that persons socialized into stultifying forms of religious fundamentalism can get out from under such inherited vocabularies simply by turning away from them. But nearly anyone who has been through such a process will confirm that this move is just the opening gambit in a long and arduous path to overcoming such deeply ingrained vocabularies.

This concern with Rorty's "minimalism," as Taylor puts it, leads some philosophers to wonder whether Rorty can make sense of the moral commitments that he and other liberal ironists are unable to relinquish. This is not a concern about being committed to ideals that one believes are contingent. If it is posed this way, I think that Rorty has a compelling response to it, as I argued in chapter 2. Nor is it an objection that depends on endorsing foundationalism in ethics. There is a vast difference between being a foundationalist, on the one hand, and being a maximalist, as Taylor uses the term, on the other. Maximalists are not looking for philosophical foundations, indubitable or otherwise, for their moral beliefs and sentiments. Rather, they are after *articulacy* about them and their origins.[8] The worry these persons have about Rorty's deflationary approach is that, if we adopt it, it leaves us less articulate about our inherited vocabularies and thus less able to relate to them as we should. We then cannot adequately understand ourselves. As Charles Guignon and David Hiley explain:

> We may agree with Rorty that moral agency need not be anchored in a foundationalist theory of the self or human nature. But we might still hold that our understanding of moral life must be anchored in an understanding of life that is deep and rich enough to make sense of why people are sometimes willing to risk everything in order to do the right thing. Such an understanding seems to be lost in Rorty's story. Even more troubling, what risks being lost is the ability to understand *oneself* in a way that captures the sense of seriousness of moral commitments, and so the ability to *be* a moral agent of the sort that Elshtain (and Rorty) take as exemplary.[9]

I concur with Taylor, Guignon, and Hiley that Rorty's minimalism threatens to leave us less articulate about our commitments and the vocabularies in which they are embedded than we should be, and so more in the dark about ourselves. Regardless of what one makes of this criticism, however, a less controversial objection lurks here as well. That is, Rorty weakens his account when he inscribes his somewhat extreme response to contingency into the very core of an ironist. One should not have to take such a controversial position in a fairly narrow philosophical debate in order to count as an ironist. An account of irony and moral commitment ought to stand apart from such parochial debates as much as possible. It is not necessary to take a controversial antirealist or realist position, or pro-metaphysics or antimetaphysics position, in order to affirm the positive roles that irony has in human life and in order to be a person who employs irony as an important element in one's ethical life. Kierkegaard's account, as I have construed it, does not place such a requirement on would-be ironists. So it has a distinct advantage over Rorty's position on this point.

In fairness to Rorty, I should point out that it is possible to set aside distracting features of his antirealist and antimetaphysics invective in order to focus on the aspects of his account of irony and moral commitment that can be considered mostly independently of these concerns. Gutting helpfully advises and employs such an approach. I also have attempted to take this approach. However, commentators who opt for this interpretive strategy must very deliberately employ it because it is frequently difficult to disentangle Rorty's insights about irony and moral commitment from his needlessly dismissive and disparaging remarks about traditional philosophical pursuits and those who still engage in them.

There is a subtler point to be made here as well about Rorty's singling out the recognition of contingency as the key feature of his ironist. By comparison, if Kierkegaardian ethical ironists are characterized by any basic recognition, it is recognition of *incongruity*.[10] Kierkegaardian ironists are persons who are especially perceptive of incongruities of various sorts, gaps between what is and what ought to be or between what is said to be and what is.

Kierkegaard uncovers something more basic about irony by construing it as negativity that recognizes and seizes on incongruity. In a most elementary sense, this description better captures what ironists do—they perceive incongruities through critical reflection. To recognize that all human communities, practices, vocabularies, hopes, and ideals are contingent, in the way that Rorty does, in a certain respect just is to recognize at least several basic incongruities in human life. First, it is to recognize the painful disparity between how we tend to think about ourselves and who and what we really are. Second, it also is to recognize the gap between (a) the strength of our convictions about the meaning and value of our own lives, the lives of our children, and of human life in general and (b) our ability to justify these convictions to just any person who might question them. Ed Mooney has in mind this discrepancy when he states, "At some point, we just have the cares that we do. Across much of our lives, they motivate justly and effectively without deep theoretical derivation."[11] Rorty correctly and helpfully points out that it is difficult for us to accept this fact. He illuminates the incongruities to which I refer here and rightly so. My point is that recognizing contingency in the way that Rorty does is a particular way of recognizing incongruity. Rorty's recognition of contingency would lose much of its force and intrigue, if it did not trade on the poignant incongruities noted here and others, of course. I think that this fact helps to reveal that Kierkegaard gets to something more fundamental in his account of irony, what we might call the core of irony. Certainly we should recognize and accept contingency wherever it is to be found. Being an ironist, however, ought not to be wholly or mostly identified with this particular, frequently debunking activity, as important as it is.

So, to sum up the line of reasoning in this section, Kierkegaard's view of irony has wider appeal and broader scope than Rorty's for several reasons. Kierkegaard's sketch of ethical irony offers us a way of combining irony and moral commitment in our lives that is a bit less peculiar and more realizable than Rorty's liberal irony. Kierkegaard's position also is not saddled with parochial concerns about the value and legitimacy of metaphysics and the overcoming of realism, as is Rorty's. It stands independently of these issues, and it is good that it does. For the fate of irony ought not to be linked to the success or failure of any agenda of this sort. Furthermore, Kierkegaard's view that irony is negativity that recognizes and seizes on incongruity gets to the bottom of what irony is and what ironists do. It accounts for the particular kind of debunking critical reflection that Rorty undertakes when he points out the various contingencies of human existence and our sometimes poignant failures as human beings to recognize and come to terms with them.

7.2   MASTERING IRONY

Kierkegaard, Rorty, and MacIntyre all recognize the volatile and potentially destructive nature of irony. For MacIntyre, the benefits that accompany irony, if there are any, do not outweigh the exceeding costs that we incur when we employ it. Consequently, MacIntyre masters irony by dispatching it altogether and solely on the basis of his negative assessment of Rorty's liberal irony. This move clearly is hasty and unwarranted. Both Rorty and Kierkegaard uncover not a few profound benefits of irony both for personal development and ethical life. Furthermore, Kierkegaard's position shows that irony is part of the warp and woof of our existence. What would human life be like, after all, if we did not, through critical reflection, recognize and seize on incongruities in our social environment? It is not as if we could *decide* not to be ironic, at least not in many respects. We just are this way at this stage in our biological and cultural evolution, and there is no turning back. As Climacus reminds us, even if persons generally are not pure ironists, every person is "basically ironical." Kierkegaard thinks our challenge, then, is to employ irony in the most beneficial ways, to promote personal development and human community through irony, not to use it to undermine these goods. Thus, from the vantage point of Kierkegaard's position, MacIntyre's outright dismissal of irony comes to seem almost incredible.

Nevertheless, MacIntyre rightly alerts us to irony's potential to undermine and destroy social goods and bonds that hold together human communities. He also helpfully reminds us that we are inherently social beings. Our projects of self-creation are made possible by our social embeddedness. They never finally culminate in radically autonomous existence. These points ought to be kept in mind.

Both Kierkegaard and Rorty, however, are well aware of the deeply social roots of human identity and agency and that pure irony is morally enervating and destructive of human community. Both recognize the need to master irony and to master it through moral commitment. For his part, Rorty acknowledges the potential cruelty of redescription and the asocial aspects of irony. That is why he circumscribes irony within the boundaries of a more ultimate commitment to liberalism. That is also why he seeks to confine asocial projects of self-creation and the cruel redescriptions that may accompany them to the privacy of personal solitude. These moves constitute Rorty's way of mastering irony.

Kierkegaard devotes a significant portion of his thesis to precisely the sort of moral critique of unbridled irony that MacIntyre briefly sketches in response to Rorty's liberal irony (as he construes it). Unlike MacIntyre, however, he seeks to recover the "truth" of irony as a controlled element in an ethical way of life. I think it is clear that Kierkegaard is fairly successful in this endeavor, as I attempted to demonstrate in chapter 5. Also, Climacus helpfully supplements and extends Kierkegaard's account of mastered irony through his explication of irony as an incognito of the ethical.

So, who offers the most helpful way to master irony? Clearly MacIntyre does not, since he hastily dispenses with irony on the basis of his critique of liberal irony. Rorty's approach suffers from the difficulties that attend his original private–public distinction. However, in fairness to him, he has modified this distinction in such a way that now it is less problematic. He leaves us with the view that we master irony through commitment to liberalism. For Rorty, this involves abhorring and opposing cruelty above everything else.[12] I concur with Rorty on this point. Firm opposition to cruelty should inform and constrict our employment of irony and redescription. Kierkegaard acknowledges this point as well, insofar as he suggests that irony's uses as an "excellent surgeon" and "disciplinarian" should be *inward* applications of it.[13] He too advises us not to wield irony cruelly, even if he does not make opposition to cruelty the defining feature of his morality.

There is something narrow and inadequate, however, about singling out a loyalty to *liberalism* as one's most basic moral commitment. There may be some, if not many, goods other than those bound up with liberalism that also should inform and set parameters for our employment of irony. Furthermore, our commitment to the good of persons and to goodness and duty themselves ought to be more ultimate than a commitment to liberalism, and it certainly should not be conflated with such a commitment.

If Rorty were to concede that a commitment to liberalism is a bit too narrow to be a singular ultimate moral commitment, he would avoid the charge, leveled at him by McCarthy, Critchley, Fraser, and others, that he irresponsibly exempts liberalism from radical critique. As his account stands, he tends to suggest that liberal societies themselves largely are not in need of thoroughgoing critique, not merely that the claim, "cruelty is the worst thing we do," is beyond cavil. But the idea that liberal societies do not need radical critiques is very problematic.

One might argue in response that Rorty simply follows out consistently the implications of Michael Walzer's plausible view that morality is "thick from the beginning, culturally integrated, fully resonant, and it reveals itself thinly only on special occasions, when moral language is turned to specific purposes."[14] If we give credence to Walzer's position, it appears that Rorty, not Kierkegaard and Adams, is on the right track since he opts for a fairly thick ultimate commitment.

Lurking in this objection is confusion about Walzer's position that needs to be sorted out and dispatched. The fact, if it is a fact, that morality is "thick from the beginning" does not imply that our most basic moral commitments should not be construed thinly. As Walzer explains:

> I want to stress . . . that "minimalism"[15] does not describe a morality that is substantively minor or emotionally shallow. The opposite is more likely true: this is morality close to the bone. There isn't much that is more important than "truth" and "justice," minimally understood. The minimal demands that we make on one another are, when denied, repeated with passionate insistence. In moral discourse, thinness and intensity go together, whereas with thickness comes qualification, compromise, complexity, and disagreement.[16]

Walzer's remarks are instructive. They seem to *confirm* Adams's and Kierkegaard's position, not to render it problematic. For what is an ultimate moral commitment, if it is not an intensely held loyalty? But if, as Walzer posits, "thinness and intensity go together," it follows that at least some of our most ultimate moral commitments ought to be and typically are thinly construed. Walzer's remarks about truth and justice make the same point. Apparently Walzer believes that when a person defines her most ultimate moral commitments, such an occasion is one of those special occasions in which moral language appropriately "reveals itself thinly." Consequently, Walzer's account does not imply that Rorty's position has an advantage over Kierkegaard's and Adams's position. If anything, it lends support to the idea, espoused by Kierkegaard and Adams, that our commitment to the good of persons and to goodness and moral obligation is an entirely appropriate ultimate commitment.

It is not the case, either, that this sort of position leads to a pale, abstract, passionless view of ethical life. For, as we have seen, there is a much thicker side to Kierkegaard's account of actuality as gift and task. Thickly construed, Kierkegaard understands commitment to the good of persons and to goodness and duty to involve earnest engagement in one's social roles and other ethical tasks of actuality. He severely criticizes those who use irony to disengage radically from these roles and from human community in general.

I conclude that Kierkegaard's position provides a better approach to mastering irony than does Rorty's. There are many reasons not to quarantine irony in a private sphere of some sort, in Kierkegaard's view, as is clear from his discussion of mastered irony. There are many other goods in addition to avoidance of cruelty and commitment to truthfulness, moreover, which constrain and inform our employment of irony and our pursuit of self-creation. Kierkegaard's position explicitly invites us to seize on these goods embedded in our social practices and roles. Furthermore, it does not confine us to an ultimate commitment that is perhaps a bit *too* narrow.[17] We clearly have leeway to evaluate critically and even radically the social practices of the liberal societies in which we live and our own personal commitments.

There is one other feature of Kierkegaard's account of mastered irony that distinguishes it from Rorty's and MacIntyre's. Kierkegaard is more attuned, if only slightly, to the benefits of irony within ethical life, in comparison to Rorty. To his credit, Rorty acknowledges that his ironist's recognition of contingency helps her to be more tolerant and civil. It also helps her become autonomous. So, Rorty recognizes that irony has important benefits for ethical life. Some of the benefits he points out, moreover, are not noticed or emphasized by Kierkegaard. There are important benefits of irony that Rorty fails to recognize, however. Kierkegaard shows us that when we turn our own irony inward we discover all sorts of inconsistencies in our beliefs, desires, and ideals, especially when we compare these to our behavior. Recognizing these disparities is a necessary first step in pruning them out of our characters. That is why he suggests that mastered irony is crucial for the promotion of "personal life."

Rorty's construal of irony leads him to miss this benefit and some other personal benefits of irony, when it is mastered. For recognizing contingency and deconstructing metaphysics have little if anything to do with recognizing personal inconsistencies. Kierkegaard recognizes and illuminates for us this personal benefit of mastered irony and other such benefits because he has a broader account of irony. To recognize personal inconsistencies is to recognize incongruities of a certain sort.

7.3 CONCLUSION

If I had to choose between Rorty's liberal irony and MacIntyre's outright rejection of irony, I would opt for Rorty's position. Rorty deserves much credit for bringing irony and its relation to moral commitment back into the purview of contemporary Anglo-American philosophy. Many of his critics argue that he takes extreme positions as he sketches his account of contingency, irony, and solidarity. I have argued that these criticisms often are unfair and even occasionally completely baseless, as they turn on uncharitable or simply mistaken readings of Rorty. There is some truth to the charge, however, that Rorty overreacts to the passing of classical foundationalism and other modernist positions. As a result, his account of irony and moral commitment is parochial in certain respects.

Kierkegaard anticipates and preempts MacIntyre by offering a more extended and more incisive critique of pure irony. He also recovers and illuminates the central place that irony has in human life, especially in ethical life. Furthermore, he probes deeper into the core of irony than does Rorty, perhaps because Rorty is preoccupied with other concerns.

We do not have to choose between Kierkegaard's and Rorty's views, however. I hope to have shown through these reflections how we can appropriate the best insights of both as we seek to understand and overcome the dualism of irony and moral commitment bequeathed to us. It is, after all, just an inherited contingency.

NOTES

INTRODUCTION

1. Jedediah Purdy, *For Common Things: Irony, Trust, and Commitment in America Today* (New York: Alfred A. Knopf, 1999), xi.
2. Purdy, *For Common Things*, 9–10.
3. Alasdair MacIntyre, *Dependent Rational Animals: Why Human Beings Need the Virtues* (Chicago: Open Court, 1999), 153–154.
4. He also briefly mentions Friedrich Schlegel's defense of irony. But he mentions Schlegel simply to show that his treatment of Rorty's position is analogous in certain respects to Hegel's critique of Schlegel's position. See MacIntyre, *Dependent Rational Animals*, 153.
5. By the year 2000, this work had been translated into at least seventeen different languages. Henceforth I will refer to this work simply as *Contingency*.
6. See Richard Bernstein, "Rorty's Liberal Utopia," in *The New Constellation: The Ethical-Political Horizons of Modernity/ Postmodernity* (Cambridge, MA: MIT Press, 1992), 283.
7. Jean Bethke Elshtain, "Don't Be Cruel: Reflections on Rortyian Liberalism," in *The Politics of Irony: Essays in Self-Betrayal*, ed. Daniel W. Conway and John E. Seery (New York: St. Martin's Press, 1992), 207. Elshtain continues to advance this criticism in a recently published and slightly modified version of this essay. See her article with the same title in *Richard Rorty*, ed. Charles B. Guignon and David R. Hiley (Cambridge: Cambridge University Press, 2003), 147. My subsequent citations of Elshtain's work, however, all refer to her first article, since she does not substantially revise her objections to Rorty's position in her more recent essay.
8. Hereafter I generally will refer to this work simply as *Postscript*.
9. Purdy, *For Common Things*, 203.

CHAPTER 1   RICHARD RORTY'S LIBERAL IRONY

1. Richard Rorty, *Contingency, Irony, and Solidarity* (Cambridge: Cambridge University Press, 1989), 73.
2. Ibid. Of course, Rorty is not saying that words or concepts within a final vocabulary cannot be internally justified by showing how they are

implied by or cohere with other words or concepts in that same vocabulary. They can be, on Rorty's view.

3. Rorty, *Contingency*, 73.
4. Ibid.
5. Gary Gutting, *Pragmatic Liberalism and the Critique of Modernity* (Cambridge: Cambridge University Press, 1999), 63–64.
6. Rorty, *Contingency*, 73.
7. Ibid., 74.
8. Michele Moody-Adams, "Theory, Practice, and the Contingency of Rorty's Irony," *Journal of Social Philosophy* 25 (1994): 212.
9. Rorty, *Contingency*, 74–75.
10. Ibid. For a helpful discussion of this controversial feature of Rorty's account, see Alan Malachowski, *Richard Rorty* (Princeton: Princeton University Press, 2002), 109–120. See also David R. Hiley, *Philosophy in Question: Essays on a Pyrrhonian Theme* (Chicago: The University of Chicago Press, 1988), 143–173.
11. Rorty, *Contingency*, 73–74.
12. Ibid., xv.
13. For more on this way of understanding Rorty's view of contingency, see Nathan Rotenstreich, "Can Expression Replace Reflection?" *The Review of Metaphysics* 43 (March 1990): 607–609.
14. Rorty, *Contingency*, 28.
15. I highlight this point because we might not be apt to conclude to the nonuniversality of something from the recognition of its contingency. Indeed, some philosophers find this move problematic. See, for example, Thomas McCarthy, "Ironist Theory as a Vocation: A Response to Richard Rorty's Reply," *Critical Inquiry* 16 (Spring 1990): 649.
16. The desire to avoid pain might be an exception to this claim. See Rorty, *Contingency*, 91, 189–198.
17. Rorty, *Contingency*, 28.
18. Ibid., 74.
19. Ibid.
20. Habermas's ongoing interest in universal validity is precisely what leads Rorty to take issue with his vision of a pluralistic, democratic society. See Rorty, *Contingency*, 67.
21. Rorty, *Contingency*, 87–88.
22. This is true of strong poets or makers as well. For my purposes, there is no significant distinction between ironists and strong poets or makers. If one thinks of strong poets as persons who write poetry or other works of literature, then there is a significant distinction between ironists and strong poets. In that case, strong poets are ironists, but ironists are not necessarily strong poets. In most cases, "strong poet" simply is a reference to "ironist" before this concept has been formally introduced in *Contingency*.
23. By antiepistemological I have in mind, for instance, Rorty's antifoundationalism and his complete rejection of criteria of choice between

final vocabularies. By antimetaphysical I have in mind, for instance, his antiessentialism and persistent invective against metaphysics. These strains in Rorty's thought can be distinguished. But they are part of a unified attempt to unsettle traditional ways of understanding the central tasks of philosophy. For more discussion of these points, see Richard Rorty, *Philosophy and the Mirror of Nature* (Princeton: Princeton University Press, 1979), 129–164, 313–394.

24. Rorty, *Contingency*, 26.
25. Ibid., 25, advances this claim in reference to strong poets before he explicitly introduces ironists and then returns to it in his discussion of ironism, 96–99.
26. Rorty, *Contingency*, 29. Rorty's reading of Nietzsche inspires his position.
27. One could have these formative and individuating experiences apart from recognizing the contingency of final vocabularies, of course. I take Rorty's point to be that the recognition of contingency makes such experiences much more likely to occur.
28. Rorty, *Contingency*, 97.
29. Ibid., 27.
30. Ibid.
31. Ibid., 75.
32. Cf. John Horton, "Irony and Commitment: An Irreconcilable Dualism of Modernity," in *Richard Rorty: Critical Dialogues*, ed. Matthew Festenstein and Simon Thompson (Malden, MA: Polity, 2001), 21, who states: "the worry, therefore, amounts only to doubts about whether I (or perhaps others) would have been happier, more content or whatever if I had been born into a different tribe, learnt a different language game, been a different sort of human being."
33. Gutting, *Pragmatic Liberalism*, 63–64.
34. Rorty denies that there ultimately is a hard and fast distinction between moral and aesthetic concerns and judgments. See Rorty, *Contingency*, 194. This point does not nullify my claim, however. He does not deny that one can distinguish between *prima facie* ethical and aesthetic elements and implications of a position. Cf. Eric M. Gander, *The Last Conceptual Revolution: A Critique of Richard Rorty's Political Philosophy* (Albany: State University of New York Press, 1999), 53.
35. Rorty, *Contingency*, 97.
36. Ibid., 120.
37. Ibid., 79–81.
38. Ibid., 97.
39. Ibid., 194.
40. For more textual evidence for the claim that Rorty takes worries about not being able to undertake quests for self-creation as ethical and not merely aesthetic concerns, see Richard Rorty, "Feminism and Pragmatism," in *Truth and Progress*, vol. 3, *Philosophical Papers*

(Cambridge: Cambridge University Press, 1998), 202–227. This essay originally was delivered as a Tanner Lecture at the University of Michigan in the spring of 1991 and was published in *The Tanner Lectures on Human Values*, vol. 13 (Salt Lake City: University of Utah Press, 1994).

41. There is one additional sense in which an ironist's worries are ethical. That is, they are resolved by measures that require the practice of certain liberal virtues, such as tolerance and openness to others. As Rorty explains, "Nothing can serve as a criticism of a person save another person, or of a culture save an alternative culture—for persons and cultures are, for us, incarnated vocabularies. So our doubts about our own characters or our own culture can be resolved or assuaged only by enlarging our acquaintance." See Rorty, *Contingency*, 80. Thus, according to Rorty, an ironist's doubts about her final vocabulary will lead her to be more tolerant and open to others, if she understands that to resolve her doubts she has to "enlarge her acquaintance."

42. Rorty, *Contingency*, xv.

43. Ibid., 120.

44. The references to a new self and personal identity here are not intended in a metaphysical sense. They are not intended to suggest any position concerning debates about what persons are, metaphysically speaking, or what is true about persons, if anything, that underwrites our believing that persons persist over time. It is not that Rorty does not have a position regarding these issues. For Rorty's views, see especially chapters one and two of his *Philosophy and the Mirror of Nature*, where he offers a deflationary position on these issues. Rather, it is simply that, for my purposes, these issues can and must be set aside. For a helpful discussion of the broadly ethical sense of personal identity that is in view here, see Bernard Williams's "Persons, Character and Morality," in *The Identities of Persons*, ed. Amélie Oksenberg Rorty (Berkeley and Los Angeles: University of California Press, 1976), 197–216.

45. Of course, persons in these situations may very well create new terms or ways of understanding themselves and others. See Rorty, "Feminism and Pragmatism," 204–205.

46. Rorty, *Contingency*, 102–103. For an interesting, related discussion of Proust, see Alain de Botton's *How Proust Can Change Your Life* (New York: Vintage Books, 1997), 117–132.

47. Rorty, *Contingency*, 78.

48. Ibid., 99.

49. Ibid.

50. Ibid., 89–90.

51. Ibid., 90.

52. Ibid.

53. Ibid., 91.

54. Ibid.

55. Rorty, *Contingency*, 74. For a helpful discussion of some difficulties that attend Rorty's adoption of Shklar's conception of liberalism, see Gander, *The Last Conceptual Revolution*, 63–114.
56. Rorty, *Contingency*, 83.
57. Ibid., 91.
58. Ibid., 91–92.
59. Nancy Fraser, "Solidarity or Singularity? Richard Rorty between Romanticism and Technocracy," in *Reading Rorty*, ed. Alan R. Malachowski (Oxford: Blackwell, 1990), 306–308.
60. Fraser, "Solidarity or Singularity," 303–313.
61. Rorty, *Contingency*, 91. Cf. Fraser, "Solidarity or Singularity," 309.
62. Fraser, "Solidarity or Singularity," 311–312.
63. Gutting, *Pragmatic Liberalism*, 62.
64. Since Rorty counts humiliation as a form of cruelty, the complete elimination of cruelty in public seems an unrealizable ideal insofar as having one's views rejected by others in public is humiliating but also unavoidable in a liberal democracy that is even remotely committed to public discourse.
65. Rorty, *Contingency*, 189.
66. Ibid.
67. Ibid., 46.
68. Ibid., 48.
69. Ibid., 54.
70. Ibid., 198.
71. Cf. Rorty, "Reply to Simon Critchley," in *Deconstruction and Pragmatism: Simon Critchley, Jacques Derrida, Ernesto Laclau and Richard Rorty*, ed. Chantal Mouffe (New York: Routledge, 1996), 42.
72. Rorty, *Contingency*, 50.
73. See, for instance, L. P. Gerson, "Philosophy, Literature, and Truth," review of *Contingency, Irony, and Solidarity*, by Richard Rorty. *University of Toronto Quarterly* 59 (Spring 1990): 449–451.

Chapter 2 The Ethics of Rortian Redescription

1. Moody-Adams, "Theory," 214–215.
2. Elshtain, "Don't Be Cruel," 206.
3. Ibid., 206–207. Cf. Bernstein, "Rorty's Liberal Utopia," 274, who states, "To suggest that the horrors and Holocausts of the twentieth century can be redescribed to 'look good' might seem to count as a *reductio ad absurdum* of his [i.e., Rorty's] position."
4. The "ultimately" qualifier is rather important. It is not that a moral judgment within a given moral vocabulary is arbitrary. It would be far too easy to criticize Rorty, if that were his position. More important, that is not his position. Rather, Elshtain means that Rorty's notion

that our final vocabularies are contingent implies that ultimately they are arbitrary—Europe could have had a very different set of moral vocabularies. Nothing in the nature of reality necessitated adopting the moral vocabularies that were adopted by Europeans.

5. Richard Rorty, "Robustness: A Reply to Jean Bethke Elshtain," in Conway and Seery, *The Politics of Irony*, 220.

6. Rorty, "Robustness," 219–220.

7. Elshtain's criticism is not a *red herring* in regard to assessing the overall plausibility and coherence of Rorty's combining in his ironist a thoroughgoing recognition of contingency and liberal moral commitments. I address this challenge to Rorty's position in the next chapter.

8. Presumably the quick and easy slide I have suggested here from "only one or a few things cannot be made to look good" to "most things *we* take to be evil cannot be made to look good" partly accounts for why Rorty does not modify AC in the following way: *almost* anything can be made to look good or bad by being redescribed.

9. Robert Adams, *Finite and Infinite Goods: A Framework for Ethics* (Oxford: Oxford University Press, 1999), 388.

10. Rorty, "Robustness," 223. The ethics to which Rorty refers is a decosmologized ethics that refuses to ground our rejection of Nazi values, for instance, in metanarratives about God or the human condition.

11. Moody-Adams, "Theory," 215, 217. Cf. Ruth L. Smith, "Morals and Their Ironies," *Journal of Religious Ethics* 26 (1998): 378.

12. Rorty, "Feminism and Pragmatism," 210. Moody-Adams has in view Rorty's essay as it was first published as a Tanner Lecture.

13. Moody-Adams, "Theory," 217–218.

14. Richard Rorty, "Truth and Freedom: A Reply to Thomas McCarthy," *Critical Inquiry* 16 (Spring 1990): 639.

15. Rorty's position on truth is notoriously difficult to pin down. The obvious truth is that Rorty almost entirely rejects all vestiges of a correspondence theory of truth. I briefly address Rorty's views on truth and objectivity in the first section of the next chapter. Suffice it to say here that it is highly unlikely that Rorty holds a position that implies even unwittingly that victimizers have a "correct" description that trumps competing descriptions. For an instructive and insightful discussion of Rorty's views on truth and justification, see Gutting, *Pragmatic Liberalism*, 15–47. See also the interesting exchanges between Rorty and other philosophers such as John McDowell, Hilary Putnam, and James Conant in Robert B. Brandom, ed., *Rorty and His Critics* (Malden, MA: Blackwell, 2000).

16. Bernstein, "Rorty's Liberal Utopia," 283.

17. MacIntyre, *Dependent Rational Animals*, 151.

18. Ibid., 150–151.

19. Ibid., 152.

20. I wonder whether there is a creeping Augustinianism in Bernstein's and MacIntyre's positions that is revealed here.
21. See James Conant, "Freedom, Cruelty, and Truth: Rorty versus Orwell," in *Rorty and His Critics*, ed. Robert B. Brandom (Malden, MA: Blackwell, 2000), 294–295, 308–309.
22. Richard Rorty, "Response to Conant," in *Rorty and His Critics*, ed. Robert B. Brandom (Malden, MA: Blackwell, 2000), 347.
23. If MacIntyre responds by suggesting that Rorty's private–public distinction is untenable, then the dispute between them will shift to that issue and not the supposed duplicity of ironists (who embrace AC).
24. For a helpful and concise summation of some standard criticisms, see Daniel Conway, "Irony, State and Utopia," in Festenstein and Thompson, *Richard Rorty*, 78.
25. Rorty, *Contingency*, 91.
26. Fraser, "Solidarity or Singularity," 312–313.
27. Richard Rorty, "Against Bosses, Against Oligarchies: A Conversation with Richard Rorty," interview by Derek Nystrom and Kent Puckett, *Prickly Pear Pamphlets*, no. 11, ed. Matthew Engelke and Mark Harris (Charlottesville: Prickly Pear Pamphlets, 1998), 60.
28. Richard Rorty, "Response to Daniel Conway," in Festenstein and Thompson, *Richard Rorty*, 91. In fairness to Rorty, this other way of construing his private–public distinction is already detectable in *Contingency*, even if it is not emphasized. See, for instance, *Contingency*, xiv–xv.
29. Rorty, "Against Bosses," 61.
30. Of course, it is possible to use a redescription in pursuit of self-creation without believing that it accurately captures what it describes. Suppose one is trying to get out from under a certain viewpoint. One might then intentionally redescribe it or certain persons who promote it in a way that is an extreme but humorous caricature of it or those persons who promote it, in an attempt to loosen its grip on one.
31. Of course, she still might be a truthful person, if she consistently says to others what she believes.
32. See John Rawls, *Political Liberalism* (New York: Columbia University Press, 1993), 59. These are the conditions that Rawls sets forth for a comprehensive doctrine to count as reasonable. Rawls also refers to the first two conditions as a comprehensive view's being (a) an exercise of theoretical reason and (b) an exercise of practical reason, respectively.
33. I have focused on the actions and words of the ironist parent and not the fundamentalist parent not because I seek to celebrate the ironist or criticize the fundamentalist but because I am concerned with the consistency of a certain component of liberal irony.

Chapter 3   Autonomy and Moral Commitment in Liberal Irony: Problems and Proposals

1. Richard Rorty, "Justice as a Larger Loyalty," in Festenstein and Thompson, *Richard Rorty*, 235.
2. Simon Critchley, "Metaphysics in the Dark: A Response to Richard Rorty and Ernesto Laclau," *Political Theory* 26 (December 1998): 812.
3. I am concerned only with Rorty's appropriation of Nietzsche here and not with whether Rorty gets Nietzsche right. So the criticisms that I consider of Rorty's Nietzschean view of autonomy solely concern Rorty's position.
4. Gerson, "Philosophy, Literature, and Truth," 450.
5. Bernard Williams, *Problems of the Self* (Cambridge: Cambridge University Press, 1973), 136–137.
6. Richard Rorty, "Truth Without Correspondence to Reality," in *Philosophy and Social Hope* (New York: Penguin Books, 1999), 37.
7. Malachowski, *Richard Rorty*, 136.
8. See, for instance, Rorty, *Contingency*, 8–9.
9. Merold Westphal, "Coping and Conversing: The Limits and Promise of Pragmatism," *The Hedgehog Review* 3, no. 3 (Fall 2001): 90.
10. Richard Rorty, "Response to Simon Thompson," in Festenstein and Thompson, *Richard Rorty*, 51.
11. See Gutting, *Pragmatic Liberalism*, 31.
12. See, for instance, Michael Devitt, *Realism and Truth* (Princeton: Princeton University Press, 1991), 204–208.
13. Gutting, *Pragmatic Liberalism*, 31–32.
14. The position Gutting commends has interesting parallels with Lynne Rudder Baker's "Practical Realism." See Lynne Rudder Baker, *Explaining Attitudes: A Practical Approach to the Mind* (Cambridge: Cambridge University Press, 1995), 220–241.
15. Hiley, *Philosophy in Question*, 146.
16. Of course, I am already standing for certain beliefs and against others when I say this.
17. Anthony Rudd, "Kierkegaard's Critique of Pure Irony," in *Kierkegaard: The Self in Society*, ed. George Pattison and Steven Shakespeare (New York: St. Martin's Press, 1998), 90.
18. Rudd, "Kierkegaard's Critique," 93.
19. Cf. Rudi Visker, " 'Hold the Being': How to Split Rorty Between Irony and Finitude," *Philosophy and Social Criticism* 25 (1999): 31.
20. Rorty, "Reply to Simon Critchley," 43.
21. Ibid., 42, 43.
22. Rorty, *Contingency*, 73.
23. I am not assuming here that all metaphysical realists endorse a correspondence theory of truth.

24. Cf. David Owen, "The Avoidance of Cruelty: Joshing Rorty on Liberalism, Scepticism, and Ironism," in Festenstein and Thompson, *Richard Rorty*, 99. For a contrary view, see Eugene Goodheart, "The Postmodern Liberalism of Richard Rorty," *Partisan Review* 63 (1996): 223–235.

25. Or as an alternative to other vocabularies that they have adopted, which were not inherited. There is no assumption here that the persons in view move directly from inherited vocabularies to liberalism.

26. Rudd, "Kierkegaard's Critique," 92.

27. Ibid.

28. Anthony Rudd, "Reason in Ethics: MacIntyre and Kierkegaard," in *Kierkegaard after MacIntyre: Essays on Freedom, Narrative, and Virtue*, ed. John J. Davenport and Anthony Rudd (Chicago: Open Court, 2001), 137.

29. Søren Kierkegaard, *The Concept of Irony with Continual Reference to Socrates, together with "Notes on Schelling's Berlin Lectures"* (Princeton: Princeton University Press, 1989), 259.

30. Rudd, "Kierkegaard's Critique," 84. In the next chapter, I discuss in much greater detail Kierkegaard's critique of pure irony.

31. Lest one think that I am not giving romantic irony its due here, note that I have in view merely romantic irony as Kierkegaard and Rudd construe it. My goal simply is to show that Kierkegaard's critique of romantic irony does not apply to Rorty's position. For an insightful discussion of romantic irony that puts it in a better light, see Charles Larmore, *The Romantic Legacy* (New York: Columbia University Press, 1996). Also, see Claire Colebrook, *Irony* (New York: Routledge, 2004), 47–71.

32. A person could meet the three initial conditions that Rorty sets forth as definitive of irony and not pursue projects of self-creation. In that case, she would not fully exemplify liberal irony.

33. John Owens, "The Obligations of Irony: Rorty on Irony, Autonomy, and Contingency," *The Review of Metaphysics* 54 (September 2000): 35.

34. Ibid., 36.

35. Ibid., 37.

36. For instance, Rawls states: "Full autonomy is realized by citizens when they act from principles of justice that specify the fair terms of cooperation they would give to themselves when fairly represented as free and equal persons." See Rawls, *Political Liberalism*, 77.

37. See section 1.3 of the opening chapter for a discussion of this view of freedom.

38. Rorty, *Contingency*, 28.

39. Ibid., 42.

40. Ibid., 43.

41. It would be more accurate to say here, "as a condition for pursuing autonomy." Rorty sometimes does not distinguish between recognizing contingency and pursuing autonomy. But these ideas are separable in

his account. For Rorty, recognizing contingency greatly facilitates the pursuit of autonomy but is not to be identified with this. One could recognize the contingency of the vocabulary that one has inherited without making any effort whatsoever to get out from under it. Furthermore, one could attempt to get out from under an inherited vocabulary without recognizing its contingency, although this task might be more difficult as a result.

42. Owens, "The Obligations of Irony," 38–39.
43. For a sampling of Rorty's views on ethnocentrism, see Richard Rorty, "Introduction: Antirepresentationalism, Ethnocentrism, and Liberalism," in *Objectivity, Relativism, and Truth*, vol. 1, *Philosophical Papers* (Cambridge: Cambridge University Press, 1991), 2, 13–14. Also, see in the same volume, "Solidarity or Objectivity," 29, and "On Ethnocentrism: A Reply to Clifford Geertz," 203.
44. MacIntyre, *Dependent Rational Animals*, 152.
45. Ibid., 153.
46. Ibid., 152.
47. See, for instance, Richard Rorty, "Moral Identity and Private Autonomy: The Case of Foucault," in *Essays on Heidegger and Others*, vol. 2, *Philosophical Papers* (Cambridge: Cambridge University Press, 1991), 193–194.
48. Moody-Adams, "Theory," 217–218, 224, draws a similar conclusion.
49. See MacIntyre, *Dependent Rational Animals*, 153–154. The passage in which MacIntyre dispatches irony is quoted at length in the Introduction.

CHAPTER 4 KIERKEGAARD ON THE PROBLEMS OF PURE IRONY

1. In 1841, when Kierkegaard defended his thesis, the *Magister* degree in philosophy was equivalent to the doctor of philosophy in other academic disciplines at the University of Copenhagen. In 1854, this distinction in title was discontinued, and those holding the *Magister* degree in philosophy simply were recognized as doctors of philosophy. See Howard V. Hong and Edna H. Hong, "Historical Introduction to Søren Kierkegaard," in *The Concept of Irony*, xii–xiii.
2. Robert L. Perkins, "What a Hegelian Fool I Was," *History of European Ideas* 20 (1995): 180. Cf. Alastair Hannay, *Kierkegaard: A Biography* (Cambridge: Cambridge University Press, 2001), 134–135, 151.
3. I must set to the side here discussion of how the concept of mastered irony illuminates Kierkegaard's pseudonymous writings and his use of pseudonyms. For helpful discussions of the former topic, see Ronald L. Hall, "The Irony of Irony," in *International Kierkegaard Commentary: "The Concept of Irony,"* ed. Robert L. Perkins

(Macon, GA: Mercer University Press, 2001): 317–346, and John Lippitt, *Humour and Irony in Kierkegaard's Thought* (New York: St. Martin's Press, 2000). In regard to the latter topic, see C. Stephen Evans, *Passionate Reason: Making Sense of Kierkegaard's "Philosophical Fragments"* (Bloomington: Indiana University Press, 1992), 1–12. See also Sylvia Walsh, *Living Poetically: Kierkegaard's Existential Aesthetics* (University Park: The Pennsylvania State University Press, 1994), 10–15. Roger Poole, *Kierkegaard: The Indirect Communication* (Charlottesville: University Press of Virginia, 1993), advances an alternative view. For discussion of general approaches to Kierkegaard interpretation, see Patrick Goold, "Reading Kierkegaard: Two Pitfalls and a Strategy for Avoiding Them," *Faith and Philosophy* 7 (July 1990): 304–315.

4. Kierkegaard, *The Concept of Irony*, 259, 261.
5. Ibid., 9. At least Kierkegaard intends that Socrates is the first well-known ironist. For a helpful discussion of Socratic irony and the shift that occurs in Kierkegaard's thinking about it, from initially taking Socrates to be a kind of pure ironist to coming to view him as an exemplary subjective thinker who effectively employs irony as an incognito for ethical passion, see Lippitt, *Humour and Irony*, 135–157. Kierkegaard articulates the former position in his thesis and the latter, more positive view of Socrates and Socratic irony in *Postscript*, under the guise of Johannes Climacus.
6. Kierkegaard, *The Concept of Irony*, 9.
7. Ibid., 11.
8. Ibid., 254.
9. Ibid., 259.
10. Allen W. Wood, *Hegel's Ethical Thought* (Cambridge: Cambridge University Press, 1990), 196. See also Merold Westphal, *History and Truth in Hegel's "Phenomenology,"* 3rd ed. (Bloomington: Indiana University Press, 1998), 138–146, 156–157, and Charles Taylor, *Hegel* (Cambridge: Cambridge University Press, 1975), 376–378, 386–388.
11. Taylor, *Hegel*, 376, 377.
12. Kierkegaard, *The Concept of Irony*, 256.
13. Ibid., 257, 258.
14. The advice that "A," the young man of the first volume of *Either/Or*, offers in regard to friendship in an essay entitled, "Rotation of Crops: A Venture in a Theory of Social Prudence," aptly illustrates this disengaged stance. See Søren Kierkegaard, *Either/Or*, 2 vols., ed. and trans. Howard V. Hong and Edna H. Hong (Princeton: Princeton University Press, 1987), 1:295–296.
15. For a helpful discussion of this point, see Rudd, "Kierkegaard's Critique," 87–91.
16. Kierkegaard, *The Concept of Irony*, 251.
17. Ibid., 253.

18. Ibid., 262.
19. There is a parallel here with a Rortian ironist's pursuit of novel self-creation, even though a Rortian ironist is not a pure ironist, as I argued in the previous chapter.
20. Kierkegaard, *The Concept of Irony*, 261.
21. Rudd, "Kierkegaard's Critique," 82.
22. Kierkegaard, *The Concept of Irony*, 249–250.
23. Ibid., 284.
24. Here (and in regard to the next criticism) Kierkegaard anticipates the argument of Judge William for the superiority of an ethical way of life over a life of ironic detachment in "The Esthetic Validity of Marriage." See Kierkegaard, *Either/Or*, 2:3–154.
25. Kierkegaard, *The Concept of Irony*, 269.
26. Ibid., 270.
27. Ibid., 253.
28. Ibid., 280.
29. Andrew Cross, "Neither Either Nor Or: The Perils of Reflexive Irony," in *The Cambridge Companion to Kierkegaard*, ed. Alastair Hannay and Gordon Marino (Cambridge: Cambridge University Press, 1998), 138–139.
30. Or, alternatively, irony is destructive of the good of personal identity. I intend here personal identity in a broadly ethical, and not metaphysical, sense.
31. Kierkegaard, *The Concept of Irony*, 276–286. Walsh, *Living Poetically*, 56–62, provides a helpful discussion of this idea.
32. Rorty, *Contingency*, 88.
33. Kierkegaard, *The Concept of Irony*, 276–277.
34. Ibid., 279.
35. The qualifier "reasonable" may allude to the fact that one does not have to accept passively, uncritically, and in total, inherited social roles and the norms that govern them in order to fulfill the task of actuality.
36. Anthony Rudd, *Kierkegaard and the Limits of the Ethical* (Oxford: Oxford University Press, 1993), 73.
37. I am referring, of course, to the judge's letters to "A." Even though these letters belong to a genre that is very different from Kierkegaard's thesis, they still come across as diffuse and philosophically complex.
38. Kierkegaard, *The Concept of Irony*, 279–280, 281, 282.
39. Such an irresponsible parent also would socialize his children into an unjust view of gender.
40. To use Rorty's terminology, such persons take contingent social conventions to be necessary. Kierkegaard does not necessarily intend common persons when he uses the phrase, "commonplace persons." For a helpful discussion of Kierkegaard's views of the common person, see Jørgen Bukdahl, *Søren Kierkegaard and the Common Man*, trans. Bruce H. Kirmmse (Grand Rapids: Eerdmans, 2001).
41. Kierkegaard, *The Concept of Irony*, 280.

42. Readers familiar with Kierkegaard's *The Sickness Unto Death* will recognize here an obvious foreshadowing of Anti-Climacus's discussion of the despair of necessity and the despair of possibility. See Søren Kierkegaard, *The Sickness Unto Death: A Christian Psychological Exposition for Upbuilding and Awakening*, ed. and trans. Howard V. Hong and Edna H. Hong (Princeton: Princeton University Press, 1980), 29–42.

43. If this claim seems overly vague, then consider these points. First, as Aristotle cautions us, we should not look for more precision in the subject matter than it permits. Second, the vagueness of this claim may be a strength in the sense that a more specific claim might unwittingly rule out ways of life that do exemplify healthy individuality. Third, in the next section I qualify Kierkegaard's position, as he does, in a way that will render it more exclusionary. Fourth, it is important, however, not to make it more exclusionary than it, in fact, is. I elaborate on this point in the next section.

44. Kierkegaard, *The Concept of Irony*, 283, 284, 285.

45. Perhaps we could put it this way. An ironist's overarching project is to realize negative freedom. However, this project devolves into numerous subprojects, so that she ultimately finds herself simply trying to overcome boredom as her immediate goal. "A" is rather forthcoming about this. In "Rotation of Crops," he clarifies that the basic principle that underlies his various tenets of social prudence is that "all people are boring." Furthermore, he claims that boredom is "the root of all evil." See Kierkegaard, *Either/Or*, 1:285. So if there is any such thing as a human *telos*, it is to escape boredom, according to "A"; and one should not expect to reach this goal through community with other persons.

46. Williams, "Persons, Character and Morality," 201.

47. Ibid., 208.

48. Ibid., 209.

49. There is reason to believe that Kierkegaard had a decisive conversion to Christianity in 1838, well before he completed and defended his thesis in 1841.

50. This is the idea that in our society "there is diversity of comprehensive doctrines, all perfectly reasonable." Moreover, this condition is not an unfortunate one that is soon to pass away, according to Rawls. It is the inevitable result of "free human reason." Therefore, since we take the free exercise of human reason to be a basic good that should be granted to all citizens, we should acknowledge that there will continue to be a diversity of reasonable comprehensive doctrines, and that this is good. See Rawls, *Political Liberalism*, 24–25*n*, 36–37.

51. I attempt to take the same kind of approach to Rorty both in regard to the divide between Rorty and theists and the divide between Rorty and philosophers who embrace forms of metaphysical realism.

52. Consider, for instance, the broadly ethical viewpoint of Judge William in volume two of *Either/Or* and the rigorous Christian viewpoint that

Kierkegaard adopts, under the pseudonym Anti-Climacus in *Practice in Christianity.*

53. I am not suggesting here, however, that in *The Concept of Irony* Kierkegaard already clearly has in mind his later distinction between ethical and ethical–religious forms of existence. I am merely suggesting that in this work there are central claims that do not depend on Christian presuppositions, and there are others that do depend on these assumptions. I am also suggesting that, although these claims often are not sharply distinguished by Kierkegaard, it is not un-Kierkegaardian to distinguish them. Even if it were, however, that would not be a good enough reason not to distinguish them, in my view.

54. Kierkegaard, *The Concept of Irony*, 280.

55. Ibid., 280.

56. Walsh, *Living Poetically*, 57.

57. In Kierkegaard's account, there is no important distinction between a romantic and a pure ironist.

58. However, Kierkegaard does not suggest that human beings have anything more than a fallible grasp of some of these norms.

59. Kierkegaard, *The Concept of Irony*, 280.

60. Ibid., 280–281. Kierkegaard's reference to a "simple Christian" who lives "far more poetically than many a brilliant intellectual" anticipates an important distinction that he offers in *Postscript*, under the pseudonym, Johannes Climacus, between simple and intellectual modes of self-realization. For a discussion of Climacus's position, see section 6.4 of chapter six.

61. For a helpful and extended discussion of these points, see Alasdair MacIntyre, *After Virtue*, 2nd ed. (Notre Dame: University of Notre Dame Press, 1984), 121–164.

62. Indeed, he himself moves back and forth between these perspectives in his critique of pure irony.

63. Kierkegaard, *The Concept of Irony*, 297.

64. Søren Kierkegaard, *The Point of View for My Work as an Author*, ed. and trans. Howard V. Hong and Edna H. Hong (Princeton: Princeton University Press, 1998), 64. For a helpful discussion of this point as it relates to Kierkegaard's account of irony in *Postscript*, see C. Stephen Evans, *Kierkegaard's "Fragments" and "Postscript": The Religious Philosophy of Johannes Climacus* (Atlantic Highlands, NJ: Humanities Press, 1983), 190–192.

65. Kierkegaard may object to this on account of his humanism as well. See Evans, *Kierkegaard's "Fragments" and "Postscript,"* 190–191.

66. It is beyond the purview of this chapter to explore this claim in detail. However, here are a few points in support of it. For starters, many persons never become aware of Christian views of God and humanity. Others experience these views as so foreign as to be unintelligible. Furthermore, many persons who do encounter Christian views also

witness such cruelty from Christians that it is nearly impossible for them to consider a Christian view of God and humanity as a plausible starting point for moral reflection on the human condition. Finally, some persons experience horrific evil in such a way that it becomes impossible for them to view the world theistically.

67. Kierkegaard, *The Concept of Irony*, 326.
68. This boundary refers to the point at which an ethical way of life passes into an ethical–religious way of life. There is well-attested precedent in Kierkegaard's writings for demarcating a boundary between these ways of life.
69. See MacIntyre, *After Virtue*, 39–45.
70. For more critical analysis of MacIntyre's interpretation of Kierkegaard and a rejoinder from MacIntyre, see Davenport and Rudd, *Kierkegaard after MacIntyre*.
71. MacIntyre acknowledges that his reading of *Either/Or* conflicts with Kierkegaard's own reflections on it in *Point of View*. See MacIntyre, *After Virtue*, 41.

CHAPTER 5   KIERKEGAARD ON MASTERED IRONY

1. Kierkegaard, *The Concept of Irony*, 324, entitles the final section of his thesis: "Irony as a Controlled Element, the Truth of Irony."
2. Kierkegaard, *The Concept of Irony*, 325.
3. Here I follow Robert Adams's discussion of moral faith. See Adams, *Finite and Infinite Goods*, 374.
4. Kierkegaard, *The Concept of Irony*, 324.
5. Kierkegaard's discussion can be taken in such a way that it applies to any person who produces a work of art, broadly construed. That is how I will take it.
6. If an artist wants to convey a breakdown in communication, then she still is trying to convey something. In that case, uncontrolled irony in her work might foil her intentions by making her work appear to convey some other, straightforward idea.
7. C. Stephen Evans, "Realism and Antirealism in Kierkegaard's *Concluding Unscientific Postscript*," in Hannay and Marino, *The Cambridge Companion*, 161. Evans has in view readers of Kierkegaard who take his use of pseudonyms to imply that everything in his pseudonymous writings is ironical. His point applies in this context as well, however.
8. Kierkegaard, *The Concept of Irony*, 324.
9. For a slightly different reading of Kierkegaard on this point, see Richard M. Summers, " 'Controlled Irony' and the Emergence of the Self in Kierkegaard's Dissertation," in *International Kierkegaard Commentary: "The Concept of Irony,"* ed. Robert L. Perkins

(Macon, GA: Mercer University Press, 2001), 305. Summers takes the phrase "let the objective dominate" partly to refer to the idea that "personal opinions and predilections have no place in the economy of the work" that an artist is creating. For a helpful discussion of Kierkegaard's views on objectivity and subjectivity, which suggests that this is not Kierkegaard's considered view of authorial objectivity, see Robert C. Roberts, "Thinking Subjectively," *International Journal for the Philosophy of Religion* 11 (1980): 71–92.

10. The sermon at the end of *Either/Or* points us to a third, alternative way of life, that is, a religious existence.

11. Kierkegaard, *The Concept of Irony*, 326 (emphasis added).

12. Kierkegaard makes this transition by focusing first on the role of irony in a poet's work, then in his life, and then in any person's life. As he notes, in making the last transition: "what holds for the poet-existence holds also in some measure for every single individual's life." See Kierkegaard, *The Concept of Irony*, 325–326.

13. Kierkegaard, *The Concept of Irony*, 326.

14. Hall, "The Irony of Irony," 342–345.

15. Ibid., 343, 344.

16. Perhaps Hall thinks that this move is necessary because he thinks that Kierkegaard clearly is an incompatibilist and that the only kind of incompatibilism is the kind that endorses the principle of alternative possibilities. However, it is possible to be an incompatibilist and also to reject the principle of alternative possibilities. For a helpful discussion of this point, see Eleonore Stump, "Intellect, Will, and the Principle of Alternative Possibilities," in *Perspectives on Moral Responsibility*, ed. John Martin Fischer and Mark Ravizza (Ithaca: Cornell University Press, 1993), 237–262. Stump's article is instructive here in another way as well. She argues that Aquinas, who is thought by many to be an incompatibilist who subscribes to the principle of alternative possibilities, is an incompatibilist who does not hold to this principle. Perhaps the same point holds true with respect to Kierkegaard. At any rate, in the absence of a convincing argument that Kierkegaard is an incompatibilist who holds to the principle of alternative possibilities, the flat assumption that he subscribes to this problematic position should not be made.

17. For starters, see Frankfurt, *The Importance of What We Care About: Philosophical Essays* (Cambridge: Cambridge University Press, 1988), 1–10. For a more recent discussion of this issue, see John Martin Fischer and Mark Ravizza, S. J., *Responsibility and Control: A Theory of Moral Responsibility* (Cambridge: Cambridge University Press, 1998).

18. Kierkegaard, *The Concept of Irony*, 329, states in the same context that irony "prevents all idol worshipping of the phenomenon." This is another way of saying that irony delivers person from uncritical social conformity or from having a servile attitude in relation to their social order.

19. Vincent McCarthy, *The Phenomenology of Moods in Kierkegaard* (Boston: Martinus Nijhoff, 1978), 29.

20. For more discussion of this claim, see section 4.2 of the previous chapter. Another way to unpack the suggested analogy here is this. Just as an artistic work devolves into an incoherent chaos of irony, if the artist who employs irony in it is not master over the irony, an individual's life likely will fail to have continuity, if she pursues a stance of total irony.

21. Kierkegaard, *The Concept of Irony*, 328.

22. Summers, " 'Controlled Irony,' " 309.

23. One might think that Kierkegaard has in mind as well a theological source of normativity and value. While it is clear that Kierkegaard does affirm such a source, he does not invoke it in this context, at least not in relation to mastered irony. For Kierkegaard associates this religious perspective with humor, not irony (not even mastered irony). That is why in the concluding paragraph he refers to it in relation to humor but not irony. He states that humor "has a far deeper positivity, since it moves not in human but in theanthropological categories; it finds rest not by making man man but by making man God-man." See Kierkegaard, *The Concept of Irony*, 329. Here Kierkegaard anticipates the distinction between irony and humor that, under the guise of Johannes Climacus, he discusses in much more detail in *Postscript*. For an insightful discussion of Kierkegaard's views on humor and his distinction between irony and humor, see Lippitt, *Humour and Irony*, 47–103.

24. As is the case with all analogies, this analogy breaks down at a certain point. If a person "lets the objective dominate" to such an extent that she becomes merely a social conformist, then she is not ironical enough (if at all).

25. Kierkegaard, *The Concept of Irony*, 326–328.

26. Ibid., 327.

27. Ibid., 326.

28. Ibid., 328.

29. Cf. Lippitt, *Humour and Irony*, 148, who states: "Kierkegaard's central claim in this section, then, can be seen as being that the *use of irony from a position of rootedness* is fundamentally different from when that irony is symptomatic of 'infinite absolute negativity.' "

30. Adams, *Finite and Infinite Goods*, 374.

31. Ibid. Adams specifically has in view moral faith. His remarks apply just as well in this context to moral commitment.

32. Adams, *Finite and Infinite Goods*, 374.

33. One might object to this interpretation on the grounds that Kierkegaard assumes a very particular and controversial view of morality in *The Concept of Irony*, namely, that morality requires taking one's actuality to be a gift and task (with all that is implied by this). If so, and if Kierkegaard suggests that this controversial view of morality is not to be treated ironically, then he holds a more restrictive position

than I allow for. It is not only moral commitment itself that is not to be treated ironically but also a controversial view of what moral commitment requires of us. My response is twofold. First, I think that we can plausibly interpret Kierkegaard's position as very similar to Adams's. In that case, Kierkegaard's view is not that we should treat some very specific verbal formulation of morality nonironically but the good of persons and goodness and moral obligation. Second, we also can distinguish between a narrow and a very broad understanding of actuality as gift and task in Kierkegaard's account. The broad view just is that morality, whatever else it requires, requires commitment to the good of persons and to goodness and duty. But one cannot truly be committed to the good of persons, if one is unconcerned about the very persons with whom one interacts in everyday life (not to mention oneself, of course). On this reading, Kierkegaard's position is not as restrictive as it might appear to be. I recognize, however, that some will not be convinced that Kierkegaard himself holds this exact position or allows for this sort of distinction between a broad and a strict view of actuality as gift and task. Whether or not Kierkegaard himself holds this precise view, it is a position that I find defensible as a Kierkegaardian position.

34. Kierkegaard, *The Concept of Irony*, 326–327.
35. I emphasize "partially" because there is no reason to think that this kind of distance requires complete transcendence of one's social roles, if that were possible.
36. It is hard to overlook the fact that these metaphors also are religious metaphors. It is beyond the purview of this chapter, however, to explore the religious implications of these metaphors.
37. Cf. Walsh, *Living Poetically*, 61.
38. Kierkegaard, *The Concept of Irony*, 327.
39. Perhaps that is one reason why Kierkegaard notes that poets who want to master irony in their individual existence need to become philosophers "to a certain degree." See Kierkegaard, *The Concept of Irony*, 325. Also, cf. Lippitt, *Humour and Irony*, 149.
40. Since I have argued above that irony is mastered through moral commitment, one might wonder how moral commitment helps a person not to be overly self-critical. There are many ways that moral commitment could help a person not be overly self-critical. First, if one is fortunate enough to be committed to others who reciprocate this commitment, then these other persons may help one not be severe toward oneself. Second, if one truly is committed to the good of others, then one will have reason not to be overly critical of oneself on account of this fact alone, if one recognizes this fact. Third, persons who employ mastered irony, who are committed to the good of others but not in a servile way, are more likely to recognize cruel and unfair criticisms of themselves from others, which often are the basis of low self-esteem. Fourth, and perhaps most to the point, the idea that irony

is controlled through moral commitment, as I defined it above, is the idea that irony is employed within the parameters of commitment to the good of persons in general, including one's *own* good. In a certain respect, then, if a person is not sufficiently committed to her own value and flourishing, she suffers from a certain incompleteness of moral commitment. If she does not have this incompleteness, her commitment to her own good should enable her to overcome the extremes of the searing negativity of irony turned inward.

41. Although MacIntyre rejects irony, he makes a similar point about the inherently social nature of critical reflection. See MacIntyre, *Dependent Rational Animals*, 155–166, especially 162.

42. Summers, " 'Controlled Irony,' " 313.

43. Ibid.

44. Kierkegaard, *The Concept of Irony*, 326.

CHAPTER 6   CLIMACUS ON IRONY AND MORAL COMMITMENT

1. Søren Kierkegaard, *Concluding Unscientific Postscript to "Philosophical Fragments,"* vol. 1, ed. and trans. Howard V. Hong and Edna H. Hong (Princeton: Princeton University Press, 1992), 501–502, 503.

2. Cross, "Neither Either Nor Or," 136–137.

3. It becomes apparent below why it is necessary to distinguish these objects of reflection in this way.

4. Evans, *Kierkegaard's "Fragments" and "Postscript,"* 82.

5. In section 6.6 below, I show that, for Climacus, in some cases immediate persons might appear to be very ethically earnest while ethical persons might seem to be nonchalant about morality by comparison.

6. Kierkegaard, *Postscript*, 135–136.

7. Cross, "Neither Either Nor Or," 144.

8. Kierkegaard, *Postscript*, 503–504.

9. Climacus has in view here a person who is posing as an ironist.

10. Kierkegaard, *Postscript*, 502n.

11. Evans, *Kierkegaard's "Fragments" and "Postscript,"* 189.

12. Kierkegaard, *Postscript*, 391.

13. Evans, *Kierkegaard's "Fragments" and "Postscript,"* 191–192.

14. Kierkegaard, *The Concept of Irony*, 326.

15. Ibid.

16. Lippitt, *Humour and Irony*, 148, 149.

17. The claim that irony is necessary for a genuinely human life.

18. Lippitt, *Humour and Irony*, 148.

19. Kierkegaard, *Postscript*, 504.

20. I add the qualifier "a slight variant" because Cross does not discuss the final section of Kierkegaard's thesis, which contains Kierkegaard's final thesis that irony is necessary for a genuinely human life.

21. Cross, "Neither Either Nor Or," 137.
22. In Cross's reading of Kierkegaard, this position is the position of an ethical person.
23. Cross, "Neither Either Nor Or," 148.
24. Ibid., 141.
25. Ibid.
26. In part one of his thesis, Kierkegaard makes this point somewhat indirectly through his Hegelian analysis of Socrates as a crucial "world-historical" figure who trailblazes the way out of immediacy.
27. Cross takes Kierkegaard and Climacus to concur on this point. See Cross, "Neither Either Nor Or," 147.
28. Cross, "Neither Either Nor Or," 147.
29. Ibid.
30. Ibid., 148.
31. Merold Westphal, *Becoming a Self: A Reading of Kierkegaard's "Concluding Unscientific Postscript"* (West Lafayette, Ind.: Purdue University Press, 1996), 24.
32. Kierkegaard, *Postscript*, 502.
33. Evans, *Kierkegaard's "Fragments" and "Postscript,"* 82.
34. Ibid., 83–84. Evans's reference to the "eternal" seems to be a reference to the "ethical infinite requirement," which he refers to as "eternal and absolute" in the same context.
35. I take it that Evans has something like this line of reasoning in mind when he posits a distinction in Climacus's account between irony as a transition zone and irony as an existence-sphere. See Evans, *Kierkegaard's "Fragments" and "Postscript,"* 191–192.
36. For discussion of this claim about irony, see section 5.2 in chapter five. One candidate for an analogue to Climacus's "ethical infinite require-ment" in Kierkegaard's thesis is Fichte's transcendental Ego, as it is understood and appropriated by certain romantic ironists, whom Kierkegaard considers exemplars of pure irony. Kierkegaard, *The Concept of Irony*, 283, refers to this concept as "the eternal *I* for which no actuality is adequate." The analogy is so loose, however, as to be unhelpful. On Kierkegaard's reading, romantic ironists become radi-cally disengaged through completely unbridled, withering negativity, not through discovering contradictions that arise from holding up social practices to the light of an absolute moral ideal. They *begin* with the *a priori* assumption that every actuality is an obstacle to be over-come in pursuit of negative freedom. Then they proceed to critique social norms and practices in order to realize this sort of freedom. For concise but helpful discussions of these issues, see Hall, "The Irony of Irony," 333–339, and Rudd, "Kierkegaard's Critique of Pure Irony," 83–86. Also, see Robert L. Perkins, "Hegel and Kierkegaard: Two Critics of Romantic Irony," *Review of National Literatures* 1 (1970): 232–254.
37. See Evans, *Kierkegaard's "Fragments" and "Postscript,"* 190–191.

38. Søren Kierkegaard, *Concluding Unscientific Postscript to "Philosophical Fragments,"* trans. David F. Swenson and Walter Lowrie (Princeton: Princeton University Press, 1941), 142–143. I have opted for this particular translation of this extended passage in *Postscript* because it more elegantly captures Climacus's distinction between philosophically inclined persons and simpler persons than does the Hong translation. In the same context of this extended passage Climacus indicates that it is not an indignity or burden for intellectually inclined persons that simple truths become complicated for them. Climacus compares a wedding of common persons to a royal wedding, which is an "event," in order to convey this point. He argues that the fact that a royal wedding is an "event" is not derogatory to the royal couple, but honors them. Analogously, the intellectual complexities that a "wise man" encounters when he reflects on simple truths are not indignities, but are indicative of something good (even if something bad, such as intellectual arrogance, can be present as well).

39. Kierkegaard, *Postscript,* 199*n*. See also 197–199.

40. Kierkegaard, *Postscript* (Swenson translation), 159. I take the somewhat obscure phrase "simple man of knowledge" to refer to a person who believes and appropriates the same simple propositions that a "simple religious man" believes and appropriates, but in a more complicated way on account of his more reflective approach to these propositions.

41. Since humor is associated with a religious way of life and some religious ways of life require grace, on Climacus's view, one might think that Climacus could not make this substitution. This supposition is confused, however. The relevant distinction here is not the distinction between irony and humor or ethical and ethical–religious modes of existence. It is the distinction between intellectual modes of self-realization and simple modes of self-realization. Both irony and humor, as elements within ethical and ethical–religious existence, respectively, are intellectual modes of self-realization, for Climacus.

42. Evans, *Kierkegaard's "Fragments" and "Postscript,"* 191.

43. Kierkegaard, *Postscript,* 502.

44. Of course, it may be the case that Climacus will not be able to remove some form of moral luck from his account no matter what measures he takes.

45. One might wonder how Climacus's position squares with Kierkegaard's claim in *Point of View* that irony is peculiar to very specific intellectual cultures. Simply stated, the discrepancy between Climacus and Kierkegaard on this point is merely apparent because in *Point of View,* Kierkegaard has in view a more complicated and reflective form of irony, that is, one that resembles or approaches *pure* irony. For an interesting and detailed discussion of the sordid and difficult episode in Kierkegaard's life, otherwise known as *The Corsair* affair, which he is reflecting on when he remarks on the peculiarity of this

sort of irony, see Hannay, *Kierkegaard: A Biography*, 317–341. See also Joakim Garff, *Søren Kierkegaard: A Biography*, trans. Bruce H. Kirmmse (Princeton: Princeton University Press, 2005), 375–411. I regret that in general I was not able to take into account Garff's magisterial biography of Kierkegaard because of the timing of its publication.

46. Kierkegaard does anticipate in his thesis Climacus's view that irony can be an outward disguise. However, he has in view publicly dissembling in order to keep certain projects and personal relations private. See Kierkegaard, *The Concept of Irony*, 251–253.

47. Kierkegaard, *Postscript*, 503.

48. There is no need to conclude that, for Climacus, it *never* is appropriate to be obviously earnest. He has in view a *pattern* of ethical existence. There can be occasions in which it is wise to depart from this general approach.

49. Kierkegaard, *Postscript*, 323.

50. For Climacus, irony is a mode of the comic.

51. Kierkegaard, *Postscript*, 504–505.

52. Evans, *Kierkegaard's "Fragments" and "Postscript,"* 193–194. Cf. Walsh, *Living Poetically*, 212, and Lippitt, *Humour and Irony*, 91–93, 145.

53. Westphal, *Becoming a Self*, 168.

54. In later writings Kierkegaard comes to be suspicious of the idea that ethical striving is mostly a matter of inward ethical passion. For an illuminating and groundbreaking discussion of the shift that occurs in Kierkegaard's thinking, see Merold Westphal, "Kierkegaard's Teleological Suspension of Religiousness B," in *Foundations of Kierkegaard's Vision of Community*, ed. George B. Connell and C. Stephen Evans (London: Humanities Press, 1992), 110–129.

55. See Susan Wolf, "Moral Saints," in *The Virtue: Contemporary Essays on Moral Character*, ed. Robert B. Kruschwitz and Robert C. Roberts (Belmont, CA: Wadsworth, 1987), 137–152.

56. Evans, *Kierkegaard's "Fragments" and "Postscript,"* 81.

57. Ibid., 81–82.

58. I recognize that some contemporary Kantian moral theorists, such as Marcia Baron, Onora O'Neill, and Barbara Herman, have argued that Kant's moral theory has the resources to overcome the objection that I have advanced here. See, for instance, Barbara Herman, *The Practice of Moral Judgment* (Cambridge, MA: Harvard University Press, 1993), and Onora O'Neill, *Constructions of Reason: Explorations of Kant's Practical Philosophy* (Cambridge: Cambridge University Press, 1989). Perhaps these same moves can be made to some extent to lend support to Climacus's position as well. I doubt that they would allay completely the concerns that I raise, however.

59. Kierkegaard, *Postscript*, 193.

60. I do not explore here why Climacus takes a different approach to pure irony than Kierkegaard. Nevertheless, three possible reasons immediately present themselves. First, Kierkegaard's thesis is his most Hegelian work, whereas *Postscript* has Kantian elements that are not present in the thesis. This fact might help to account for the explicit introduction of the "ethical infinite requirement" and the central role that it plays. It might also account for Climacus's lower estimation of responsible engagement in *Sittlichkeit*. Second, and closely related, there is good reason to think that Climacus is committed to the view that the "ethical infinite requirement" is written into the fabric of human nature or the structure of reality in such a way that persons usually come to discover it. Evans takes Climacus to hold this position. In the context of clarifying Climacus's position, he notes: "It is possible for the individual to discover his superiority as the individual over the relative cultural patterns handed down to him, which is at bottom the discovery of man's eternal character and destiny, and then to misuse this self-understanding." See Evans, *Kierkegaard's "Fragments" and "Postscript,"* 192–193. Not to belabor the point, but would not a pure ironist be a bit suspicious of the idea that she had discovered "man's eternal character and destiny," as over against the "relative cultural patterns" passed down to her? At any rate, this conviction of Climacus's might help to account for his different approach. Third, Climacus is working within the parameter of a theory of stages of spheres of existence, a theory that Kierkegaard had not worked out when he wrote his thesis.

CHAPTER 7   IRONY AND MORAL COMMITMENT: CONCLUDING REFLECTIONS

1. I fully recognize that there are other accounts of irony and moral commitment that are worthy of consideration. Also, I am not claiming that Rorty's and Kierkegaard's positions are better than all the rest. I am in no position to make or justify such a claim. So, I do not necessarily disagree, for instance, with Elshtain's intimation that Camus is a better ironist than Rorty. The idiosyncrasies of my circumstances and interests helped my project take the particular focus that it has.
2. Perhaps that is why Rudd thinks he can use Kierkegaard's critique of romantic irony also as an adequate critique of Rortian irony. Rortian irony minus a commitment to liberalism, however, is a very truncated and much more objectionable position.
3. For the sake of simplicity, henceforth I will refer to such a person as a "Kierkegaardian ethical ironist." Also, I will assume that such a person attempts to employ irony as an incognito for her ethical passion, as Climacus suggests she should, since she can do this without subscribing to Climacus's stringent moral views.

4. Thomas McCarthy, "Private Irony and Public Decency: Richard Rorty's New Pragmatism," *Critical Inquiry* 16 (Winter 1990): 361. Cf. McCarthy, "Ironist Theory," 644, where he refers to this position as Rorty's "all-or-nothing approach to philosophy."

5. Evans, "Realism and Antirealism," 170.

6. Sometimes Rorty does accentuate this more pragmatic sort of critique of metaphysicians and epistemologists. This critique is difficult to sustain, however, if those who engage in these pursuits conscientiously fulfill their obligations to others.

7. Charles Taylor, "Rorty and Philosophy," in Guignon and Hiley, *Richard Rorty*, 158–159.

8. For more discussion of this point, see Charles Taylor, *Sources of the Self: The Making of the Modern Identity* (Cambridge, MA: Harvard University Press, 1989), especially 3–107.

9. Charles Guignon and David R. Hiley, "Introduction," in Guignon and Hiley, *Richard Rorty*, 38.

10. Cf. Westphal, *Becoming a Self*, 165–169. I grant that Climacus's ironists and ethicists also are characterized by recognition of the "ethical infinite requirement." But I have in view what I take to be the least objectionable and most compelling sort of ironist conceived in Kierkegaard's writings, namely, the ethical person of Kierkegaard's thesis who employs mastered irony and who also utilizes it as an incognito (like Climacus's ethicist).

11. Edward Mooney, *Selves in Discord and Resolve: Kierkegaard's Moral Religious Psychology from "Either/Or" to "Sickness Unto Death"* (New York: Routledge, 1996), 74.

12. I am not ignoring Rorty's endorsement of truthfulness. As he recognizes, this is not what distinguishes his moral perspective from other positions. So, for simplicity's sake, I set it aside here.

13. Of course, Kierkegaard himself struggled to bridle his ironic temper in this way.

14. Michael Walzer, *Thick and Thin: Moral Argument at Home and Abroad* (Notre Dame: University of Notre Dame Press, 1994), 4.

15. Of course, Walzer has a kind of "minimalism" in view that is different from and not to be confused with Taylor's "minimalism."

16. Walzer, *Thick and Thin*, 6.

17. I reiterate that I am referring to Kierkegaard's position as I have construed it. If we give a much more central place to the irreducibly religious aspects of Kierkegaard's position, it quickly threatens to become narrower than Rorty's and loses its broader appeal.

BIBLIOGRAPHY

Adams, Robert Merrihew. *The Virtue of Faith and Other Essays in Philosophical Theology*. Oxford: Oxford University Press, 1987.
———. *Finite and Infinite Goods: A Framework for Ethics*. Oxford: Oxford University Press, 1999.
Allen, Jonathan. "The Situated Critic or the Loyal Critic? Rorty and Walzer on Social Criticism." *Philosophy and Social Criticism* 24 (1998): 25–46.
Anderson, Charles W. "Pragmatism and Liberalism, Rationalism and Irrationalism: A Response to Richard Rorty." *Polity* 23 (Spring 1991): 357–371.
Arneson, Richard J. "Review of *Contingency, Irony, and Solidarity*, by Richard Rorty." *The Philosophical Review* 101 (April 1992): 475–479.
Baier, Annette C. *Postures of the Mind: Essays on Mind and Morals*. Minneapolis: University of Minnesota Press, 1985.
———. *Moral Prejudices: Essays on Ethics*. Cambridge, MA: Harvard University Press, 1994.
Baker, Lynne Rudder. *Explaining Attitudes: A Practical Approach to the Mind*. Cambridge: Cambridge University Press, 1995.
———. "Philosophy *In Mediis Rebus*." *Metaphilosophy* 32 (July 2001): 378–393.
Bellinger, Charles K. "Kierkegaard's *Either/Or* and the Parable of the Prodigal Son: Or, Three Rival Versions of '*Three Rival Versions*.' " In *International Kierkegaard Commentary: "Either/Or, Part II*," ed. Robert L. Perkins, 59–82. Macon, GA: Mercer University Press, 1995.
———. *The Genealogy of Violence: Reflections on Creation, Freedom, and Evil*. Oxford: Oxford University Press, 2001.
Bencivenga, Ermanno. "The Irony of It." *The Philosophical Forum* 25 (Winter 1993): 125–133.
Bernstein, Richard J. "One Step Forward, Two Steps Backward: Richard Rorty on Liberal Democracy and Philosophy." *Political Theory* 15 (November 1987): 538–563.
———. "Rorty's Liberal Utopia." In *The New Constellation: The Ethical-Political Horizons of Modernity/Postmodernity*, 258–292. Cambridge, MA: MIT Press, 1992.
———. *The New Constellation: The Ethical-Political Horizons of Modernity/Postmodernity*. Cambridge, MA: MIT Press, 1992.
Brandom, Robert B., ed. *Rorty and His Critics*. Malden, MA: Blackwell, 2000.

Bukdahl, Jørgen. *Soren Kierkegaard and the Common Man.* Translated by Bruce H. Kirmmse. Grand Rapids: Eerdmans, 2001.

Colebrook, Claire. *Irony in the Work of Philosophy.* Lincoln, NE: University of Nebraska Press, 2002.

———. *Irony.* London: Routledge, 2004.

Collins, James. *The Mind of Kierkegaard.* Princeton: Princeton University Press, 1983.

Conant, James. "Freedom, Cruelty, and Truth: Rorty versus Orwell." In *Rorty and His Critics,* ed. Robert B. Brandom, 268–342. Malden, MA: Blackwell, 2000.

Connell, George. *To Be One Thing: Personal Unity in Kierkegaard's Thought.* Macon, GA: Mercer University Press, 1985.

———. "Judge William's Theonomous Ethics." In *Foundations of Kierkegaard's Vision of Community,* ed. George B. Connell and C. Stephen Evans, 56–71. London: Humanities Press, 1992.

Connell, George B. and C. Stephen Evans, eds. *Foundations of Kierkegaard's Vision of Community.* London: Humanities Press, 1992.

Conway, Daniel W. "Taking Irony Seriously: Rorty's Postmetaphysical Liberalism." *American Literary History* 3 (1991): 198–208.

———. "Thus Spoke Rorty: The Perils of Narrative Self-Creation." *Philosophy and Literature* 15 (1991): 103–110.

———. "Irony, State and Utopia: Rorty's 'We' and the Problem of Transitional *Praxis.*" In *Richard Rorty: Critical Dialogues,* ed. Matthew Festenstein and Simon Thompson, 55–88. Malden, MA: Polity, 2001.

Conway, Daniel W. and John E. Seery, eds. *The Politics of Irony: Essays in Self-Betrayal.* New York: St. Martin's Press, 1992.

Critchley, Simon. "Deconstruction and Pragmatism—Is Derrida a Private Ironist or a Public Liberal?" In *Deconstruction and Pragmatism: Simon Critchley, Jacques Derrida, Ernesto Laclau and Richard Rorty,* ed. Chantal Mouffe, 19–40. New York: Routledge, 1996.

———. "Metaphysics in the Dark: A Response to Richard Rorty and Ernesto Laclau." *Political Theory* 26 (December 1998): 803–817.

Cross, Andrew. "Neither Either Nor Or: The Perils of Reflexive Irony." In *The Cambridge Companion to Kierkegaard,* ed. Alastair Hannay and Gordon D. Marino, 125–153. Cambridge: Cambridge University Press, 1998.

Davenport, John J. and Anthony Rudd, eds. *Kierkegaard After MacIntyre: Essays on Freedom, Narrative, and Virtue.* Chicago: Open Court, 2001.

De Botton, Alain. *How Proust Can Change Your Life.* New York: Vintage Books, 1997.

Deutscher, Max. *Subjecting and Objecting: An Essay in Objectivity.* Oxford: Blackwell, 1983.

Doyle, James. "Moral Rationalism and Moral Commitment." *Philosophy and Phenomenological Research* 55 (January 2000): 1–22.

Dunning, Stephen N. *Kierkegaard's Dialectic of Inwardness: A Structural Analysis of the Theory of Stages.* Princeton: Princeton University Press, 1985.

Elshtain, Jean Bethke. "Don't Be Cruel: Reflections on Rortyian Liberalism." In *The Politics of Irony: Essays in Self-Betrayal*, ed. Daniel W. Conway and John E. Seery, 199–217. New York: St. Martin's Press, 1992. (Republished in a slightly modified form in *Richard Rorty*, ed. Charles B. Guignon and David R. Hiley, 139–157. Cambridge: Cambridge University Press, 2003.)

Evans, C. Stephen. *Kierkegaard's "Fragments" and "Postscript": The Religious Philosophy of Johannes Climacus*. Atlantic Highlands, NJ: Humanities Press, 1983.

———. *Passionate Reason: Making Sense of Kierkegaard's "Philosophical Fragments."* Bloomington: Indiana University Press, 1992.

———. "Kierkegaard's View of the Unconscious." In *Kierkegaard in Post/Modernity*, ed. Martin J. Matustik and Merold Westphal, 76–97. Bloomington: Indiana University Press, 1995.

———. "Realism and Antirealism in Kierkegaard's *Concluding Unscientific Postscript*." In *The Cambridge Companion to Kierkegaard*, ed. Alastair Hannay and Gordon D. Marino, 154–176. Cambridge: Cambridge University Press, 1998.

Evans, C. Stephen and Merold Westphal, eds. *Christian Perspectives on Religious Knowledge*. Grand Rapids: Eerdmans, 1993.

Ferguson, Harvie. *Melancholy and the Critique of Modernity: Søren Kierkegaard's Religious Psychology*. New York: Routledge, 1995.

Ferrara, Alessandro. "The Unbearable Seriousness of Irony." *Philosophy and Social Criticism* 16 (1990): 81–107.

Ferreira, M. Jamie. *Transforming Vision: Imagination and Will in Kierkegaardian Faith*. Oxford: Oxford University Press, 1991.

———. "Faith and the Kierkegaardian Leap." In *The Cambridge Companion to Kierkegaard*, ed. Alastair Hannay and Gordon D. Marino, 207–234. Cambridge: Cambridge University Press, 1998.

Festenstein, Matthew. "Richard Rorty: Pragmatism, Irony and Liberalism." In *Richard Rorty: Critical Dialogues*, ed. Matthew Festenstein and Simon Thompson, 1–14. Malden, MA: Polity, 2001.

Festenstein, Matthew and Simon Thompson, eds. *Richard Rorty: Critical Dialogues*. Malden, MA: Polity, 2001.

Foelber, Robert E. "Can a Historicist Sustain a Diehard Commitment to Liberal Democracy? The Case of Rorty's Liberal Ironist." *The Southern Journal of Philosophy* 32 (1994): 19–48.

Frankfurt, Harry. *The Importance of What We Care About: Philosophical Essays*. Cambridge: Cambridge University Press, 1988.

———. *Necessity, Volition, and Love*. Cambridge: Cambridge University Press, 1999.

Fraser, Nancy. "Solidarity or Singularity? Richard Rorty between Romanticism and Technocracy." In *Reading Rorty*, ed. Alan R. Malachowski, 303–321. Oxford: Blackwell, 1990.

———. "From Irony to Prophecy to Politics: A Response to Richard Rorty." *Michigan Quarterly Review* 30 (Spring 1991): 259–266.

Gaita, Raimond. *A Common Humanity: Thinking About Love and Truth and Justice.* New York: Routledge, 2000.

Gander, Eric. *The Last Conceptual Revolution: A Critique of Richard Rorty's Political Philosophy.* Albany: State University of New York Press, 1999.

Garff, Joakim. *Søren Kierkegaard: A Biography.* Translated by Bruce H. Kirmmse. Princeton: Princeton University Press, 2005.

Gerson, L. P. "Philosophy, Literature, and Truth." Review of *Contingency, Irony, and Solidarity,* by Richard Rorty. *University of Toronto Quarterly* 59 (Spring 1990): 449–451.

Goodheart, Eugene. "The Postmodern Liberalism of Richard Rorty." *Partisan Review* 63 (1996): 223–235.

Goold, Patrick. "Reading Kierkegaard: Two Pitfalls and a Strategy for Avoiding Them." *Faith and Philosophy* 7 (July 1990): 304–315.

Gouwens, David J. "Kierkegaard on the Ethical Imagination." *Journal of Religious Ethics* 10 (Fall 1982): 204–220.

———. *Kierkegaard's Dialectic of the Imagination.* New York: Peter Lang, 1989.

———. *Kierkegaard as Religious Thinker.* Cambridge: Cambridge University Press, 1996.

Green, Ronald M. *Kierkegaard and Kant: The Hidden Debt.* Albany: State University of New York Press, 1992.

Guignon, Charles B. and David R. Hiley. "Biting the Bullet: Rorty on Private and Public Morality." In *Reading Rorty,* ed. Alan Malachowski, 339–364. Oxford: Blackwell, 1990.

———, eds. "Introduction: Richard Rorty and Contemporary Philosophy." In *Richard Rorty,* 1–40. Cambridge: Cambridge University Press, 2003.

———. *Richard Rorty.* Cambridge: Cambridge University Press, 2003.

Gurewitch, Morton. *The Ironic Temper and the Comic Imagination.* Detroit: Wayne State University Press, 1994.

Gutting, Gary. *Pragmatic Liberalism and the Critique of Modernity.* Cambridge: Cambridge University Press, 1999.

Hall, David L. *Richard Rorty: Prophet and Poet of the New Pragmatism.* Albany: State University of New York Press, 1994.

Hall, Ronald L. *Word and Spirit: A Kierkegaardian Critique of the Modern Age.* Bloomington: Indiana University Press, 1993.

———. *The Human Embrace, The Love of Philosophy and the Philosophy of Love: Kierkegaard, Cavell, Nussbaum.* University Park: The Pennsylvania University State Press, 2000.

———. "The Irony of Irony." In *International Kierkegaard Commentary: "The Concept of Irony,"* ed. Robert L. Perkins, 317–346. Macon, GA: Mercer University Press, 2001.

Hallie, Philip P. *The Scar of Montaigne: An Essay in Personal Philosophy.* Middletown, CT: Wesleyan University Press, 1966.

———. "Scepticism, Narrative, and Holocaust Ethics." *The Philosophical Forum* 16 (Fall/Winter 1984–85): 33–49.

Hannay, Alastair. *Kierkegaard.* New York: Routledge, 1982.

————. *Kierkegaard: A Biography*. Cambridge: Cambridge University Press, 2001.

Hannay, Alastair and Gordon D. Marino, eds. *The Cambridge Companion to Kierkegaard*. Cambridge: Cambridge University Press, 1998.

Hardwick, Charley D. and Donald A. Crosby, eds. *Pragmatism, Neo-Pragmatism, and Religion: Conversations with Rorty*. New York: Peter Lang, 1997.

Hare, John. *The Moral Gap: Kantian Ethics, Human Limits, and God's Assistance*. Oxford: Oxford University Press, 1996.

Hegel, Georg William Friedrich. *Phenomenology of Spirit*. Translated by A. V. Miller. Oxford: Oxford University Press, 1977.

————. *Lectures on the History of Philosophy*. Vol. 1, *Greek Philosophy to Plato*. Translated by E. S. Haldane. Lincoln, NE: University of Nebraska Press, 1995.

Herman, Barbara. *The Practice of Moral Judgment*. Cambridge, MA: Harvard University Press, 1993.

Horton, John. "Irony and Commitment: An Irreconcilable Dualism of Modernity." In *Richard Rorty: Critical Dialogues*, ed. Matthew Festenstein and Simon Thompson, 15–28. Malden, MA: Polity, 2001.

Jackson, Timothy P. "Kierkegaard's Metatheology." *Faith and Philosophy* 4 (January 1987): 71–85.

————. "The Disconsolation of Theology: Irony, Cruelty, and Putting Charity First." *Journal of Religious Ethics* 20 (1992): 1–36.

Jordan, Jeff and Daniel Howard-Snyder, eds. *Faith, Freedom, and Rationality: Philosophy of Religion Today*. Lanham, MD: Rowman & Littlefield, 1996.

Kemp, Kenneth W. "The Virtue of Faith in Theology, Natural Science, and Philosophy." *Faith and Philosophy* 15 (October 1998): 462–477.

Kierkegaard, Søren. *Concluding Unscientific Postscript to "Philosophical Fragments."* Translated by David F. Swenson and Walter Lowrie. Princeton: Princeton University Press, 1941.

————. *Purity of Heart is to Will One Thing*. Translated by Douglas V. Steere. New York: Harper & Row, 1956.

————. *Journals and Papers*. 7 vols. Edited and translated by Howard V. Hong and Edna H. Hong, assisted by Gregor Malantschuk. Bloomington: Indiana University Press, 1967–1978.

————. *The Sickness Unto Death: A Christian Psychological Exposition for Upbuilding and Awakening*. Edited and translated by Howard V. Hong and Edna H. Hong. Princeton: Princeton University Press, 1980.

————. *Either/Or*. 2 vols. Edited and translated by Howard V. Hong and Edna H. Hong. Princeton: Princeton University Press, 1987.

————. *The Concept of Irony with Continual Reference to Socrates, together with "Notes on Schelling's Berlin Lectures."* Edited and translated by Howard V. Hong and Edna H. Hong. Princeton: Princeton University Press, 1989.

————. *Practice in Christianity*. Edited and translated by Howard V. Hong and Edna H. Hong. Princeton: Princeton University Press, 1991.

Kierkegaard, Søren. *Concluding Unscientific Postscript to "Philosophical Fragments."* Vol. 1. Edited and translated by Howard V. Hong and Edna H. Hong. Princeton: Princeton University Press, 1992.

———. *The Point of View for My Work as an Author.* Edited and translated by Howard V. Hong and Edna H. Hong. Princeton: Princeton University Press, 1998.

Kirmmse, Bruce H. *Kierkegaard in Golden Age Denmark.* Bloomington: Indiana University Press, 1990.

———. "Socrates in the Fast Lane: Kierkegaard's *The Concept of Irony* on the University's Velocifère: Documents, Context, Commentary, and Interpretation." In *International Kierkegaard Commentary: "The Concept of Irony,"* ed. Robert L. Perkins, 17–99. Macon, GA: Mercer University Press, 2001.

Kolenda, Konstantin. "Misreading Rorty." *Philosophy and Literature* 15 (1991): 111–117.

Kruschwitz, Robert B. and Robert C. Roberts, eds. *The Virtues: Contemporary Essays on Moral Character.* Belmont, CA: Wadsworth, 1987.

Larmore, Charles. *The Romantic Legacy.* New York: Columbia University Press, 1996.

Lillegaard, Norman. "Judge William in the Dock: MacIntyre on Kierkegaard's Ethics." In *International Kierkegaard Commentary: "Either/Or, Part II,"* ed. Robert L. Perkins, 83–111. Macon, GA: Mercer University Press, 1995.

———. "Thinking with Kierkegaard and MacIntyre about the Aesthetic, Virtue, and Narrative." In *Kierkegaard After MacIntyre: Essays on Freedom, Narrative, and Virtue,* ed. John J. Davenport and Anthony Rudd, 211–232. Chicago: Open Court, 2001.

Lippitt, John. *Humour and Irony in Kierkegaard's Thought.* New York: St. Martin's Press, 2000.

Lovibond, Sabina. "Feminism and Pragmatism: A Reply to Richard Rorty." *New Left Review* 193 (May/June 1992): 56–74.

MacIntyre, Alasdair. *After Virtue,* 2nd ed. Notre Dame: University of Notre Dame Press, 1984.

———. "Review of *Contingency, Irony, and Solidarity,* by Richard Rorty." *Journal of Philosophy* 87 (December 1990): 709–711.

———. *Three Rival Versions of Moral Enquiry: Encyclopaedia, Genealogy and Tradition.* Notre Dame: University of Notre Dame Press, 1990.

———. *Dependent Rational Animals: Why Human Beings Need the Virtues.* Chicago: Open Court, 1999.

Mackey, Louis. *Kierkegaard: A Kind of Poet.* Philadelphia: University of Pennsylvania Press, 1971.

Malachowski, Alan, ed. *Reading Rorty.* Oxford: Blackwell, 1990.

Malantschuk, Gregor. *Kierkegaard's Thought.* Edited and translated by Howard V. Hong and Edna H. Hong. Princeton: Princeton University Press, 1971.

Marino, Gordon D. "Is Madness Truth, is Fanaticism Faith?" *International Journal for the Philosophy of Religion* 22 (1987): 41–53.

———. "The Place of Reason in Kierkegaard's Ethics." In *Kierkegaard After MacIntyre: Essays on Freedom, Narrative, and Virtue*, ed. John J. Davenport and Anthony Rudd, 113–127. Chicago: Open Court, 2001.

Martinez, Roy. *Kierkegaard and the Art of Irony*. Amherst, NY: Humanity Books, 2001.

Matuøtík, Martin J. and Merold Westphal, eds. *Kierkegaard in Post/ Modernity*. Bloomington: Indiana University Press, 1995.

McCarthy, Thomas. "Private Irony and Public Decency: Richard Rorty's New Pragmatism." *Critical Inquiry* 16 (Winter 1990): 355–370.

———. "Ironist Theory as a Vocation: A Response to Rorty's Reply." *Critical Inquiry* 16 (Spring 1990): 644–655.

McCarthy, Vincent. *The Phenomenology of Moods in Kierkegaard*. Boston: Martinus Nijhoff, 1978.

McCumber, John. *Philosophy and Freedom: Derrida, Rorty, Habermas, Foucault*. Bloomington: Indiana University Press, 2000.

McDowell, John. "Towards Rehabilitating Objectivity." In *Rorty and His Critics*, ed. Robert B. Brandom, 109–123. Malden, MA: Blackwell, 2000.

Mehl, Peter J. "Moral Virtue, Mental Health, and Happiness: The Moral Psychology of Kierkegaard's Judge William." In *International Kierkegaard Commentary: "Either/Or, Part II,"* ed. Robert L. Perkins, 155–182. Macon, GA: Mercer University Press, 1995.

———. "Kierkegaard and the Relativist Challenge to Practical Philosophy (with a New Postscript)." In *Kierkegaard After MacIntyre: Essays on Freedom, Narrative, and Virtue*, ed. John J. Davenport and Anthony Rudd, 2–38. Chicago: Open Court, 2001.

Melkonian, Markar. *Richard Rorty's Politics: Liberalism at the End of the American Century*. Amherst, NY: Humanity Books, 1999.

Moody-Adams, Michele. "Theory, Practice, and the Contingency of Rorty's Irony." *Journal of Social Philosophy* 25 (1994): 209–227.

———. *Fieldwork in Familiar Places: Morality, Culture, and Philosophy*. Cambridge, MA: Harvard University Press, 1997.

Mooney, Edward. "Kierkegaard on Self-Choice and Self-Reception: Judge William's Admonition." In *International Kierkegaard Commentary: "Either/Or, Part II,"* ed. Robert L. Perkins, 5–31. Macon, GA: Mercer University Press, 1995.

———. *Selves in Discord and Resolve: Kierkegaard's Moral-Religious Psychology From "Either/Or" to "Sickness Unto Death."* New York: Routledge, 1996.

———. "The Perils of Polarity: Kierkegaard and MacIntyre in Search of Moral Truth." In *Kierkegaard After MacIntyre: Essays on Freedom, Narrative, and Virtue*, ed. John J. Davenport and Anthony Rudd, 233–263. Chicago: Open Court, 2001.

Morreall, John. *Comedy, Tragedy, and Religion*. Albany: State University of New York Press, 1999.

Morris, T.F. "Kierkegaard's Understanding of Socrates." *International Journal for the Philosophy of Religion* 19 (1986): 105–111.

Mouffe, Chantal, ed. *Deconstruction and Pragmatism: Simon Critchley, Jacques Derrida, Ernesto Laclau and Richard Rorty.* New York: Routledge, 1996.

Muecke, D.C. *The Compass of Irony.* London: Methuen and Company, 1969.

Nagel, Thomas. *Mortal Questions.* Cambridge: Cambridge University Press, 1979.

———. "Review of *Ethics and the Limits of Philosophy*, by Bernard Williams." *Journal of Philosophy* 83 (June 1986): 351–360.

Nehamas, Alexander. *Nietzsche: Life as Literature.* Cambridge, MA: Harvard University Press, 1985.

———. *The Art of Living: Socratic Reflections from Plato to Foucault.* Berkeley and Los Angeles: University of California Press, 1998.

———. *Virtues of Authenticity: Essays on Plato and Socrates.* Princeton: Princeton University Press, 1999.

Neiman, Alven. "Ironic Schooling: Socrates, Pragmatism and the Higher Learning." *Educational Theory* 41 (Fall 1991): 371–384.

Nussbaum, Martha C. "Skepticism About Practical Reason in Literature and the Law." *Harvard Law Review* 107 (Fall 1994): 714–744.

———. "Transcendence and Human Values." *Philosophy and Phenomenological Research* 64 (March 2002): 445–452.

Olesen, Tonny Aagaard. "Kierkegaard's Socratic Hermeneutic in *The Concept of Irony*." In *International Kierkegaard Commentary: "The Concept of Irony,"* ed. Robert L. Perkins, 101–122. Macon, GA: Mercer University Press, 2001.

O'Neill, Onora. *Constructions of Reason: Explorations of Kant's Practical Philosophy.* Cambridge: Cambridge University Press, 1989.

Owen, David. "The Avoidance of Cruelty: Joshing Rorty on Liberalism, Scepticism and Ironism." In *Richard Rorty: Critical Dialogues*, ed. Matthew Festenstein and Simon Thompson, 93–110. Malden, MA: Polity, 2001.

Owens, John. "The Obligations of Irony: Rorty on Irony, Autonomy, and Contingency." *Review of Metaphysics* 54 (September 2000): 27–41.

Pattison, George. *Kierkegaard: The Aesthetic and the Religious.* New York: St. Martin's Press, 1992.

———. "Beyond the Grasp of Irony." In *International Kierkegaard Commentary: "The Concept of Irony,"* ed. Robert L. Perkins, 347–363. Macon, GA: Mercer University Press, 2001.

Pattison, George and Steven Shakespeare, eds. *Kierkegaard: The Self in Society.* New York: St. Martin's Press, 1998.

Perkins, Robert L. "Either/Or/Or: Giving the Parson His Due." In *International Kierkegaard Commentary: "Either/Or, Part II,"* 207–231. Macon, GA: Mercer University Press, 1995.

———. "What a Hegelian Fool I Was." *History of European Ideas* 20 (1995): 177–181.

———, ed. *International Kierkegaard Commentary: "The Corsair Affair."* Macon, GA: Mercer University Press, 1990.

———, ed. *International Kierkegaard Commentary: "Either/Or, Part I,"* Macon, GA: Mercer University Press, 1995.

———, ed. *International Kierkegaard Commentary: "Either/Or, Part II."* Macon, GA: Mercer University Press, 1995.

———, ed. *International Kierkegaard Commentary: "Concluding Unscientific Postscript."* Macon, GA: Mercer University Press, 1997.

———, ed. *International Kierkegaard Commentary: "The Concept of Irony."* Macon, GA: Mercer University Press, 2001.

Phillips, Hollibert E. "The Ironist's Utopia: Can Rorty's Liberal Turnip Bleed?" *International Philosophical Quarterly* 32 (September 1992): 363–368.

Piety, Marilyn Gale. "The Place of the World in Kierkegaard's Ethics." In *Kierkegaard: The Self in Society*, ed. George Pattison and Steven Shakespeare, 24–42. New York: St. Martin's Press, 1998.

———."Kierkegaard on Rationality." In *Kierkegaard After MacIntyre: Essays on Freedom, Narrative, and Virtue*, ed. John J. Davenport and Anthony Rudd, 59–74. Chicago: Open Court, 2001.

Poole, Roger. *Kierkegaard: The Indirect Communication.* Charlottesville: University Press of Virginia, 1993.

Purdy, Jedediah. *For Common Things: Irony, Trust, and Commitment in America Today.* New York: Alfred A. Knopf, 1999.

Putnam, Hilary. *The Many Faces of Realism: The Paul Carus Lectures.* Peru, IL: Open Court, 1987.

Quinn, Philip L. "Kierkegaard's Christian Ethics." In *The Cambridge Companion to Kierkegaard*, ed. Alastair Hannay and Gordon D. Marino, 349–375. Cambridge: Cambridge University Press, 1998.

Rawls, John. *A Theory of Justice.* Cambridge, MA: Harvard University Press, 1971.

———. *Political Liberalism.* New York: Columbia University Press, 1993.

Riley, Denise. *The Words of Selves: Identification, Solidarity, Irony.* Stanford: Stanford University Press, 2000.

Roberts, Robert C. "Thinking Subjectively." *International Journal for the Philosophy of Religion* 11 (1980): 71–92.

———. "Sense of Humor as a Christian Virtue." *Faith and Philosophy* 7 (1990): 177–192.

———. "Kierkegaard, Wittgenstein, and a Method of 'Virtue Ethics.' " In *Kierkegaard in Post/Modernity*, ed. Martin J. Matustik and Merold Westphal, 142–166. Bloomington: Indiana University Press, 1995.

———. "Existence, Emotion, and Virtue: Classical Themes in Kierkegaard." In *The Cambridge Companion to Kierkegaard*, ed. Alastair Hannay and Gordon D. Marino, 177–206. Cambridge: Cambridge University Press, 1998.

Rorty, Amélie Oksenberg, ed. *The Identities of Persons.* Berkeley and Los Angeles: University of California Press, 1976.

Rorty, Richard. *Philosophy and the Mirror of Nature*. Princeton: Princeton University Press, 1979.

———. *Consequences of Pragmatism*. Minneapolis: University of Minnesota Press, 1982.

———. *Contingency, Irony, and Solidarity*. Cambridge: Cambridge University Press, 1989.

———. "Truth and Freedom: A Reply to Thomas McCarthy." *Critical Inquiry* 16 (Spring 1990): 633–643.

———. *Essays on Heidegger and Others*. Vol. 2, *Philosophical Papers*. Cambridge: Cambridge University Press, 1991.

———. "Freud and Moral Reflection." In *Essays on Heidegger and Others*. Vol. 2, *Philosophical Papers*, 143–163. Cambridge: Cambridge University Press, 1991.

———. "Introduction: Antirepresentationalism, Ethnocentrism, and Liberalism." In *Objectivity, Relativism, and Truth*. Vol. 1, *Philosophical Papers*, 1–17. Cambridge: Cambridge University Press, 1991.

———. "Moral Identity and Private Autonomy: The Case of Foucault." In *Essays on Heidegger and Others*. Vol. 2, *Philosophical Papers*, 193–198. Cambridge: Cambridge University Press, 1991.

———. *Objectivity, Relativism, and Truth*. Vol. 1, *Philosophical Papers*. Cambridge: Cambridge University Press, 1991.

———. "On Ethnocentrism: A Reply to Clifford Geertz." In *Objectivity, Relativism, and Truth*. Vol. 1, *Philosophical Papers*, 203–210. Cambridge: Cambridge University Press, 1991.

———. "Postmodernist Bourgeois Liberalism." In *Objectivity, Relativism, and Truth*. Vol. 1, *Philosophical Papers*, 197–202. Cambridge: Cambridge University Press, 1991.

———. "Solidarity or Objectivity." In *Objectivity, Relativism, and Truth*. Vol. 1, *Philosophical Papers*, 21–34. Cambridge: Cambridge University Press, 1991.

———. "The Priority of Democracy to Philosophy." In *Objectivity, Relativism, and Truth*. Vol. 1, *Philosophical Papers*, 175–196. Cambridge: Cambridge University Press, 1991.

———. "Robustness: A Reply to Jean Bethke Elshtain." In *The Politics of Irony: Essays in Self-Betrayal*, ed. Daniel W. Conway and John E. Seery, 219–223. New York: St. Martin's Press, 1992.

———. "Reply to Simon Critchley." In *Deconstruction and Pragmatism: Simon Critchley, Jacques Derrida, Ernesto Laclau and Richard Rorty*, ed. Chantal Mouffe, 41–46. New York: Routledge, 1996.

———. *Against Bosses, Against Oligarchies: A Conversation with Richard Rorty*. Interview by Derek Nystrom and Kent Puckett. Prickly Pear Pamphlets, ed. Matthew Engelke and Mark Harris, no. 11. Charlottesville: Prickly Pear Pamphlets, 1998.

———. "Feminism and Pragmatism." In *Truth and Progress*. Vol. 3, *Philosophical Papers*, 202–227. Cambridge: Cambridge University Press, 1998.

———. "Human Rights, Rationality, and Sentimentality." In *Truth and Progress.* Vol. 3, *Philosophical Papers*, 167–185. Cambridge: Cambridge University Press, 1998.

———. "Rationality and Cultural Difference." In *Truth and Progress.* Vol. 3, *Philosophical Papers*, 186–201. Cambridge: Cambridge University Press, 1998.

———. "The End of Leninism, Havel, and Social Hope." In *Truth and Progress.* Vol. 3, *Philosophical Papers*, 228–243. Cambridge: Cambridge University Press, 1998.

———. "The Very Idea of Human Answerability to the World: John McDowell's Version of Empiricism." In *Truth and Progress.* Vol. 3, *Philosophical Papers*, 138–152. Cambridge: Cambridge University Press, 1998.

———. *Truth and Progress.* Vol. 3, *Philosophical Papers.* Cambridge: Cambridge University Press, 1998.

———. "Education as Socialization and as Individualization." In *Philosophy and Social Hope*, 114–126. New York: Penguin Books, 1999.

———. "Ethics Without Principles." In *Philosophy and Social Hope*, 72–90. New York: Penguin Books, 1999.

———. "Failed Prophecies, Glorious Hopes." In *Philosophy and Social Hope*, 201–209. New York: Penguin Books, 1999.

———. "Globalization, The Politics of Identity, and Social Hope." In *Philosophy and Social Hope*, 229–239. New York: Penguin Books, 1999.

———. *Philosophy and Social Hope.* New York: Penguin Books, 1999.

———. "The Banality of Pragmatism and the Poetry of Justice." In *Philosophy and Social Hope*, 93–103. New York: Penguin Books, 1999.

———. "Trotsky and the Wild Orchids." In *Philosophy and Social Hope*, 3–20. New York: Penguin Books, 1999.

———. "Truth Without Correspondence to Reality." In *Philosophy and Social Hope*, 23–46. New York: Penguin Books, 1999.

———. "Response to Conant." In *Rorty and His Critics*, ed. Robert B. Brandom, 342–350. Malden, MA: Blackwell, 2000.

———. "Response to McDowell." In *Rorty and His Critics*, ed. Robert B. Brandom, 123–128. Malden, MA: Blackwell, 2000.

———. "Justice as a Larger Loyalty." In *Richard Rorty: Critical Dialogues*, ed. Matthew Festenstein and Simon Thompson, 223–237. Malden, MA: Polity, 2001.

———. "Response to Daniel Conway." In *Richard Rorty: Critical Dialogues*, ed. Matthew Festenstein and Simon Thompson, 89–92. Malden, MA: Polity, 2001.

———. "Response to David Owen." In *Richard Rorty: Critical Dialogues*, ed. Matthew Festenstein and Simon Thompson, 111–114. Malden, MA: Polity, 2001.

———. "Response to John Horton." In *Richard Rorty: Critical Dialogues*, ed. Matthew Festenstein and Simon Thompson, 29–32. Malden, MA: Polity, 2001.

Rorty, Richard. "Response to Simon Thompson." In *Richard Rorty: Critical Dialogues*, ed. Matthew Festenstein and Simon Thompson, 51–54. Malden, MA: Polity, 2001.

Rotenstreich, Nathan. "Can Expression Replace Reflection?" *The Review of Metaphysics* 43 (March 1990): 607–618.

Rothleder, Dianne. *The Work of Friendship: Rorty, His Critics, and the Project of Solidarity.* Albany: State University of New York Press, 1999.

Rudd, Anthony. *Kierkegaard and the Limits of the Ethical.* Oxford: Oxford University Press, 1993.

———. "Kierkegaard's Critique of Pure Irony." In *Kierkegaard: The Self in Society*, ed. George Pattison and Steven Shakespeare, 82–96. New York: St. Martin's Press, 1998.

———. "Reason in Ethics: MacIntyre and Kierkegaard." In *Kierkegaard After MacIntyre: Essays on Freedom, Narrative, and Virtue*, ed. John J. Davenport and Anthony Rudd, 131–150. Chicago: Open Court, 2001.

Rumble, Vanessa. "Eternity Lies Beneath: Autonomy and Finitude in Kierkegaard's Early Writings." *Journal of the History of Philosophy* 35 (January 1997): 83–103.

Scott, John Finley. *Internalization of Norms: A Sociological Theory of Moral Commitment.* Englewood Cliffs, NJ: Prentice-Hall, 1971.

Smith, Ruth L. "Morals and Their Ironies." *Journal of Religious Ethics* 26 (1998): 367–388.

Søltoft, Pia. "Ethics and Irony." Translated by Stacey E. Ake. In *International Kierkegaard Commentary: "The Concept of Irony,"* ed. Robert L. Perkins, 265–287. Macon, GA: Mercer University Press, 2001.

Strawser, Michael. *Both/And: Reading Kierkegaard from Irony to Edification.* New York: Fordham University Press, 1997.

Stump, Eleonore. "Libertarian Freedom and the Principle of Alternative Possibilities." In *Faith, Freedom, and Rationality: Philosophy of Religion Today*, ed. Jeff Jordan and Daniel Howard-Snyder, 73–88. Lanham: Rowman & Littlefield, 1996.

Summers, Richard M. "'Controlled Irony' and the Emergence of the Self in Kierkegaard's Dissertation." In *International Kierkegaard Commentary: "The Concept of Irony,"* ed. Robert L. Perkins, 289–315. Macon, GA: Mercer University Press, 2001.

Talisse, Robert B. "A Pragmatist Critique of Richard Rorty's Hopeless Politics." *The Southern Journal of Philosophy* 39 (2001): 611–626.

Taylor, Charles. *Hegel.* Cambridge: Cambridge University Press, 1975.

———. *Philosophical Arguments.* Cambridge, MA: Harvard University Press, 1995.

———. "Rorty and Philosophy." In *Richard Rorty*, ed. Charles B. Guignon and David R. Hiley, 158–180. Cambridge: Cambridge University Press, 2003.

Taylor, Mark C. *Kierkegaard's Pseudonymous Authorship: A Study of Time and the Self.* Princeton: Princeton University Press, 1975.

———. *Journeys to Selfhood: Hegel and Kierkegaard.* New York: Fordham University Press, 2000.

Thompson, Simon. "Richard Rorty on Truth, Justification and Justice." In *Richard Rorty: Critical Dialogues*, ed. Matthew Festenstein and Simon Thompson, 33–50. Malden, MA: Polity, 2001.

Thulstrup, Niels. *Kierkegaard's Relation to Hegel*. Translated by George L. Stengren. Princeton: Princeton University Press, 1980.

Van Hook, Jay M. "Caves, Canons, and the Ironic Teacher in Richard Rorty's Philosophy of Education." *Metaphilosophy* 24 (January/April 1993): 167–174.

Visker, Rudi. " 'Hold the Being' How to Split Rorty Between Irony and Finitude." *Philosophy and Social Criticism* 25 (1999): 27–45.

Vlastos, Gregory. *Socrates, Ironist and Moral Philosopher*. Ithaca: Cornell University Press, 1991.

Walsh, Sylvia. "Kierkegaard and Postmodernism." *International Journal for the Philosophy of Religion* 29 (1991): 113–122.

———. *Living Poetically: Kierkegaard's Existential Aesthetics*. University Park: The Pennsylvania State University Press, 1994.

———. "Living Poetically: Kierkegaard and German Romanticism." *History of European Ideas* 20 (1995): 189–194.

Walzer, Michael. *Spheres of Justice: A Defense of Pluralism and Equality*. New York: Basic Books, 1983.

———. *Thick and Thin: Moral Argument at Home and Abroad*. Notre Dame: University of Notre Dame Press, 1994.

Westphal, Merold. *Kierkegaard's Critique of Reason and Society*. University Park: The Pennsylvania State University Press, 1991.

———. "Kierkegaard's Teleological Suspension of Religiousness B." In *Foundations of Kierkegaard's Vision of Community*, ed. George B. Connell and C. Stephen Evans, 110–129. London: Humanities Press, 1992.

———. "Christian Philosophers and the Copernican Revolution." In *Christian Perspectives on Religious Knowledge*, ed. C. Stephen Evans and Merold Westphal, 161–179. Grand Rapids: Eerdmans, 1993.

———. *Becoming a Self: A Reading of Kierkegaard's "Concluding Unscientific Postscript."* West Lafayette, IN: Purdue University Press, 1996.

———. *History and Truth in Hegel's "Phenomenology,"* 3rd ed. Bloomington: Indiana University Press, 1998.

———. "Kierkegaard and Hegel." In *The Cambridge Com panion to Kierkegaard*, ed. Alastair Hannay and Gordon D. Marino, 101–124. Cambridge: Cambridge University Press, 1998.

———. "Coping and Conversing: The Limits and Promise of Pragmatism." *The Hedgehog Review* 3, no. 3 (Fall 2001): 73–92.

———. "Kierkegaard, Socratic Irony, and Deconstruction." In *International Kierkegaard Commentary: "The Concept of Irony,"* ed. Robert L. Perkins, 365–390. Macon, GA: Mercer University Press, 2001.

Williams, Bernard. *Problems of the Self*. Cambridge: Cambridge University Press, 1973.

———. "Persons, Character and Morality." In *The Identities of Persons*, ed. Amélie Oksenberg Rorty, 197–216. Berkeley and Los Angeles: University of California Press, 1976.

Williams, Bernard. *Ethics and the Limits of Philosophy.* Cambridge, MA: Harvard University Press, 1985.

Wisdo, David. *The Life of Irony and the Ethics of Belief.* Albany: State University of New York Press, 1993.

Wolf, Susan. "Moral Saints." In *The Virtues: Contemporary Essays on Moral Character*, ed. Robert B. Kruschwitz and Robert C. Roberts, 137–152. Belmont, CA: Wadsworth, 1987.

———. "A World of Goods." *Philosophy and Phenomenological Research* 64 (March 2002): 467–474.

Wood, Allen W. *Hegel's Ethical Thought.* Cambridge: Cambridge University Press, 1990.

Young, Phillips E. "The Irony of Ironic Liberalism." *International Studies in Philosophy* 29 (1997): 121–130.

INDEX